New Letters Reader II

An Anthology of Contemporary Writing

Edited by DAVID RAY
with JUDY RAY

A *New Letters* Book
University of Missouri—Kansas City

1984

Publication of this edition is supported by a grant from the National Endowment for the Arts, a federal agency. We are also grateful for support from the Missouri Arts Council.

New Letters magazine is published quarterly. Subscriptions for individuals or gifts are: $15 1 year; $25 2 years; $50 5 years. Library rates are: $18 1 year; $30 2 years; $60 5 years.

Second class postage paid at Kansas City, Mo.

New Letters
University of Missouri—Kansas City
5100 Rockhill Road
Kansas City, Mo. 64110

ISBN 0-938652-08-7   ISSN 0146-4930
©Copyright 1984 The Curators of the University of Missouri
All Rights Reserved

VOLUME 50   WINTER/SPRING 1984   NUMBERS 2 & 3

New Letters Reader II

CONTENTS

7 Editorial

FICTION and ESSAYS:

11	The Sheller	E. M. BRONER
39	The Executive Touch	JAMES B. HALL
65	The Fields of Golden Glow	JACK CONROY
79	Bambi	HENRIETTA WIEGEL
95	St. Louis Woman	ISHMAEL REED
99	The Penny	PAUL GOODMAN
102	The Psychiatrist	DAVID RAY
115	This	H. E. FRANCIS
141	Father's Day	HARRY ROSKOLENKO
153	Recycle	THOMAS ZIGAL
173	Macabre	CYRUS COLTER
191	Father and Daughter	WALTER LOWENFELS
201	Each New Springtime, Each New Summer	JAMES McKINLEY
221	White the Bones of Men: Asian Poets React to War	BEN W. FUSON
249	Separate Courses	HENRY H. ROTH
265	The Dying of Frank Oldmixon	WYATT WYATT

POETRY:

29	Three Poems	WILLIAM STAFFORD
31	Bones	ROGER PFINGSTON
32	The Gentlemen in the U-Boats	SHARON OLDS
33	Merry Christmas!	ELDER OLSON
34	Two Poems	JOSEPH BRUCHAC
35	Studies From Life	MARTHA DICKEY
36	Hardy Street	STEPHEN DUNNING
37	The Limits of the Town	ELIZABETH WRAY
38	Ultima Thule Hotel	GEORGE HITCHCOCK
55	Texas Indian Rock Art	DAVE OLIPHANT
56	Two Poems	VASSAR MILLER
58	The Empty Chair	J. J. MALONEY
59	Weldon Kees	LARRY LEVIS

60	Semper Eadem	DEREK WALCOTT
61	Friday Evening	D. M. THOMAS
62	Two Poems	JOHN TAGLIABUE
63	Putsch—1923	ROBERT WILLSON
64	In The Beginning	JONATHAN GRIFFITH
76	Entering Time in a House Photographed by Walker Evans	ROBERT GIBB
85	Fayetteville Dawn	JOHN CLELLON HOLMES
86	Two Poems	DAVID PERKINS
87	"R.S.V.P."	G. N. GABBARD
88	Chickens in San Francisco	WILLIAM DICKEY
89	Upon the Bible Belt	JOHN CAIN
90	Farmer	LUCIEN STRYK
91	A Dead Woman's Eyes	JULES SUPERVIELLE
	(Translated by Geoffrey Gardner)	
92	My Moon Girl	TOBY OLSON
93	Introduction	HEATHER WILDE
94	Three Poems	JOHN KNOEPFLE
104	Alice Braxton Johnson	MICHAEL S. HARPER
105	November	JONATHAN HOLDEN
106	Three Poems	CHARLES G. BELL
107	The Marble Distances	BYRON VAZAKAS
108	A Day in the Sun	JOHN LOGAN
109	Shelby County, Indiana, February, 1977	G. E. MURRAY
110	Photocopied Garments	PATI HILL
114	Missing Now 5 Days	GEOF HEWITT
127	Four Poems	ETHERIDGE KNIGHT
129	Duchamp's Nude	CRYSTAL MacLEAN FIELD
130	Card Island or Cod Island?	ISABELLA GARDNER
131	Liv	PHILIP BOOTH
132	Two Poems	WILLIS BARNSTONE
134	Rain	JORGE LUIS BORGES
	(Translated by Willis Barnstone)	
134	Widow	FELIX POLLAK
136	Two Poems	TOM HANNA
137	Nothing To Remember You By	JAN GAUGER
138	Lloyd Reynolds, Calligrapher	ALBERT BELLG
140	Haiku from the Japanese Masters	
	(Translated by Lucien Stryk and Takashi Ikemoto)	
163	Two Poems	A. R. AMMONS
164	Four Poems	E. L. MAYO
166	The Best Dance Hall in Iuka, Mississippi	THOMAS JOHNSON
167	Morning Raga	ROBERT SLATER

169	End of the War in Merida	ANTHONY OSTROFF
170	Four Poems	MBEMBE (MILTON SMITH)
182	A Short Novel	PETER EVERWINE
183	Two Poems	HUGH MacDIARMID
184	The Day After the Election	DAN JAFFE
184	Why the Eskimos Never Answer Their Letters	M. T. BUCKLEY
185	Some Modern Good Turns	DENNIS DIBBEN
185	On Being Native	DAVID BUDBILL
186	Ballet Under the Stars	ROBERT J. STEWART
186	dazzled	ARTHUR SZE
188	Why Not?	LINDA PASTAN
188	Poem for My Wife	MICHAEL SHERIDAN
189	Root River	DAVID KHERDIAN
190	My Mother	JAMES T. McCARTIN
213	Things To Do Around Taos	KEN McCULLOUGH
215	The Artist's Intention	A. G. SOBIN
216	Characters in Motion	JOSEPHINE JACOBSEN
216	The Lifting	RALPH J. MILLS, JR.
217	Two Poems	VICTORIA McCABE
218	Wind	JOHN W. MOSER
218	Rain For Two Days	ROBERTA PALEY
219	Two Poems	ELLIOTT COLEMAN
220	After Our War	JOHN BALABAN
239	Metaphors	SALLY McNALL
239	To Frank	DAVID V. QUEMADA
240	Round Lake	JANET KAUFFMAN
241	Two Poems	GREG FIELD
242	Absent Star	QUINTON DUVAL
243	She Pleads Guilty	ADRIAN OKTENBERG
244	Satyr	MARYA MANNES
244	Your Father Is Awake Shaking	OLIVIA MARTIN
245	Consolation	JIM BARNES
245	After Fire	KEN FIFER
246	Two Poems	ALFRED STARR HAMILTON
247	Lilac Feeling	RICHARD EBERHART
248	poem for a "divorced" daughter	HORACE COLEMAN
258	Two Poems	DUFF BIGGER
259	Barbie	HAROLD WITT
260	Luz de Corral	CHARLES ITZIN
262	Cattails	GREG KUZMA
263	Girl Floating On Air	MARY CROW
264	Note In A Bottle	GERALD McCARTHY

Haiku by Richard Wright

In the falling snow
    A laughing boy holds out his palms
  Until they are white

    With a twitching nose
      A dog reads a telegram
    On a wet tree trunk

Standing in the field
    I hear the whispering of
  Snowflake to snowflake

    Make up your mind snail
      You are half inside your house
    And halfway out

I am nobody
    A red sinking autumn sun
  Took my name away

Calligraphy by Lloyd J. Reynolds

Editorial

When we designed *New Letters* in 1971, I turned to Lloyd J. Reynolds, calligrapher, teacher, and poet, for our logo and main titles because I had for years admired his work and everything he stood for, and I wanted the magazine to reflect that feeling. Lloyd had a Zen outlook, and his calligraphy hinted of a better world than that bespoken by the smokestacks of the industrial revolution—a world of subtle balance and harmony. All Lloyd J. Reynolds' work had grown out of a deep and abiding interest in human creativity, ecology, and peace. And though I wanted our magazine to avoid soapbox oratory and art that is too shrill, I did not want us to be a part of a widespread mockery of serious concern with the world's fate. Lloyd admired the Arts and Crafts movement, which encouraged everyone to anchor his own life as an example of concern for the world: lifestyle and aesthetic choice are always political expressions, as are sneers and smiles. We too wanted to smile, encourage, endorse the best in everyone. If we sometimes got bogged down in chores and sometimes were discouraged by the multitude of problems facing publishers today, especially those with shoestring support, we will no doubt be forgiven by those who know of those problems or have shared them in their own creative endeavors.

The purpose of a magazine is to bring the best work to the best audience. We have tried to do that, and have also turned to National Public Radio, with our radio edition, New Letters On The Air, to extend that audience, to reach listeners who might be less informed about the literary scene but are nevertheless open and responsive to poetry, stories, and statements that seem relevant to their lives. We have been touched when a listener has discovered a poet while driving across Nebraska or pausing amidst housework. We value readers and listeners alike, as well as the poets, musicians, fiction writers, photographers and graphic artists who provide work worthy of attention. Of course we confess a special fondness for those who help keep our efforts alive in an age when all arts organizations must beg for patronage.

During these years of publication as a quarterly magazine, special issues of *New Letters,* or collections of material from several issues, have been published subsequently as books. Such volumes include: *Richard Wright: Impressions and Perspectives* (University of Michigan Press); *Two Novels* by Natalie L. M. Petesch, which was retitled *Seasons Such As These* (Swallow Press), *From A to Z: 200 Contemporary American Poets; Collected Poems of E. L. Mayo*; *India: An Anthology of Contemporary Writing,* and the two retrospective anthologies, *New Letters Reader I* and *Reader II* (all from Ohio University Press). We hope these book editions will give this varied and excellent work longer life on the shelves of homes and libraries.

Lloyd J. Reynolds taught children to write Zen poems, "weathergrams," calligraphy on strips of grocery sack. Then they tied the poems to trees in the forests to await the thaw that would bring new readers. And that is what we have attempted with *New Letters.* If such acts seem frivolous in a year when our tax dollars are used to 'encourage democracy and prosperity' by gunning down doubting peasants, if our billions of dollars can buy helicopters and the bullets that sprout from their bay gunneries, yet fill no belly, build no school, cure no tumor, curtail no population explosion save by summary execution, then we can only grieve and feel the guilt and inadequacy we know to be widely shared. And yet we feel that medieval monks and philosophers in retreat have served history perhaps as well as its heroes; they at least, along with poets and musicians and, yes, clowns and dancers, have vividly enunciated the need for a better world. They built no bombs. And when television came along they did not allow themselves to be trotted out for the talk shows to lie on cue. In 1984, with Doublethink the strange logic of our time, there are many who praise those of our dependants who murder fewer this month than last. No doubt it is easier to lie to faceless multitudes than to a single friend or reader.

Art speaks of these realities, with understatement to be sure. But who could bear the truth unedited?

We feel fortunate to have survived to Orwell's long-dreaded year (I first read his most famous novel when the last two digits of its title were reversed), and we are aware that a baker's dozen years add up to a ripe old age for a little magazine. We cannot, as E. M. Cioran put it, speaking of the ambition of artists and philosophers, "sow Doubt into the entrails of the globe . . . " nor keep "the multitude from wallowing in the compost heap of certitudes." That would be a big order indeed for a little magazine, with its small community of volunteers and its editor assailed with his own doubts. But neither have we been, we hope to say, a part of the lamentable certitude which makes the work of the writer and artist even more difficult than their labors to harness the creativity within.

—DAVID RAY
University of Missouri—Kansas City, 1984

*A fame
that is to last
a thousand years
will rise after
an unappreciated life
is past*

TU FU

The Sheller

E. M. Broner

It is feeding time for the gulls, sandpipers and pelicans. A man in tan shorts whose pressed hem has become unpressed throws bread to the gulls. The sandpipers walk daintily into the surf, pecking momentary holes in the sand. Pelicans diving for fish are long under water.

She walks the beach, does Mrs. Calumet. From heel to toe shells are crunched, her soles scratched by gastropods. The Florida Cerith, a miniature Siamese tower, drills into her heel. The slipper shells collect between her toes. She picks up a red-veined slipper, turns it over, sees the pearly half-ledge, discards it, thinking someone else's heavy tread broke the other half of the ledge. It is not Mrs. Calumet's first mistake.

No letters arrive, along with the Key news. No phone calls vibrate. At her window Australian pines drop their cones. An albino cat mews to be let in, becomes frantic to go out again. From her window a blue heron perches on the wooden pilings.

She forgot to put the sand dollars into the sun. They are on the coffee table, like uncut cooky dough, with their five petals and five slashes cut into the off-white uneven circle. They are molding. Green almost obliterates the daisy-shape. The green speckles, like poppy-seed, the slight hump of the animal. It is offensive to her to see that spreading mold. She turns it over.

The shapes are inclusive on the flat back, like claws, fronds, like clusters of leaves. They remain upside-down on her coffee table.

All is upside down—the diving birds, the sand dollars and her day. For the sun is too hot to sun in, she discovered, lying on the sand, the sugary-white sand, that first day of arrival and burning her eyelids so that she had to wear sunglasses for a week. She looked puffy-lidded and Oriental, but then, when the puffiness went down, the lids shriveled and she became older like these leathery retirees around her.

So she covers herself tightly in the sun, with a green overpriced cotton hat from the shopping center near Sarasota.

If she shells, she stoops, rising suddenly, and far down on the public beach she thinks she sees green, moving slowly towards her, expanding brightly, her own light-green hat, walking on a stick, on branches of legs. There are no eyes under the hat. The mouth is smiling; no, sneering.

There is another green hat tickling, like a blade of grass at the back of her neck. Years ago. A green paper crown cut out of bunting. Under it straggles a green-dyed mop, the strands separating over the shoulder, curling on a nylon curtain, dyed light green, over a green dress, whose cap sleeve is visible as is the pinkish arm through the gossamer curtain. The hands are folded on the lap. The pink lips—is it the color film, too brownish?—are slightly separated and the light sparkles on a bit of a tooth. What has come into her head with the shimmering green queen? Is it Halloween? A St. Patrick's Day affair?

She stumbles over spiny shells, spiky shells, abalone fish scales, shells stuck inside of other shells until she is at her own efficiency apartment with its indoor-outdoor green carpeting (for grass in winter climates, for grass in sandy ones). She pulls the drape cord against the sun and the aquamarine Gulf, purple further out where the sandy bottom is not visible.

She glues scallop shells to driftwood.

"Elmer's Glue," said the crackly voices at the art club. "That makes it really stick."

They glue their shells and sell each other their own arrangements.

Mrs. Calumet glues a white scallop shell with its fin-like projections next to a red-ribbed scallop shell. The coloring is fading from the red shell as the shell dries, so Mrs. Calumet sprinkles water on the shell and bluish-grey appears under the red. She fancies selling the shells with a circulating spray, a pump that will wet them and keep their sea color. The two shells, white and the damp bluish-grey under red, are turned sideways, facing the center. There, slightly elevated, is the most beautiful scallop of the beach—a sherbety peach with white edges and projections like whiskers.

The room darkens, a squall storm coming up. Rain—and more of her shells drying outside!

A storm is at another cottage. She reads, in a lettered rather than scripted hand: "You always hear seagulls and boats' horns and a little repair work on the docks in the morning. Right now the foghorn is booming every few seconds:
B-o-o-o-o-o-om
  B-o-o-o-o-o-om
    B-o-o-o-o-om
      B-o-o-o-om

"Pardon me, but due to an unquiet rest last night, the author of these reminiscences has just fallen asleep. Therefore, in the author's stead, I bring this odyssey to a close. Fin."

The same cabin, some years before "the author" could write, could only print, could only print capital letters, Mrs. Calumet had a record of THE WEEPING WILLOW, THE SEAGULLS, THE PRETTY CLOUDS, THE DARK ROOM.

THE WEEPING WILLOW rested on tall grass, crayoned red-green-yellow-blue-green. The trunk was shaped like an ice-cream cone and colored black-brown. The willow leaves were each a separate color, red-yellow-black-green, alternating. THE SEAGULLS were plants of gulls with wings like leaves, with head and beak of flowers. THE PRETTY CLOUDS was more conventional, with purple - aquamarine - green - yellow - black crayoned clouds above. In the same order of color, flowers sprouted below. THE DARK ROOM had red dark walls, dark blue drapes, purple rug, dark green lamp, brown lamp cord, huge brown electric outlet. Although Mrs. Calumet has now opened her drapes, in the light of the squall it is still THE DARK ROOM.

To the tune of "Swanee River," ("The home of Stephen Foster," said the billboards on her way from New York to Florida), the oldies had sung: "Now we are gathered for Barney Greenstone, who's sixty-three."

He was also the baby of the group, a bouncy, overweight baby boy. They cuddled him, treasured him, would have glued him on driftwood to set their own memories of ten, twenty years before. He was also the only Jew on Dolphin Key, wide-spaced teeth, mustache, aggressive stomach and all. He aggressed towards Mrs. Calumet and said, with hairy mouth, aerated teeth, "We are well-met/ Mrs. Calumet."

He invited her into the pool of his condominium. But he was so busy greeting people at both the shallow and deep ends of this small pool, and introducing her, that she had no chance to swim. Mr. Greenstone is very social.

He called to take her to Marina Jack's. They will view the sunset from that ideal spot, but he has been busy greeting people before he picks her up and they miss the sunset, park too far from the restaurant and have a several-block walk. They do have a table overlooking the water, but no streaked sky or dramatic sun. It is better when twin lights go on above and then shimmering into the water. It is better when the green turtle soup arrives. It is not better when Barney talks about his *netsuke*. It is not better when he drives her back to his condominium to show them to her, Japanese toggles, behind an ornate glass case, each dwarfed, humped, gargoyle, each scowling big-headed miniature, each peasant carrying miniature fruit or a miniature baby. It is not better when Barney reads her their papers from Japan, the history of each one and of the man who carved them. He goes to get her a glass of wine. Mrs. Calumet is fast asleep on his couch, not leaning or stretching out, but sitting stiffly, head erect and snoring.

The jingle shells around her jingle. They are common in these warm waters. She holds them in her palm, a monochromatic study from pearly white, mottled middle-bluish grey to dark grey, about or less than an inch, none regular, no flat or smooth circles. She has collected ten earred-ark shells, heavy, clumsy, thickish things, strongly ribbed, irregularly marked, a sudden rich black around the edge or to one side—splattered on, like tar. The earred ark is less clumsy upside down with its fluted, toothed hinge line.

Those smooth ears of shells. The sun through the baby's ear, a red sun for the baby has a port-wine stain, "Nothing serious, just not cosmetic," and, when her hair finally grows, she never allows her ears to show.

The squall storm is over. Light mottles on the front ground of Australian pines, cleaning their own grounds with their fir needles. The sun mottles in her eye, and there is the baby by that flecked light, ears projecting, eyes squinting, green gingham dress faded in the snapshot, green rattle faded in her mouth, the background, over the edge of the yellow-lined carriages, is splotches of greens and yellows and not recognizable.

The baby stretching on the couch. 1952. "How big? Soooo big!" The baby, not yet strong enough to sit alone, leans over the balancing weight of her buddha stomach and thickly diapered bottom. She has fallen backwards in the yellow-lined carriage. Her mouth is spread, her ears are spread, her hands hug each other. The belly button winks and all holes of cheek, elbow and knee dimple.

That was when Mrs. Calumet had gained too much weight. She is in red jeans, red-checkered shirt, her thick hair fastened back so she won't loose it on baby, her legs filling the jean pants, her hips filling the pockets, her breasts, milk-filled, stuffing the red-gingham shirt. She has fatty pouches under her cheeks, although a young woman then.

In a black-and-white picture she has her red shawl over one shoulder; it is dark grey in the picture. Her hair is very black, pinned in place, for she is nursing. There is the soft black of new baby's hair against her hand; there is the receiving blanket which is white, there is the black cord of watchband against the wrist, the white sparkling face of watch, the lipstick 1950's red, a beauty mark on her left cheek which could be black, brown or red; there is the Macy's plaid pull-out couch losing a button. There is the infant's fist lost on the hill of the breast; there is the nipple, a circle around the mouth. No one is reading the time on the watch. *He* has long since disliked both faces—that of time and her own. The baby was born on St. Valentine's Day and the nurses passed out heart-shaped cookies.

She has a two-burner efficiency kitchen behind the blinds and reaches over her head to the shelves for a plate. She bought cheese and fruit at the supermarket but the cheese is sweating and the fruit is molding. She is still fighting those fatty pouches under her cheeks. There is a scramble, on her hand, a leap, a scream. Who screamed? It could not have been that big South American cockroach that screamed. She chases it with a wet beach towel, slams it, kills it over again and again. It was killed but she could not let it go, not the tiniest quiver of the legs, the antennae, the wings. It is curled and small when she flushes it down the toilet.

Barney's car drives up and he laughs at her breathless account of the hunt and the bagged game. He will take her to the Ringling Museum. It is still hot out. She puts on her green sun hat, a towel dress in greens and blues that she has worn every summer for ten years. She needs no bra for her breasts have not been milk-filled in many years.

"I can't identify everything," she tells Barney. He can, for, with his condominium, he purchased *Golden Nature Guide*, 475 Marine Subjects in Full Color.

She can identify people along the beach. They are, besides the oldies, a few grandchildren, bikini'd, golden rather than leathered, and, surprisingly, there are the Amish, bonneted, bearded, suspendered, sitting near the hot-dog stand picnic tables in the hot sun. Do the Amish, through their beards and bonnet crowns, look at the smooth flesh of the bathers? Do those old men with white shirts and black pants see a colorful world beyond them, under the palms, away from the garish red of hotdogs, the falsely-colored orange drink? Do they see that world of blue, green, brown of eye, pink of lips, curve of hips? Mrs. Calumet's cheek.

Mrs. Calumet's cheek is to be scratched. On the day of the visit. It is to be a thin red vein of a scratch as on the slipper shells; it is to be a thin rib of blood along her shell of cheek. The nail will catch her cheek, the bitten, jagged nail so that the mark on the cheek will not be a straight line, but a dot-dashed one where the nail is or is bitten away. Mrs. Calumet's face will have the scowl of Barney's *netsuke*. In a broken whirl, in sun that seems to glare from bits of mirror, Mrs. Calumet will strike back at the attacker and catch the corner of an eye with her own sharp, mist-pink nailpolish, and will pull that eye Oriental.

Barney turns into the hot sun of the Ringling Museum. They walk through a transplanted Roman villa, gauche not grand, into the art gallery. Circus-like paintings, crowd-catching biblical scenes are playing. A particular repeated theme is Judith with the Head of Holofernes. There are large paintings of Rubens' bulging bodies from his body factory. There are those three rings of biblical scenes, everything visible from the top of the bleachers. There is Barney, stomach bouncing, hairs of mustache blowing as he explains, as he explains. Mrs. Calumet becomes thirsty and irritable.

"I can't write, I can't speak," said the loose-leaf sheet which Mrs. Calumet found after the first disappearance. "I no longer think. Feeling and pictures have taken over. Now Mrs. Kennedy is pregnant with an eleventh child and there are the constant assassinations, assassinations as common as births. I cry & mother weeps, tears falling on my head in her lap. I don't understand and therefore no words, no logical, comprehending words come to calm me. I am 16 & it is unfair that people at 16 must think about the country's fate, must experience the pain. ('Damnit,' says my friend Joel after I say, 'We don't get to miss school; all that for nothing.')

"Come, Hades, give me a taste of your medicine. Cure me of the life force. And last week at Chris' I tried your medicine, powerful Hades. And mother found me and laughed and screamed,

'You are sick. If I had the money I'd put you in an institution,' and I, in my pain, hear her laughing scream, and she slaps me to show me how much she loves me, and the doctor on the radio tells of slapping Kennedy to hear a heart beat and the pulse, and he hands the stethescope to Mrs. Kennedy to listen."

Barney goes into the carpentry shop to buy Mrs. Calumet a Coke. There is a box for dimes on top of the refrigerator. He helps himself, puts in his dimes and carries out the bottles. The guard stops him, so they drink the Cokes in the carpentry shop.

They drive back, Barney one-handed, holding the hand of Mrs. Calumet. The waves are high and there are the high-pitched cries of the sandpipers. Barney parks the car at her rented efficiency and walks with her along the beach. Waves implode, a dull thud as of thunder. Later they slam against the groins that jut out from each beach home, the pilings recently built to stop the loss of the beach.

"That's $40,000 worth of pilings," says Barney. "I don't know if the Gulf takes away more than it gives."

Shells are piled against each wooden beach barrier. There are the most delicate fingernail pink of shells, spirals of shells, jellyfish shimmering on the sand. When the sea recedes the shells are left behind like buttons on a mattress. Black-headed gulls stand on the water's edge. Barney and Mrs. Calumet find the brackish smell of tar on their sandals. She will not let Barney come into the apartment for he has tar between his toes. They stretch out on the steps and wiggle their toes at each other. In the greening evening, their toes are like seaweed.

Mrs. Calumet remarks on the Spanish moss on a neighbor's trees.

"Like lace shawls," says Mrs. Calumet.

"Like cannibals," says Barney. "They eat up the trees."

Moon shells are drying on the stoop, each a carnivore that had engulfed and smothered other shellfish. Barney studies them with his porpoise eyes, and there is the Shark Eye staring back at him.

Mrs. Calumet is proudest of her Florida Fighting Conches

with their pagoda tops, the orange, golden, purple, pearly interiors. She has found a West Indian Fighting Conch, also. Barney wants her to return with him to the condominium.

"Not *netsuke*," he promises, "I have the largest conches in the Crafts Club, twelve-inch Queen Conches, fourteen-inch Emperor Helmets. I have Giant Tuns. Fig Shells."

As she sits there, she again becomes sleepy and yawns. He is hurt and puts on his sandals. She is yawning too hard to apologize, but does wave as he drives away.

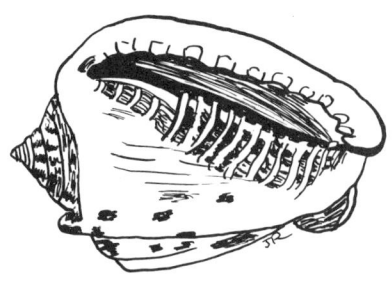

"NO THING UNITES US," said the outside of the airmail envelope, still capitals, no matter where or when the voyage overseas. But why write to say that? The yawning brought tears to Mrs. Calumet. The daughter had written to say more, a visit was pending, impending, rending.

Mrs. Calumet kept several ugly yet fascinating shells. One huge thing had barnacles all over it. One was a thick corroded white oyster shell. There was sand cementing small shells together. She kept a piece of sponge. And she kept letters, those corrosive letters.

"Was in Hawaii. Pretty uptight."

From some country whose postmark was obliterated: "There's a cat on my lap listening. The light is dim after/before the rain. One auburn cow in all this green. Super sonic crickets. Ducks birds sounding well. Everything that's still appears to be moving."

Months later, another card: "One day a person entered a room feeling confused. I am nowhere. What can I do? A person answered saying when one is nowhere there is nothing to say and nothing to confuse. One is nowhere."

Another card. From Hungary? The Soviet Union? "Honesty is emptiness."

The daughter, like her father, had seen the face of time and thought it her mother's own face, and had fled them both.

Those oldies on the Key fled too, never speaking to a young one. Even their leases, Barney had told her, banned children under fifteen years of age. The few long hairs they saw hitched down on their way to Ft Lauderdale or were coming for a bit of warmth down a little ways from Atlanta. The old drivers would grip the wheels of their cars the tighter, not to suddenly swerve upon them. They only trusted, in this Dolphin Key, those dolphins that leapt by in schools early mornings or the blue heron, cormorants, pelicans and gulls. They put these symbols on the doors of their houses, metal arching gulls, wrought-iron ships, tarpoons and dolphins.

The next morning Barney is by.

"Breakfast?" he asks.

"I have strawberries," she says, "cantaloupe, eggs."

"No," says Barney, "waffles, bacon, sausages." He smiles. It is a joyous thought, all that forbidden food, as were the clams and lobsters from Marina Jack's.

They drove to a Howard Johnson in Tampa. A few young traveling families were seated, one child asleep with his head on his mother's lap.

Mrs. Calumet had brought down a few books with her. She had, in effect, moved. Not too many books because even when the package was marked Books they were expensive to ship. She took her photo albums, under Books, also. There at the beginning of the imitation-leather album with golden tooling are her spread arms, her black velveteen, sleeveless blouse, her hair that looks like black velveteen, her light Northern skin, white flared shirt with large black polka-dots. On one knee is her daughter's head, her daughter's arms hugging that knee, the little girl's black hair a little bluer than the sleeveless black velveteen blouse that is its backdrop, the mouth closed but upturned, the eyes soft, the ears protruding, the port-wine stain almost as red as the red knee socks. Mother and daughter are kneeling in the grass.

When had the sad pictures begun? The portents? The one with the red-knitted hat that fastened under the chin, the red knitted sweater with large white pearl buttons, where she is seated on a furry pony and the pony's face, under its harness, is worried, not knowing who is on the saddle, on its velveteen red blanket with silver stars? The little girl is clutching her own hands rather than the reins. Her face is almost serious enough to be grim. Or the picture in front of that screened-in cabin by the lake, long ago? The wind is blowing. The mother's hair is piled in curls on top of her head, in an old-fashioned style. The daughter's hair has loosened from the pony tail. She is holding something, a tube? A game? Mrs. Calumet thinks it might be a frozen ice-cream drumstick. The mouth is twisted—worry? The sun in her eyes? Or just eating the drumstick? Mrs. Calumet cannot remember. Or there is the girl, younger still, on a park bench. A friend, a boy friend of Mrs. Calumet, took the photo. Mrs. Calumet is in the background: a tiny part of her rounded cheek, slender nose, a bit of her red-lipsticked smiling mouth, three or four upper teeth. In front of Mrs. Calumet's head is her daughter's, eye large and round with worry or fear or resentment of the photographer. Her brows are knitted. The mouth is definitely in pain, the hair in need of combing. The dress is neatly ironed, the press marks showing on the cap sleeve.

In a photo when she was about six the front upper teeth are missing. Is that smile gay or impish or malicious? Mrs. Calumet never knew, would never know.

At the Howard Johnson more than menus, waffles, sausages, coffee, pats of butter, encapsulated marmalade, were the old people. Seated were a round-bellied, jowled man, bulldog face, and his prune-faced wife. With the wife everything tightened to a scrunch, with him everything was loosened.

Another old man was tight-faced, a stretched-skinned man with cheekbones cutting through the skin. Out of the window a barrel of an old man with tiny feet went skimming along the sidewalk.

They had heard two couples talking in the lobby, while they awaited their table.

"You can't trust California for the earthquakes," said one old man, it didn't matter which couple.

"You can't trust Florida for the sudden freeze," said the other old man.

"Trust Arizona," said an old lady holding her purse handles. "It cools down at night in Arizona and you can sleep."

They all agreed.

"Looking all over," they said, "for a place to sleep."

Barney is listening, amused.

"Nobody dies in Florida," he tells Mrs. Calumet.

Mrs. Calumet will look down into the water. It will be clear. She will see depressions under her eyes. She will see the skin around her eye, left eye, is becoming cracked like mud. Too much sun? She will see several chins, or is it a slight hanging of skin under the chin? And a slight, light growth of colorless hair on the chin that she will not be able to see in the dark efficiency apartment and, therefore, cannot pluck. Her forehead will be drying and lining. Her bathing cap will be pulled off and hurled away. Her hair will be pulled down towards the water. Her mouth will be open above the water, stretched so wide the loose skin of the chin is taut. Soon her upper teeth will be covered by her upper lip as she will sink towards the water.

Barney has a surprise for her. A pen shell, a huge gross ugly thing that he unwraps for her at the Howard Johnson table. It's almost a foot long, rough-shelled, fragile, but, inside, shines as if it were oil in sunlight, with glowing golds, bluish greens, purplish blues and silver.

"I have another," Barney says, "Even larger. You're not depriving me of anything. Take it."

But does she want it?

"Do you want to watercolor with me on one of the other Keys?"

"I don't have paint or paper."

"You know me, old Barney from DIT?"

"I know MIT. What's DIT?"

"Detroit Institute of Technology."

"How do I know you?"

"You know me well enough so that it will come as no surprise after we pay the bill, leave the fifteen percent, that I came prepared with paper and watercolor paints."

They paint at the beach. She paints the froth of waves left against the groins of pilings, froth meringue, chiffon-jello. She paints the shells spilled to one side, the twinkling froth, sinking into the shell pile. She paints chips of shells, holes in bells. She paints brown seaweed, light-green sea lettuce clinging like thin rubber.

He paints a little boy with a fishing pole, a little Black boy with a pail of worms, leaning over the bridge connecting the Keys. He paints the boats moored there. He paints an Amish man sitting on a rocking chair on the bridge.

There is a sudden bark. She drops her brush into the sand.

"Did my dog scare you?" asks the passing man. "She's exuberant this morning."

Her leg is bitten in a few minutes, the mean bite of a red ant.

He takes her to a cocktail party given at the Crafts Club. She is a new neighbor, maybe a permanent one, and he is her escort. The drinks are too strong. The men all look and sound like W. C. Fields to Mrs. Calumet. The women are like sandkeeping machines, sweeping their men, flattening the whitening hair, tying their ties, dampening their faces, keeping their men in working order.

The men, freed of work, become like the lives their women

have always had to lead, frivolous, useless, full of crafts but not crafty, filling the time with the body its own floating rubber tube in the condominium pool, changing clothes several times a day for changing social events.

No one hears the news or talks of it. No one reads the paper, or talks of it, except for the listing of plays at the Ringling Museum, of movies in Tampa or Sarasota, of religious services or visiting dignitaries to their Keys.

They discuss shelling with Mrs. Calumet, who is on vacation — looking for employment, preferably in the area, preferably in office management. Only one man in the group works and he has to pay for it by missing the boating excursions, the craft classes and the cocktail parties or swims in the heated pool.

They are proud that Mrs. Calumet has gathered a fairly rare gastropod, an olive shell with unusual markings, for the shell had cracked and repaired itself. The shell, which she carries in her purse for luck, is passed about.

Mrs. Calumet's hand will press down on the hair that is floating like seaweed, and, that, through the greenish water, is brown, not blue-black. Under water the strands separate as the strands of that St. Patrick's Day mop. Mrs. Calumet will press down more. Bubbles will appear, and Mrs. Calumet will move her legs away from the scratching hands, the kicking legs. Mrs. Calumet will punch at the opened brown eyes, the gasping mouth, the stalk of neck. Mrs. Calumet's hand and face will become tired. The lines along her cheek will groove more deeply, the mouth will turn downwards in strain.

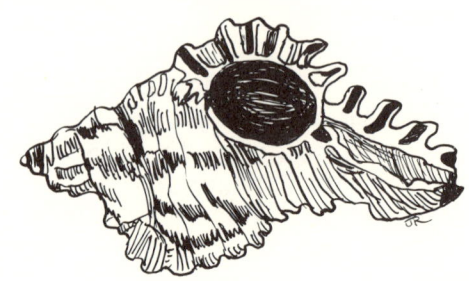

One of the red-swollen-nosed gentlemen of the Crafts Club is speaking to her.

"Your name's been bandied about, yes indeed, bandiieeeed about."

Mrs. Calumet is flattered. In this world she is twenty years younger than Barney, the baby.

"Come here, youngster," says Barney.

She is his exhibit, his seashell on driftwood, his enameled copper earrings and cufflinks that he exhibits in the Crafts Members Gift Shop.

Mrs. Calumet will shell, walking as she always does, head down, early mornings or early evenings. She is becoming acquisitive and annoyed at another sheller's turkey wing or lovely pinkish tellin.

As she will walk head down, there will be an obstinate shadow before her that will not move. She will step to one side; so will the shadow. She will look up into the eyes of a shadowed green sun hat, a bikini, a sneering smile, a daughter.

"I wondered where . . . I wondered when . . . " says the mother.

"No where," says the daughter.

"Have you eaten?" asks the mother.

"Same mother," says the daughter.

"Same daughter?" asks the mother.

They go into the efficiency. The daughter is a vegetarian so never mind the tuna or lamb chops. Now somebody to share the fruit, the soft avocado, somebody for a green salad. She wishes the daughter would wash up, comb her hair, her lustreless, not blue-black hair. She wishes her daughter would take off the mother's green sun hat.

The mother rinses her hands, standing on the indoor-outdoor carpeting that extends from the wall kitchen into the bathroom.

Once there was a pink birthday plastic comb with a pink-framed mirror and a pink bow in the daughter's hair. The pink comb combed the black bangs. The eyes were looking at the mirror, the collar was frilled and fading into the neck. What color was that collar, that dress? The mouth was opened in concentration, almost a smile at the mirror.

The mother can hear the Gulf, regular, splashing against the piles. They eat the salad, the fruit. The daughter laughs.
"I'm into meat again," she says.
"I can't please you," says the mother.
"That's right," says the daughter.
The night is full of: "Which of us is the kid? Are you afraid? Who's your boyfriend this time? One of the oldies? One of the soft-bellied Santa Claus oldies? What worries you — my power or lack of it?"
Who is talking? Mrs. Calumet cannot always tell.

Once she had read in a datebook, when she was wondering about the where and wherefore of her daughter, in a degenerating scrawl of a hand: "I love you, I think, love me, if you do, I want to protect and shelter you from anything that might hurt you, disrupt your thoughts."
The mother was profoundly moved, but never learned to whom the letter was addressed.
"You gave up my love and pretended that fifteen-year-old chicks are incapable of love, you ass, you cruel bastard, bastard, you weak selfish coward, and I still love you."

"I still love you," Mrs. Calumet says to her daughter.
All the pain in the drawers of her bedroom, all that pain that groaned with the opened drawer, the pain of the notebooks, filled with drawings of drawn women. Later, from another land, the drawings are crying, the eyes have tears but the tears have become hearts, pearls, seashells. The drawings are in a lovely, hand-bound book (bound by her nowhere-bound daughter) from India. They are on soft paper and the ink of the Indian fantasies has spread slightly.

There will be a bite under water, the mouth will turn on the mother's arm and bite it until the hand lets go of the hair. The daughter will slowly ascend to the surface, floating upwards, while the mother will rub the tooth marks in her arm. Slowly, slowly the daughter will walk the water back to shore, back to the efficiency that housed a night of accusation. The daughter will pick up her mother's sun hat and put it on her wet hair.

The mother will be left, bereft. They had drowned each other first in tears and then had almost drowned each other. The daughter will leave wearing the mother's favorite towel dress and the mother's overpriced light-green sun hat. The daughter's thumbs will work the road. The oldies will pass her by until a Ft. Lauderdale (probably) bound, long-haired blond boy will stop. The mother will watch from behind the Australian pines, from behind the neighbor's trees being consumed by Spanish moss.

"Where to?" the boy will ask.

"Where ever," the daughter will say.

Last shot. Window down, daughter staring straight ahead to the bridge connecting Dolphin Key to the other Keys. The daughter's mouth will be widely smiling.

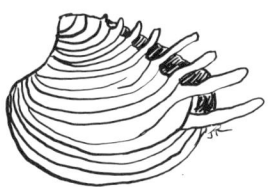

The mother is now a retiree. The mother is now an oldie.

"What *do* these young people want? What *do* they want?"

There is a shadow on her upper lip. The hairs there are darkening. Will her stomach thicken? Should she attach herself to Barney? Would two retireds be less tired? Would the sun be enough to make up for loss of life? Would she spend her time gardening, trying to grow rose bushes in this sandy, salty soil, leaving the bushes in planters and bringing them in every night? Would she mother those thorny bushes as she could never adequately protect from sand and wind her daughter?

Was intent to murder equal in the eyes of God to the commission of murder?

The insults, the vile insults, the slaps, the slaps returned, the punch, punch revisited, the flailing, kicking, scratching, uprooting of hair, ripping at cheeks, the attempts to destroy the photographs of face, in the water that left no footprints of place.

Mrs. Calumet is still at the road, staring past departure. Had she wheeled that yellow-lined carriage into the Gulf? Was she strangling that baby with her red scarf when she nurtured her? Was she pressing that face into her chest to keep the nose from breathing?

All of that happened in the moment of immersion. At that pushing down of the head, through the water, all albums were spilled, snapshots cracked. Ink ran from all letters, stamps loosened, envelopes opened. She has destroyed the present, but, much worse, the past.

Did some sea once surface her, crack her against pilings, shuck her, leave her with these other empty shells of people?

She will spend the rest of her time slapping the tiniest quiver of memory that appears, the tiniest feather, wing of thought she will crush, and, if necessary, crush again.

A car comes down the road. Mrs. Calumet's vision is blurred. It honks. Noisy Barney. Her green hat comes out of the car. Her green and blue towel dress comes walking towards her.

"No more assassinations," says the daughter.

Three Poems

WILLIAM STAFFORD

Friend Who Never Came

It has not been given me to have a friend
so steady the world becomes an incident
and all else leads us both to that event
when glances cross while two fates depend.
It has not been given. A life will end
somewhere at random, silent of rest, silent
that might have whispered another world and bent
this one around us. Here is my farewell, friend
who never came: There was a morning in June,
when I was young, and a family just from the farm
parked by our yard, not knowing what to do.
The daughter trembling lay—"Sunstroke last noon,"
they said. They soothed her, drove slowly on. The harm
had been in her eyes. They rolled, once—"I was for you."

Sometimes in the sun today I glimpse that world in the blue.

A Song of Widows and Orphans

I

Lincoln said, "Open hand"—
invaded the Sudetenland.
Wilderness, unfolding leaf—a charge
that fell toward Gettysburg

II

Along a hedge a bullet sang,
"Cold spring in Normandy."
A flute told a drum and a drum told
a bird, "War is the same all over the world."

The Spirit of '75

Far at the edge of our land—
"San Clemente" it's called—
beyond the monstrous cloud
above Los Angeles
(you can fly there by Golden West)
a crippled president stands
staring at the waves
and bearing the weight of a pardon.

Joseph is in the pit.
Mary, they have your son.
The ides of time have come—
   Erlichman, Haldeman.

We have tried to clear the scene.
Till early morning we talk—
where did it all go wrong?
In prisons all over the land
they wake up one by one:
"I meant to do right, always;
they led me, someone else led me."
   What have you done with my son?
   Erlichman? Haldeman?

Beyond that mushroom of smog
that hangs between the hills
above a most beautiful land,
and beyond that widest sea—
it couldn't be farther away—
where the crippled president stands,
they are starting up war again.
   What did you do with my sons,
   Erlichman, Haldeman?

I will climb a mountain and wait.
With little pieces of wood
I will keep a fire all night
and look in it till dawn.
Mitchell and Mardian,
Nixon, and all the rest—
and his wife looking at us—
I will hold it all till it clears
and I can look into eyes again,
    Erlichman, Haldeman.

Bones

Roger Pfingston

> " . . . the stony bone that can't be bribed,
> the sad bone that never gets any love . . . . "
>   Vicente Aleixandre
>   *(Translated by Lewis Hyde)*

Today, dear one, I attempt the impossible:
I'm going to love your bones,
I mean love your bones so they will know
that they've been loved, so your flesh
will simmer with jealousy, melt and merge
with your bones, be one with your bones
and know how cold your bones have been
without love. Are you ready? Can we do this?
It may not be easy, it may be that bones
remain without love for their own good,
it may be they can't withstand
the pressures of love, the infectious heat
of love, it may be that bones can only make it
with the hard mouth of Death. Nevertheless
today I'm going to love your bones,
beginning, of course, with your flesh . . .

The Gentlemen in the U-Boats

Sharon Olds

Yes, this is what they wanted—
to be underneath the surface of the sea
at night, in the blackness, green light of the
instruments glaring up at their chins,
gathering in the stubble on their jaws,
glittering over the curved mantle of their
eyeballs. This is the place. The smell is of
diesel oil, toilets, bilge, mildew,
sweat. It's a hundred and twenty degrees,
the black bread is white with fur,
they haven't been above water for days,
the lights are always burning, bilge-pumps whirring,
diesels throbbing, toilets overflowing,
they will probably be killed, and it is all worth it
to be here, now, in the depths, in the dark,
coming up in the path of a convoy—
sixty ships. Their pupils sharpen to
tiny points, like black dogs
running in circles faster and faster.
In the reek of feces, jism, bile,
their elegant hands hovering over the
levers, they rise and break the surface on a
starry night, the sea glistens,
there is nothing on their minds but beauty as they fire.

Merry Christmas!

Elder Olson

Santa Claus lies dead across the chair,
Shrunk to his elements—cap, suit, boots, and beard—
His swollen imposture ended, again exposed
As merely one more customary lie
Of all our numberless customary lies;
A myth I lent my substance; in itself
A dead thing that had never been alive;

Fitting saint of a false universe
Of false trees glittering with false fruits, false snow,
Of cozy uninhabitable pasteboard towns,
Paper bells, tin angels, plastic elves
—Tinselled pretence, mostly tomorrow's trash.
What? —Tell us cold is warm and dark is bright
When all about us, in the freezing night—?

Pack him away. We make myths, they make us;
Mere images of human hopes and fears,
Having only such power upon us as we give them,
Yet having such power, such power—pack him away,
Saint Liar, Saint Hypocrite. Did I "make the children happy?"
Must we deceive, then, to bring happiness?
—Then happiness itself is a deceit.

How is it that creatures craving truth
Contrive these lies, live these lies, at last
Are lived by these lies? Must such lies be told
Because the truth is more than we can bear?
O all our history, all our history!
O intolerable last error of Oedipus:
Better be blind than see what we must see.

Two Poems

JOSEPH BRUCHAC

City Wind
. . . a bear song

The sign of one feather
means power
But in this wind
drawn through city streets
thin thread
through a steel needle
only a wisp of smoke
& the ash from an incinerator
drifts down to touch my forehead...

And I dream the dance
of buffalo hooves,
of wingbeats
that can shatter stone.

Rembrandt: Two Self Portraits

I. (1637)

At thirty-one, he wore
an earring of silver,
his cap was black,
his lips half pursed
as if to belie
the feelings in those eyes.
About his neck
there was a jewel,
his hands could not be seen.

II. (1660)

At fifty-four
all jewels were gone,
the jaunty cap
replaced by one
sagging and pale
as his own face.
his lips, less set,
seem ready for a sigh
and in his hands
the pallette and brushes
with which he saw
himself at last.

Studies From Life

MARTHA DICKEY

I'm looking through the paintings of Arthur Dove
his storms
the idea of storms
as seen from storm's eye.
Storms he knew, having left his family
for the woman he loved
to live with her in a small boat
on the ocean, the galley so low
they could not stand upright.
In winter when the storms got bad
they went inland to paint
the idea of storms.

Hardy Street

Stephen Dunning

We flew down hill on our Flexible Flyers,
Ned and me, aiming to skate
on Waverly Pond. Trying to leap-frog
Ned stuck his skate in my butt, drawing blood.

    Bawling, skates still on, my sled
    dragging behind, pathetic I climbed
    the long hill home. Ma was miffed:
    How could that happen? *Who* cut your corduroys?

Early that summer we learned to eat
baby cucumbers cool from dark earth.
We stripped them white with Scout knives,
swallowed them slippery right on the spot.

    The axles of our depression car
    rested on blocks. Two step treads
    led to the rumble seat. Them scaled
    I had castle, cockpit and fort.

I buried the nickle I got for lying
in front of the hedge on Hardy Street.
First day of school we dug that treasure,
Ned and me, and walked to Thompson's.

    I bought the Butterfinger, waxy,
    yellow and blue. I sized it true,
    scored its middle with my thumbnail,
    and broke it fair. Ned took picks.

All Fall I tugged at brown stockings, getting them
snug to my knickers. Ned managed long pants.
The crows came early, taking white branches;
skaters came late to the pond.

The Limits of the Town

Elizabeth Wray

No one taught you to keep moving.
You just did. Growing up on the Plains
where mobile homes prayed
deliverance from tornados every spring.
You just did. Like the paranoid brunette,
always packed for the next bus out,
knowing her hair was too dark
and her skin too pale to hold up
to the exotic murders of LA. And anyway,
the mean-mouthed detective would testify
to all the one night mistakes she'd ever made.

You get used to it after awhile.
You learn to say a room's a room.
You buy furniture that folds into boxes with your books
and instructions for shipping out.
The thing about belonging's
there's no such thing.

You learn to see what bothers every town.
You read the faces that avoid your own, intense streets
that run one way and out. What disperses
every crowd wears some vague uniform
nobody notices.
                    Back in your room
you hear a creak, a rustling, another.
You tell yourself it's the trees, it's your neighbors
passing in the hall.
                    On your way out
an arm folds into yours like it belongs.
You don't look. So much has tried to claim you.
You walk faster. You pass the limits
of the town and breathe relief.
Every town is occupied, you say.
What walks in time with you tightens its **grip**.

Ultima Thule Hotel

George Hitchcock

philodendrons rotting the carpet
the bellman picking his nose

in the lobby elephant-ears
in the powder-room no pets

no women no guests after ten p.m.
cooking in rooms is forbidden

considerations of health prohibit
random expectoration

the armchairs are spavined
the desk clerk pours corrosive

sublimate in every bathtub
the awnings rot the corridors reek

of gin and garlic the tenants
rattle in their cells like dry beans

in a gourd yet the rooms are all full
reservations won't be honored

book early or don't come at all
this is the end this is Armageddon

in leatherette the party favors
have exploded your number is up

your credit card lies dead
under an egg-stained napkin

The Executive Touch

A Story By

James B. Hall

ALLIED HIDE & SPECIALTY CO., INC.
1 TANNERY ROW
PENNINGTON, ILLINOIS

20 March 1972

(Mrs.) Barbara Blakey
2223 Country View Terrace
Pennington, Illinois

My Dear Barbara:

    This letter conveys my heartfelt condolences to you, to Ed's immediate family in California, and to your boys who probably do not fully understand all that has happened. Enclosed, also, are three checks which pertain to your late husband's all too tragic severance from ALLIED H + S.

    First, Barbara, I want you to know all of us felt the funeral ceremonies were exactly right: dignified, tasteful, well managed. The large, non-Company "town" attendance confirmed Ed's value to our little community. I, myself, had not fully realized the extent of his personal involvement: Indian Guides, Little League, and no less than three Pennington service clubs, including Rotary of which he was past-president. These organizations will miss Ed Blakey's cheerful, affirmative presence. To me, Ed's "outside" interests again underscored the vital role of our company executives in bringing forth good community relations. In Pennington, this was not always the case. Also, I hope you think one big AH + S "All-Employees" blanket of carnations entirely appropriate and not an hour passes that I do not ask the searching question, "How shall AH + S ever replace our good soldier Ed Blakey?"

Why our Lockheed "Lodestar" crashed in West Virginia only a few miles from our newest tannery remains a mystery. The government team and our more flexible Flight-ops group under A. K. Carver are still investigating. No doubt the unexpected change in local, mountainous weather contributed. In any event, Barbara, AH + S maintenance work is always well in excess of minimum FAA standards. Those of us who also flew regularly in line of duty had the greatest confidence in both the Lockheed and her crew. Personally I doubt if the whole story will ever be known. Given the facts, I suppose we must accept the accident as one of life's necessary, tragic happenings.

The three checks enclosed are for you and your sons. The first check covers Ed's full month's salary (and allowances) even though the airplane crashed on 5th March. The second check of $15,000.00 will come as a pleasant surprise. Ed did not know it, but two years ago I contracted an "Accidental Death In Flight" program--at no cost to Company personnel. You and your family are beneficiaries of this company foresight. In addition, a third check of $4,000.00 is an administrative token of appreciation, a bonus for Ed's past services. My personal wish is that this amount be dedicated to the future education of your two sons. I hope you agree.

Meanwhile, I understand you will stay on in Pennington. I hope you will keep in touch. If problems arise, do not hesitate to call on me, just as though I were in fact a Godfather to Robbie and Mark. Oh yes, I nearly forgot to mention a minor item: two checks carry "Waiver Certificates" which are self-explanatory; our legal counsel routinely requires this sort of endorsement in all such cases.

            Very sincerely yours,

            J. KELLY JOHNS
            President, and General Manager

Blind Carbon Copies to:
- Maurice Cohen, Finance
- Hack Bronson, Legal

ALLIED HIDE & SPECIALTY CO., INC.
1 TANNERY ROW
PENNINGTON, ILLINOIS

20 March 1972

(Mrs.) Gustave Lyons
R. F. D. Box 113
Millburgh, Illinois

Dear Mary:

It now being two weeks since the funeral I send my personal condolences. Enclosed find two (2) checks to cover your husband's terminal pay and allowances with AH + S for which he flew so many years.

I regret sincerely I could not attend Gus's funeral services at the United Methodist in Millburgh. Unfortunately, without consultation, Ed Blakey's services were scheduled here in Pennington at the same hour. I felt a prior obligation to accompany Mrs. Blakey and her two young boys to their father's funeral. I did, however, get out to Millburgh and personally left the Company's "All-Employees" spray of roses at the funeral home. Although less personal, I believe the closed-casket procedure was the best thing because all our men were pretty well bruised in the crash. In any event, I was with you at Millburgh in spirit.

The two checks enclosed are for you. The first check covers Gus's regular two-week pay period (and allowances) even though the airplane crashed on 5th March. The second check of $10,000.00 will come as a pleasant surprise. Gus did not know it, but two years ago I contracted an ADIF program--at no cost to company personnel. You are the beneficiary of this company foresight. I hope this little lift will provide additional financial security for you in the years ahead. Oh yes, I nearly forgot one minor item: the two checks carry "Waiver-Certificate" which are self-explanatory; our legal counsel routinely requires this sort of endorsement in all cases of termination.

As regards the probable causes of the crash, I can add nothing to what you have already read in the local newspaper. Company maintenance procedures are always well above minimum FAA requirements; unforeseen weather conditions all across Appalachia doubtless were a contributing factor. Probably we shall never know the precise truth.

In conclusion, I want you to know that all of us are going to miss Old Gus up there in the left seat of the Lodestar. He was a superb pilot; he knew the Lockheed well. Always cheerful, cooperative, and a fine man in every way, the Company will not soon find his replacement. Gus will be missed. I understand he was born and raised near Millburgh. I hope you think it fitting he should be laid to rest in the family plot.

Feel free to consult with me personally on any problems which may arise.

Sincerely yours,

J. KELLY JOHNS
President, and General Manager

bcc: Finance + Legal

ALLIED HIDE & SPECIALTY CO., INC.
1 TANNERY ROW
PENNINGTON, ILLINOIS

20 March 1972

(Mrs.) Ralph Shambrough
c/o Mr. Art Henderson, Apt. 12
5000 S.W. 59th Terracette
South Miama, Florida

Dear Mrs. Shambrough:

    This letter conveys my heartfelt personal condolences to you and to Ralph's immediate family. Also I enclose two checks.

    First, however, let me state that I agreed wholeheartedly with your decision to leave Pennington immediately after the funeral services. It was very considerate of Mr. Henderson, Ralph's old friend from cadet days, to bring his trailer to Illinois in order to move your household goods to his apartment in Miami. You are young. You will soon make a new life for yourself in--I confess-- a more interesting area than Pennington, Illinois.

    Although in his first civilian job, Ralph flew only a six-month probationary period for AH + S, he was well-liked, always cheerful, and showed great promise as a "Flying Executive." Although only twenty-eight years old, Ralph had excellent military (jet) experience and already had lived a full, exciting life. He brought a new military alertness and tone to our whole aircraft operation. He will be missed.

    The check enclosed is for you. The check covers Ralph's regular pay as of March 5. Included also is a Company-paid ADIF insurance check for $6,000.00, which will come as a pleasant surprise. You will note a self-explanatory "Waiver-of-Claims" certificate on the reverse of the check to be signed upon deposit.

    I hope these tokens of our appreciation for Ralph's past services help you across the rough spots ahead.

                                               Yours truly,

                                               J. KELLY JOHNS
                                   President, and General Manager

MEMORANDUM

C O N F I D E N T I A L

TO: Sheldon Thomas, Vice President, Personnel

Dear Shell--

   This Memorandum (CONFIDENTIAL) in part confirms our prior discussion as regards replacements for: 1) Ed Blakey; 2) the two Lodestar pilots.

   1. RE NEW SALES MANAGER:

   Now I don't want to imply anything bad about the deceased, but let's learn something from the facts. Namely, our new Sales Manager must:

   a. Must <u>know</u> all product lines from our twelve tanneries, through our finish-plants and right on to final customer satisfaction. Blakey didn't. That's why I kept putting his ass on our airplanes, to get him out of Pennington and <u>to our production centers</u>.

   b. Must show 101 percent loyalty to AH + S management. Blakey didn't. More than once I asked him directly how much <u>company time</u> his Indian Guides, Little League and/or Rotary was costing me. I won't bore you with his justifications; I state unequivocally that Ed Blakey lacked a sense of proportion.

   c. Must be <u>cost</u> and <u>profit</u> <u>conscious</u>. Blakey wasn't. I grant his figures always <u>looked</u> good but the sales-costs for his so-called "Incentive Program for Excellence" contributed more to his personal popularity in the field than it put pure cowhide profits on our ledgers. In short, all of us carried both him <u>and</u> his "incentive" concepts. He was lucky to be so well known in Pennington--which is a very, <u>very</u> small town.

   Finally, I want to see final interviews with young, aggressive, straight <u>men</u> who won't whine and bitch just because it's a weekend and the weather is a little sour over West Virginia. On practically every flight this past three months I practically ordered Blakey to get on the Lodestar. A man that won't fly anyplace at any time won't well. Anything.

   Looking ahead: we will recruit a replacement <u>outside</u> AH + S: <u>do not promote from within</u>. That way we would only get another Blakey, small-bore.

   As a matter of courtesy I will ask Mr. Oaker for his New York recommendations. He owns other industrial interests and he gets around in both production and merchandising circles. I attach my own list of possible replacements. You may want to contact any or all of them in a preliminary way. I already gave you my new lower salary range for the job. Fringe as negotiated, of course.

   Now: let's get our new man aboard in thirty (30) days. A good Jew who knows leather might be the ticket, but no Californians. Not again!

2. RE NEW PILOT REPLACEMENTS:

Pretty much accept Carver's recommendations on replacements. Again, we can learn something from the facts.

Gus was all right, but not much of an instrument pilot. He was Senior pilot because in the old days he walked out of the cornfield to fly a single-engine Fairchild for the previous company owners--well before my time. We paid him plenty for sloppy flying, a "know-it-all," taciturn attitude which some customers found not easy to take. And all of us were aware of his drinking habits. At the very least our new Senior must be able to say "Sir" to a potential buyer without making it a Supreme Court case re discrimination.

Looking ahead: we will promote from our present list, at an <u>appropriate salary savings</u> (commensurate with Carver's judgment). In addition, our new man should have the potential of Executive Leadership and the ability to take over from A. K. Carver, if it comes to that.

Re: Shambrough. No comment.

We might pick up a well-trained youngster who has been laid-off by United or TWA. If he's local to Pennington, so much the better. No more military types, please.

On balance, I see this terrible accident gives us a chance to restudy our basic concepts (and costs) of AH + S <u>versus</u> Utilization of Executive Aircraft.

Okay, let's crank it up.

Cordially,

J. K. J.

MEMORANDUM

CONFIDENTIAL and HAND DELIVER

TO: Maurice Cohen, Vice President, Finance

Dear Murray:

I dictate this at midnight, trying to clean up the mess of 5 March. Here are some suggestions and facts (CONFIDENTIAL and HAND DELIVER) on the financial aspects.

1. ACCIDENTAL DEATH IN-FLIGHT PROGRAM WITH EQUITY INDEMNITY (recap):

From prior conversations and Voucher Request Forms you know my decision on reimbursing next-of-kin was as follows:

```
Blakey  .. .. .. .. .. .. ..    $19,000.00
    NB: in two checks, one ostensibly for an "Education" program
Gus Lyons  .. .. .. .. .. ..     10,000.00
    NB: no minor children now alive
Shambrough .. .. .. .. .. ..      6,000.00
                                 ----------
    TOTAL                        $35,000.00
```

Since our specially negotiated contract with Equity Indemnity was to insure any and all (undesignated) company personnel aboard (maximum $250,000 per occurrence) at $40,000.00 per head, AH + S will collect $120,000.00, and no questions asked. Thus we take down a favorable balance on this item of $85,000.00

Murray, I hope there is some way you can reflect that amount as operating profit in the current year. I could use it for--as you know-- wholesale hide prices are killing us.

2. LOCKHEED "LODESTAR" N- 770 (recap):

I can be brief about that turkey: Legal confirms your suggestion of the revised depreciation concept. That's a break. Good work. On insurance, Legal advises we are free and clear on any so-called reimbursement at alleged "fair-market value." So we go for the whole amount, and no questions asked.

Our coverage also has a provision for on-board _added_ equipment. Since Gus burned it all on the side of a mountain, let's confirm that everything reasonable was "aboard." Two such items: first, A. K. Carver had purchased some fancy new radio navigational gear, but--as is increasingly usual with him--had not yet got the stuff installed in the Lockheed. Let's say all of it _was_ installed, even though you have to predate a Work Order if questioned. Since we will never buy another Lodestar, let's cash-out that specialized gear now. Secondly, let's claim Blakey took with him on that last trip quite a few of his fancy sales-promotion kits--which he may have, for all I know. AH + S has plenty of cowhides tied up in that fancy little project and I strongly suspect our replacement sales manager had damned well better have some fresh approaches to a great many things around here. So let's peddle a few of those kits to the insurance carrier. You handle it.

Looking ahead: I have had two opinions about our Operations (Aircraft): first, the Lockheed was about all Gus could handle. Therefore Carver allowed the sub-qualifications of one man to hinder a necessary company upgrading of our total flight Operation. Furthermore, we have been disappointed about the high maintenance costs on the Locky, not forgetting the fact that Carver actually wanted to replace both engines (Dallas Airmotive).

Secondly, our very tragic accident of the 5th of March now allows us to consider the question of a possible upgrading of the quality of all AH + S Executive Aircraft.

You have my Memorandum to A. K. Carver on this important issue.

I permit myself to say the following: A. K. Carver had better see this juncture in AH + S Operations (Aircraft) as an opportunity. At last, we need not bend our mature, managerial judgments to a situation we inherited from a previous, local, family-owned, two-horse tannery.

3. AIRCRAFT ACCIDENT and AH + S LIABILITY (Recap):

Legal worked up an appropriate "Waiver-of-Claim Certificate" for the reverse side of all next-of-kin checks. Legal doubts if such waivers are worth a damn in court but they may discourage plaintiff actions.

Legal is also of the opinion (I do not agree) that the Blakey woman might have a case, especially before a Pennington jury, on the grounds that I knew for a fact that the weather was sour, extraordinary late hour of departure, etc. Apparently the pilots have no case at all for either they contributed negligence or they failed to exercise due caution.

I expect no static.

You received carbon copies of my check-transmittal letters (20 March); I hope these well-calculated letters help smooth things over. Please make certain, personally, that those waivers come back to you duly signed.

Additional thought: contact your counterpart at the insurance office by telephone and confirm that they are under no circumstances to contact the next-of-kin. Their contract is with AH + S. The amounts we paid out are solely my executive decision. I think our settlements were fair and reasonable and in one case a little excessive for as you know Ed Blakey was on his way out. In other words, I want no post-payment awkwardness to cloud our future ADIF program. You handle it.

In conclusion, as we look down the road ahead, AH + S is now able to get stronger replacements for both Blakey and Gus Lyons, at a salary savings. Secondly, we cash-out an obsolete aircraft, and certain "inventories" aboard at the time while taking down a favorable cash balance of $85,000 on our little AIDF program. Finally, we can now re-think a new concept for all AH + S executive aircraft.

Well, it's late. I'm headed for the barn.

J. K. J.

MEMORANDUM

TO: A. K. Carver, Director of Operations (Aircraft)

Dear A. K.

I am turning down your recent policy suggestion to schedule AH + S aircraft for executive use only during daylight hours.

An airplane is no good on the ground. The cumulative expenses of grounding both personnel and aircraft at nightfall would be prohibitive. I am aware that some companies--not our competition--follow the scheduling policies which you ably suggest.

Al, I'm as sorry as you are about Gus's bad luck; I know you flew with him a long time in the Fairchild. Nevertheless, we have to rise above these things and carry on.

In this spirit please forward at your earliest convenience your recommendations for the acquisition of newer, possibly more appropriate equipment to replace the Lockheed. You may wish to recommend we step up to executive-jet aircraft. Faster, more efficient aircraft would give us a needed edge on our competition, but against this most of our plants, aside from Pennington and Mercer City, are in relatively isolated areas all across the Eastern Seaboard. Are company airstrips and/or nearby county facilities appropriate for business jets?

A. K., I will read your realistic list figures and recommendations with considerable interest.

In closing, let me express a firm conviction: <u>all</u> AH + S aircraft are extensions of the Executive/Sales thrust of your Corporation. All aircraft and flying personnel must hustle with the rest of us. Therefore short-notice flights at AH + S are routine. If we are not present <u>first</u> at the Sales-Opportunity Point, then all of us might as well remain grounded at the home office here in Pennington, Illinois. Time is of the essence in modern marketing. It is a fact: I ordered the Lodestar, crew, and passenger to report at once to our newly acquired plant in West Virginia. I had to do so on the evening of 5 March. I will do so again.

I expect your management of AH + S aircraft to implement the above goals each and everyday.

                                      Very cordially yours,

                                      J. KELLY JOHNS
                            President, and General Manager

Blind carbon Copies:
    - Maurice Cohen, Vice President, Finance
    - Seldon Thomas, Vice President, Personnel

ALLIED HIDE & SPECIALTY CO., INC.
1 TANNERY ROW
PENNINGTON, ILLINOIS

29 March 1972

Mr. Allen Oaker, Chairman-of-the-Board
Smyth-Oaker Investment Trust, Ltd.
505 Fifth Avenue
New York, New York

Dear Allen:

    By now you have read the press accounts and have heard my preliminary telephone report of the AH + S Lockheed "Lodestar" accident not far from our newly acquired tannery at Healdsboro, West Virginia, at about 20:00 hours, 5 March 1972. This is a letter of clarification.

    Regards the proximate cause of the accident, I confirm the flight was duly authorized (Pennington to Healdsboro, direct) and at this time the investigation is not conclusive. Two facts must be stated: first, the Lockheed carried an Instrument Landing System, including glide path (and DEME); the strip at Healdsboro had only a radio beacon. That tannery being a recent acquisition, our flight crew was not entirely familiar with the field. Secondly, in deteriorating weather conditions, pilot error is indicated. They burned it approximately <u>five</u> miles short of the runway.

    I also lost Ed Blakey. Ed was a very gung-ho type. He flew off on short notice to be in West Virginia for a morning new-product (suede) conference. At the time I asked him if a telephone call and forwarded suede samples would not suffice. Ed wanted personally to see the new suede-run. So.

    Regards follow-up action, I report the following:

    a. The search for my new Manager of Sales (vice president) is underway. All of us out here wish to recruit outside AH + S: bring in new blood. If you have any personnel suggestions via your New York contacts, please advise.

    b. My two pilots are being replaced.

    c. Loss of the aircraft, added, equipment, and certain inventory items are adequately covered by insurance. After routine survivor disbursements, our ADIF program brings in approximately $80,000.00

    d. Regards long-range planning, I see this unfortunate accident as an opportunity to upgrade my sales management and also to upgrade pilot personnel. Finally, I am now in a position to take a hard look at the overall efficiency of all our aircraft operations.

On the final point, I solicit your usual astute advice. Your subsidiary is located in the middlewest; our present tanneries and finish-plants are widely scattered. All-weather aircraft operation is a necessity. What would you think of going to jet equipment?

Beyond the above merely local issues, you will be pleased to know your company has moved steadily ahead in the specialty-leather field, with sales currently 8 percent ahead of last year. The cost reduction program you ordered when I took over out here is now paying dividends. I anticipate an even greater share of the market in the next eighteen months.

As to Company-Community relations, the turnout for Blakey's funeral tells us his talent for community relations was both timely and has served its purpose. Doubtless he created the new AH + S "image" in this small town. At last the old-line, family ownership of this business is now virtually forgotten.

The "new" AH + S being a fact, I look forward to more fruitful company-community relationships, a genuine Partnership for Progress.

On a more personal note, I find small-town life a little stultifying, as does my wife Lou. Still there are small-town rewards, most notably the close, lasting ties which one inevitably builds. And, as always, there is an interesting job to do.

Faithfully,

J. KELLY JOHNS
President, and General Manager

Smith-Oaker Investment Trust, Ltd.
505 Fifth Avenue
New York, New York

Dear Johns:

    Off to Bermuda for ten days work/vacation with British interests. Nevertheless, want to answer your recent report of 29 March (about your aircraft accident).

    You state my company lost on twin-engined airplane, two pilots, one Sales Manager, plus some "inventory" and still made money. I don't know how you did it, and I don't care. Don't try to bootleg the $80,000.00 into your <u>operating</u> profits.

    By inference you have repeatedly complained about Mr. Ed Blakey, but because Pennington is a small town you lacked the guts to fire him. So you got a break: go out and find yourself a better man. I have no New York suggestions for a middlewestern based vice-president of Sales--in leather, or anything else.

    Whether you upgrade your executive fleet of airplanes or not is entirely your decision. If a jet will make money, buy it; if it eats you up later, that's tough. Don't ask for a dime of financing from this end. I'd say exactly the same thing to any of my companies.

    I remember Gus Lyons. A couple of times he flew me from Teeterboro out to Pennington. Very white hair, and chewed unlighted cigars. I thought he added a note of down-home cussedness to the whole proceedings. Sorry you lost him.

    You state my subsidiary AH + S is making money. That's why I moved in on that down-at-the-haunch, family-run picnic in the first place. That's exactly why I hired you to run it. For your future health and welfare I suggest you continue same. Your expenses are still out of line in comparison to industry-wide practice.

    If you don't like Pennington, Illinois, say so. I can always find someone else who either does, or will lie to me about it.

    I've got to leave.

                                            Thanks for the info.

                                                  J. Oaker

At Home
2223 Country View Terrace
Pennington, Illinois
5 April 1972

Mr. J. Kelly Johns, President
ALLIED HIDE AND SPECIALTY COMPANY, INC.
1 Tannery Row
Pennington, Illinois

Dear Kelly,

    Only a month ago this evening I got the terrible telephone call from our local radio station, wanting to know did I have any information about the airplane crash in West Virginia. It was Ed and poor Gus, and Bob Shambrough. Now I am now pretty much "at home"; the neighbors have just been wonderful. The boys are fine.

    I write to thank you for your thoughtfulness about the three checks. You are generous to pay the full monthly salary; the $15,000.00 really was totally unexpected. Edward never mentioned such a program to me, so I doubt if he, himself, knew about it. The "bonus" of $4,000.00 for the education of our two sons is a splendid suggestion. I have signed the checks (and the waivers) and have opened a bank account in the name of our sons. When they are older you may rest assured I shall tell them the name of their benefactor. Our heartfelt gratitude.

    Looking back on it, I also feel the funeral services were exactly as Edward might have wished. The cards and condolences from all who knew him--including <u>all</u> of his Little Leaguers--are testimony of the high esteem in which he was held not only by the community of Pennington but also by his wonderful sales organization and their wives.

    Surely Edward was a kind, generous man. The future was all before him.

    I appreciate your willingness to be of further help. I will come past your office a little later this spring to "talk things over," when my future plans are more settled.

    Again, thank you for all you have done for us.

    Sincerely yours,

    Barbara Blakey

R. F. D. Box 113
Millburgh, Illinois
7 April 1972 (a Friday)

Dear Mr. Kelly Johns,

Rec'vd the two checks. They are cashed. Thanks a lot.

You weren't the only one that missed Gus's funeral. Since they buried the Big Man in town at the same time, most of the Company people went to his if at all. Except for the hangar bunch. They came out here. Everybody. Maybe you like a closed-casked funeral, but I do not. Now I'll always have to remember Gus the way he was when he was called out on short notice that afternoon.

Which brings me to some points I want to make. I notice you ordered Gus paid from the first to the 14th (normal two-weeks pay); a big outfit like AH + S could have paid the whole month. But as Gus said, "Why, naturally they skin everything." That's what happened all right.

I signed your insurance check on the back not having much other choice. But I know and Gus knew it wasn't absolutely necessary to take off at five p.m. for a someplace in West Virginia he'd only been to once before and that one time in broad daylight. But you would have them go so they went. Gus called me at home from the telephone in the hangar and said, "Don't hold your breath on this one. Don't know when we'll get back." Well, that's what he was paid for, I guess.

And I will say this. The newspapers always claim a "pilot error." I will always think this one was caused by that high-time, right-hand engine. If they was at altitude, in the overcast, and say the blower went out, was there anyplace else to come down except on a mountain? Maybe Gus wasn't the best on instrument flight but I never did know him to be off any five miles on an approach. Gus knew the whole U.S., and it's not like him to be lower than any mountain, unless he knew for sure.

Well, what's past is past. If Gus had his choice he would always have flown during daylight hours as he observed you pretty much manage to do yourself.

Well thanks for the two checks and I've said in writing what's on my mind. And my name is not Mary, it's Maxine, and always was.

Yours truly,

Maxine Lyons

(Mrs.) Maxine Lyons

ALLIED HIDE & SPECIALTY CO., INC.
1 TANNERY ROW
PENNINGTON, ILLINOIS

8 April 1972

(Mrs.) Gustave Lyons
R. F. D. Box 113
Millburgh, Illinois

Dear Maxine Lyons:

    I received your letter of 7 April and advise since you have signed and cashed the settlement checks Mr. Lyon's salary account and his connection with the above-named company is terminated.

    I have read carefully your thoughts on the possible causes of that tragic accident which saddened company personnel and the Pennington community. Nothing in the FAA or our own Company accident investigation reports substantiates your opinions.

                          Very truly yours,

                          J. KELLY JOHNS
                   President, and General Manager

NEW LETTERS

A magazine of fine writing   *Edited by David Ray*

Fiction by Robert Day & Daniel Curley

"The Ludwig Poems" by Robert Peters

& many others

Texas Indian Rock Art

after a text by W. W. Newcomb
on work of Lula & Forrest Kirkland

DAVE OLIPHANT

It is always a guy like this,
with a damaged heart from childhood,
his bout lost to rheumatic fever,
dizzied by hiking with a heavy pack,
picks up pen, shoulders the past,
over river & crag totes to us its record.

And sure enough, the wife he takes
drives the car, explores with Kodak, cooks,
keeps a journal, loses a heel, meets a lizard,
runs in high wind through ocotillo thickets,
slips in mud, falls on rocks, her back
injured, yet lifting as ever, his soft believer.

To camp on the banks of the Rio Grande,
they burned their way by nesting wasps,
passed through a tunnel of roosting bats,
the sickening smell a nasty breeding stench,
drawings made, not worth the travel there — nights,
animal growls & screams prowling, circling round.

Reduced to luke-warm water, a few bites
fixed by flashlight, cramped, sun-burned,
done-in from crawling boulders & trash,
they enter at last a cave called "Comanche,"
the air icy cool, a cold cistern too, hats
for drink, though only the sharing could quench.

Two Poems

Vassar Miller

The Sun Has No History

The sun has no history,
the leaves keep no diary.
That bird on that limb feels no nostalgia,
nor did the bird on that limb feel the slosh of our feet,
my sister's and mine, in the worn wash tub,
nor did the hot wax of the air take the imprint
of my aunt's chuckling voice,
"Land sake's! You all sing it like a dirge"
Revive Us Again, which she has heard lively.
No, because days are sculptured from space,
shaped out of sizzling motes,
hammered from heat-waves.

Seasons repeat themselves,
babble syllables innocent of order.
Hours leave no fingerprints
for sleuths of memory to trace.
Last year camouflages itself
under the light of this instant
slanting upon me who comb
the green of this bush,
the red of that bloom,
the stuff of clouds overhead here
turning to me forever
the familiar faces of strangers.

The sun has no history.
Only I, bearing
my Adam and Eve on my back,
dragged under, dragged down may leap
up to the saddle of hope.

Roger Pfingston

Tedium

Here in this landscape of limbo,
men and women walking like trees,
where the mind slumps as limp as a leaf,
where the heart reverts from a metaphor into a pump,
I ruminate much upon sleep
counting the hours in yawn.

Love, that most delicate flower,
silts in this air where the winds
blow from the wastes of boredom
over the dunghills of shrug,
poisoned by sighs of indifference,
polluted by stench of neglect.

I weave you a welcome mat
out of nettles and thorns,
embroidered with broken glass.
Come back: you merit better than this
half-pretense at my own death-trap!

The Empty Chair

J. J. MALONEY

In the hallway where I sit
On a burnished wooden bench
(which, incidentally, my contours do not fit)
I hear the mumbled pontifications from within,
The shuffling of papers to and fro.
The paper rustle that I hear,
The sound of sweating lives caught
In the hands of civil service men.

The oaken door through which I'll pass
Would somehow be much better made
If made of glass.
The outer man I am must tread
Into the Parole Board's dread
Cabalistic conclave of those
              with God's authority.

The door is dated, made of wood and brass,
   creaks inward at the timorous touch
     of time-cowed hands—
Closes at each exit with disquieting finality.

I hesitate beside that door,
Like a virgin going to a whore.
The years spread
        like pennies on the table
That we finger and drop to hear them ring
     such a hollow ring!

Reluctant as I was to come,
    more reluctant now am I to leave.
Through that window on the left I see
   a vignette of the world I came
        to talk about.

They're coughing now, hinting that I leave,
But first I'll tarry just a bit
        a little more.

At the door I stop to take a final look
    at my fate now left behind me
        propped
            in the empty chair.

Weldon Kees

LARRY LEVIS

10 p.m., the river thinking
Of its last effects,
The bridges empty. I think
You would have left the party late,

Declining a ride home.
And no one notices, now,
The moist hat brims
Between the thumbs of farmers

In Beatrice, Nebraska.
The men in their suits
Bought on sale, ill fitting,
The orange moon of foreclosures.

And abandoning the car!
How you soloed, finally,
Lending it the fabulous touch
Of your absence.

You'd call that style—
To stand with an unlit cigarette
In one corner of your mouth,
Admiring the sun on Alcatraz.

Semper Eadem
Derek Walcott

And there is the desert but no one marches
except in the pads of the caravans,
there is the ocean but the keels incise
the precise old parallels,
there is the blue sea above the mountains,
but they scratch the same lines
in the jet trails,
the politicians plod without imagination
circling the sombre gardens
the fountains dry in the forecourt,
the grigri palms desiccating
dung pods, like goat's crud,
the same lines are ruled on the whitepapers,
the same steps ascend Whitehall,
and only the name of the fool changes
under the plumes of the tricorne
for the regimental parades,
revolving around, in rythmn
on the brazen mouths of the tubas,
why are the white eyes of the beautiful,
unmarked, sleekskinned children
in the uniforms of the country
bewildered and shy,
or are white as terror
with pride being beaten gently
into their minds?
They were truer, the old songs,
when the king lived far away,
when the veiled queen, her girth
as comfortable as cushions
held the orb and the careful admonitions,
we wait for the changing of statues,
we stand at parade.
Here he comes, now, here he comes,
the victor, in a black crowd

with the sleek waddling seals of his cabinet,
they are waddling up the dais
and the wind puts its tail
between its legs, the haunches
of the mountains and hides,
and a wave coughs once,
abruptly. Who will name this silence
respect? Those hoarse hosannas,
awe? That tin-ringing tune
and the pumping circular horns,
the new world? Find a name
for that look on the faces
of the electorate. Tell me
how it all happened, and why
I said nothing.

June 1973

Friday Evening

D. M. Thomas

You are on the train crawling across country towards me.
I am in the car driving to a half-way station.
You are switching on the overhead reading-light.
I am switching on the car sidelights.
You are losing yourself in a book.
I am losing myself in a poem.
I know this road like the palm of your hand.
To give up is as desperate as to go on.
You lean your head on the glass, speckling with rain like sperm.
I switch on the wipers.
Dusk deepens.
The station will always be there to meet us,
Unable to go even when the last train is in,
Even when the sun flickers low, a waiting-room fire.

Two Poems
John Tagliabue

Archilochos:

" . . . Keep some measure in your joy—
or in your sadness during / crisis
that you may understand man's up-and-down life."

    O yes   O yes
    We've lived long enough to know how true that is,
        up and down, up and down,
    many deep depressions, — but then again those
        curves like a woman's breasts!
    The good life returns to us in perfect weather or
        perfect pleasure
        nipples showing.

Debussy And Proust

The Customs Seal on my travel bag
    almost faded,
        looking like a miniature of an old map,
the old vaccination mark on my left arm almost faded,
    the dim moon in the morning sky,
    the memory of so many days
    and nights and flowers come
    and gone almost faded;
before you go, map of God on the fading body of the dancer,
mark of acceptance by the international officer,
    ancient body of an insect on a leaf,
    before you go I want to just
    mention you, repeat your names,
    say the alphabet from A to Z,
want to say as long as I can remember I will
    murmur prayers and the reverence
    of things past.

Putsch—1923

Robert Willson

Too many B's buzz in Munich:
Bürgerbräu, Bavaria, Blitz,
Bier, Blut und Brudern—
All this is Nazi noise.

The funny man in morning coat,
Like Chaplin amid the Kops,
Brandishes a pistol and drones
Of völkisch dreams, baiting Reds and Jews.

Suddenly he holds them, stung
To silence by his artful alliteration;
Men weep, then blurt out "Führer!"
In defiant alcoholic strains.

Bitten by a lust to hate
The sodden burghers, brothers now,
Swell in the streets to find
Brown shirts, bludgeons, boots.

In The Beginning

Jonathan Griffith

When my father and I dug
fence posts to hold our farm in,
the holes looked
as if a snake had looped itself
and followed us uphill.
I shivered.
There was a wind.
He said we needed to hurry.
The frost had already settled.
I tried to count the holes behind us
and heard him groan.
I wanted to know
if at the last the snake
would rise to greet us. I half-
expected him to chop its head.
Each stroke brought him closer.
I wanted him to dig faster,
to have it out.
When he struck bottom,
I was afraid to look
down the hole.
I was rooted to the spot
though he had already hefted
pick and shovel
calling my name—Jonathan.
Its sound woke me
into an element,
cold, deep, absolutely clear.

The Fields of Golden Glow

JACK CONROY

The story-and-a-half house in which I was born had two dormer bedrooms at the head of a steep flight of stairs, and in one of these I slept on a narrow cot with my brother Tom, three years older than I, and within hand's reach across the room my sister Margaret, three years my junior, occupied a similar cot. Our mother seemed to turn out Conroys at three year intervals. Her first husband, Joseph McKiernan, was killed in the mine. Two little girls had died very young, and their graves, like that of their father, were marked only by pine headboards in the miners' section of Huntsville graveyard. These soon rotted away so that all traces of the graves were lost after my mother, the widow McKiernan, was married to a handsome boarder named Tom Conroy and moved with him to Monkey Nest camp near Moberly. In those days, the seven-mile journey to Huntsville was difficult for a family without a "rig" and there always seemed to be things to do for the living more urgent than caring for the graves of the dead. Father and Mother brought with them four McKiernan children, two boys and two girls.

When I was about five I was tormented by a persistent dream in which my hands and legs seemed to have turned to dough, and I was incapable of moving them. This, I surmised in later years, was induced by poor circulation in the affected limbs. There was no room to turn in the narrow bed, and hardly room to stand up except in the center of the tiny room. Frequently, too, herds of snorting and jostling cows invaded my dreams, pushing into the two downstairs rooms and stomping into the leanto kitchen, pushing aside or trampling on Conroys and McKiernans with their sharp hooves. I needed no dream books to enable me to deduce that these were phantasms of the cattle that grazed in the sparse pasture surrounding our small, fenced-in domain. (My mother was an intelligent and rather well-read woman, but she had areas of credulity. She often consulted dream books and heeded their interpretations. From a Moberly drug store we each year obtained a calendar dispensed by some patent medicine company. On it the weather for each day was predicted by a series of flag signals. Though these predictions more often than not proved to be erroneous for our location, Mother never lost faith in the essential accuracy of the forecasts. All sorts of nostrums and cure-alls were advertised in magazines to which we subscribed—*Comfort*, *Woman's World* and *Hearth and Home* among them—and Mother tried a good many of them, though we could ill-afford the expenditure. One, I recall, was called Liquidzone, and it did make you feel good. I'm sure now that it contained a large percentage of alcohol. It was a paradisaical era for unscrupulous medical fakirs, little or no restrictions being placed either on claims or contents.)

The cows never actually broke into our house, but they did breach the rickety fence and devastated Mother's carefully-tended garden. There were seven children to feed—four McKiernans and three Conroys—and miner's wages were low. Boys usually joined their fathers in the mine at 12 or so. Joe McKiernan was about 14 and Everett McKiernan a little older when they accompanied their stepfather to the Monkey Nest. Their underworld bondage was short: Joe was killed by a fall of rock before he was 18 and Everett's kidneys were so badly crushed when a fractious mule crowded him on the mine cage that he never recovered. I can remember him sitting backward on a chair somehow to ease his pain. The doctor called it Bright's Disease, and sometimes gave him a draught of laudanum when the pangs became extremely sharp. Father bought a lot in Sugar Creek Cemetery, and Joe was the first to be buried there. Everett was not long behind.

Mother searched for food as for a treasure. The garden helped, and there was a small pasture in which she usually managed to keep a milch cow retired as superannuated from some farmer's herd. Our rented holding was part of a vast and not clearly-defined area owned by the Smith Heirs of Lincoln, Nebraska. It included forest, pasture, and farming lands. On it Mother found a variety of usable plants for salads and greens. She believed, with Ralph Waldo Emerson, that a weed is a plant for which no use has yet been found. Hunting for blackberries and gooseberries often turned into a pleasant outing, with lunch in the woods beside a spring that never ceased bubbling up clear, cold water.

Though the vast domain of the Smith Heirs gave us considerable maneuvering space, there was always the temptation to venture into the richer realms of neighboring farmers. Neighboring, but not to us very neighborly. For most of them, folks from the mines were about as acceptable as gypsies who had a bad reputation for trickery in horsetrading, swindling methods of fortune telling, and outright stealing of anything movable. Sugar Creek, which had its headwaters at the graveyard and the adjacent church and school house, meandered through some of the farms. Using the trees fringing it as cover, we stealthily slunk along the creekbed. Blackberries and gooseberries grew more luxuriantly there, and in the Fall there would be hazelnuts, hickory nuts and walnuts. Mother's code sternly forbade our appropriating field crops or orchard fruits. The farmers seemed to enjoy an opulence unknown to us, and we were content with the lees of their abundance—the berries and nuts they disdained.

In addition to the menace of having a farmer detect and chase us, there was the threat of bulls that grazed in the pasturelands. They usually appeared to be grazing placidly and contentedly, but now and then there were stories of a farmer or some member of his family having been gored to death by one on a rampage. Mother, with her habitual prissiness, always referred to them as "gentleman cows" and insisted we follow suit. We were somewhat less refined when she was out of earshot, and I remember my brother Tom repeating a jingle he had picked up from one of the Gravitt boys:

> "Of all the beasts that roam the woods,
> I'd rather be a boar.
> I'd curl my tail up over my back
> And frig forever more."

The Gravitt boys lived somewhere off in the woods. While the elders sometimes worked in the mines, they lived an amorphous existence between mining and farming. They hewed white oak ties for the railroad, cut cordwood for sale in Moberly, and trapped and fished. It was not unusual to see one of the boys pass by our house with two or three possum or coon skins slung over his shoulder. All in all, a most satisfactory sort of existence, we thought. The children might show up at Sugar Creek School at the beginning of the term, but soon stopped coming. There were no truancy laws in the school district, or, if there were, they did not seem to be enforced. We envied the Gravitts for their casual way of life, and also for their possession of lurid dime novels celebrating the exploits of such characters as Young Wild West, Diamond Dick, Old King Brady, and Nick Carter. They sometimes generously lent us a copy or two. These we secreted outdoors, knowing that such literature would surely be on Mother's *Index Librorum Prohibitorum*. Assuming some of the fictional personalities, we dramatized their adventures with many improvisations of our own. Sister Cora selected the male role of Kit Carson, brother Tom was sufficiently daring as Diamond Dick, while, though young for the part, I was permitted to function as the Cheyenne Kid.

Our playground was a pasture to which we appeared to have some sort of legitimate access—it was part of the Smith Heirs vast demesne. Cows and horses fed in the pasture, and their ownership was never clearly recognized by us. At times we even presumed to mount some of the more docile nags and gallop about in pursuit of redskins or outlaws. Down the hill from our house, which fronted on a rutted dirt road, stretched the two-room wooden houses of Monkey Nest Camp in a rough semicircle. The camp had been born when the Monkey Nest Mine shaft was sunk; its slow death began when the veins of coal began to dwindle and narrow and the Eagle Mining Company (the mine was officially the Eagle Mine, though always called Monkey Nest by the miners and townspeople) found its operation no longer profitable for an enterprising outfit. Several local entrepreneurs worked the mine at intervals for a few years. Then it was abandoned to the bats and the noxious black damp gas which is fatal to anyone venturing into it.

The camp houses were frugally built of cheap yellow pine boards set upright. The boards also served as the inside walls; there was no plastering. A partition reaching only to the height of the outside walls divided the houses into two rooms. There was no ceiling and above the naked rafters could be seen. A roaring fire could not provide enough warmth in wintertime; in summertime the houses were hot as the hubs of hell. There had been about a dozen when the mine was going full blast. As the fortunes of the Monkey Nest declined, so did the camp's buildings. A few were torn down for lumber. One was burned down, it was suspected, when hoboes camped in it and built fires for warmth and cooking. Farmers put three or four on rollers and hauled them away for barns or dwellings. Two were joined to make a suitable dwelling after lathes and plastering were applied to the inside walls and ceilings installed.

Our somewhat more substantial house survived. I say "ours" because it seemed to belong to us by right of long habitation. It, too, was part of the Smith Heirs holdings. Our only contact with our mysterious absentee landlords was through a Moberly realtor named A. B. Little, to whom we paid the rent. He professed to know almost as little of the Smith Heirs as we did. He merely collected the rent from the various tenants, royalties from the mines and other revenues and forwarded them, less his commission, to Lincoln, Nebraska. Our Irish parents still had old country misgivings about absentee landlords.

Each morning I observed a ritual by tumbling out of bed and assessing the outer world through the four-paned window that faced East. A great many years later I was to be reminded of this habit by Thomas Hood's lines:

"I remember, I remember
The house where I was born,

The little window where the sun
Came peeping in at morn;
He never came a wink too soon
Nor brought too long a day."

In Summer the prospect from my little window was especially pleasing. A field across the road stretched away to the railroad tracks about half a mile away. It was still called the Tramway because sometime beyond the memories of us youngsters, a railroad spur running to a mine in Happy Hollow had traversed it. We occasionally came across the rotting end of a tie or a rusted spike, but little trace of the railway line remained. In Summer the entire field was bathed with a lambent light from fields of golden glow, a bright yellow flower cursed as a weed by farmers but esteemed by us as a conveyor of beauty and gladness.

A footpath extending from the road in front of our house to the Wabash railroad tracks leading to Moberly bisected the Tramway diagonally. It was our principal outlet to the outer world, for few of the miners had any other mode of transportation than Shank's mare. Watching from the upper window, we could follow Mother's progress as she walked toward town. The smaller children soon vanished in a gilded sea of bloom, the stalks of golden glow surmounting their heads. We had our own name for most flowers, not having access to precise botanical information. Thus, the dog-tooth violet was our Easter (just Easter, not Easter *lily*), the spring beauty was the pink stripe, and the black-eyed Susan was (without malice prepense) the niggerhead. It was many years before I learned the true name of the golden glow, which we always called the yellow bell.

Among the high-rising stalks we trampled out secret rooms, secure from adult intrusion or inspection. We produced circuses with attractions such as Jo Jo the Dog-Faced Boy (my brother Tom embellished with moss and pokeberry juice) and trained dogs who never responded to orders very satisfactorily. A regular feature at twilight we called "watching the yellow bell," based on the golden glow's habit of closing its petals for the night.

If we were feeling particularly adventurous, we'd follow the Tramway path clear to the railroad tracks but stand back somewhat in fear. Freight trains with a rush and roar hurtled past, their boxcars marked by strange-sounding names from faraway places. One type of boxcar carried a picture of a small, sun-bonneted girl wearing wooden shoes and brandishing a broom or club, accompanied by the legend: "Old Dutch Cleanser Chases Dirt." We always counted these, and there were often as many as ten or fifteen on one train. The engineer or trainmen might wave at us, condescendingly and majestically it seemed to us. If hoboes dropped off as the trains slowed down to enter the yards, we hastily withdrew into the nearby yellow bell patch. Railroad bulls sometimes chased the free-riding passengers, usually with angry shouts infrequently punctuated by pistol shots aimed above the fugitives' heads. Down the tracks in a brush-shrouded ravine could be seen a "jungle" where hoboes cooked their mulligan stews in tin cans and washed their clothes and themselves in a handy slough. Usually the bulls respected this sanctuary, but when they were feeling mischievous or had gargled a good bit of moonshine readily obtainable from illicit stills in the adjacent woods, they might chase the bums away.

The detrained tramps ordinarily headed for Moberly, but a few of them might follow the path across the Tramway and hit the back doors of the camp. They probably had heard that there was a mining camp across the fields and were relying on the traditional generosity of coaldiggers. Mother had a theory that bums had a system of signals they left on fences or gates to indicate to their brethren what kind of reception might be expected within. I have since read, perhaps in the memoirs of the international super-tramp, A. No. 1, that such signals did indeed exist. Some warned of belligerent dogs or hostile housewives, while a drawing depicting an angel's wings signified that a sympathetic woman dwelt in the house so marked.

One evening as sister Cora, brother Tom and I squatted in our nook among the stalks of golden glow, watching the "yellow bell" fold its petals, a grizzled face surmounted by a shock of wild hair thrust itself into the opening. It unmistakably belonged to a tramp, a species against which we had been repeatedly warned.

"Hello, kids," said the bum, thrusting himself into our theater.

Frozen with apprehension and horror, we did not answer.

"Wish I had me a pistol," he pursued. "I'd let some daylight into that son-of-a-bitchin' dick that come tarry-hootin' into our camp. Kicked over our mulligan can, pissed on our fire, and shot holes in our bindles. He'll get it! He'll get it, all right, one of these days!"

His appearance was frightening enough, but his profane language was blood-curdling.

We hastily arose and stood in stunned silence as he lurched off in the direction of the camp. Dusk was gathering as we approached our house and heard Mother talking to somebody inside. Brother Everett was off in Arkansas cutting timber, brother Joe had walked into town, and Father must be at his job of firing shots after the other miners had left the shaft.

We saw the bum sitting at the kitchen table as we entered. He still looked angry and was glowering as Mother bustled about, apparently preparing to feed him. She never turned a tramp away hungry, and I have thought since that the sign of the angel's wings must have been carved on our gatepost.

"My husband is a little sick with a cold. Nothing serious," Mother explained.

Then she walked into the front bedroom and asked: "How do you feel now, Tom?" "I feel pretty good, Liza," a gruff voice answered. It was pitched in a low key, but to us it was embarassingly clear that Mother was answering herself. She was really a good mimic, but this test would appear to be too much for her histrionic powers.

"Is your husband sickly, ma'am?" our guest inquired as Mother came back to the kitchen.

"Oh, no! He's really a strong man. Just a little cold." Then she added: "Over six feet tall and strong as an ox."

A quizzical smile flickered over the bum's whiskers, but he addressed himself seriously to his plate of food until it was all consumed. He wiped the plate with a crust of bread, and ate it with evident gusto. As he departed he said:

"Thank you very kindly, ma'am. You've got a good heart which many people don't in this goddamn world. Your husband is a lucky man to have such a fine wife and a good cook to boot. Don't it get dark early, though."

"Mammy! He knew! He knew!" we chorused. (When small, we always call our parents Mammy and Pappy.)

Mother leaned weakly against the doorjamb. "Maybe he did and maybe he didn't. He looked real *mean*, but maybe he's not at all. Just looking for work and far away from home." We noticed that she locked all the doors and tried the window latches.

The workers in Monkey Nest Mine comprised a miniature United Nations. There were English, Welsh and Irish immigrants made up the majority, but Italy was well represented and so were France and Germany. Not all the miners lived in the camp by any means. Paths threaded through the surrounding woods, leading to small houses occupied by Monkey Nesters and their usually large families. Such homes were self-contained, not depending upon the services of electricity, gas or water from outside sources. Coal oil (kerosene) provided illumination, heating and cooking depended upon firewood readily available in the forest for the cutting. Spring water could be tapped in most locations. It was customary to enlist the aid of a "water witch," a person (almost always a man) supposedly endowed with occult powers of divination. The water witch's tool was a forked stick, a fork held in each hand and the stem upward. When the stem bent strongly downward toward the ground as the water witch walked about, it was held to be an indication that water was not far beneath. This, then, was the proper place to dig a well.

Randolph County had been settled by Virginians who brought their attitudes and place names with them. The region is still called "Little Dixie" with good reason. And in the games we played in the pasture commons between our house and the camp, overseas echoes from the British Isles survived. We sang of dukes and Bonnie Prince Charlie without knowing exactly who these strangers were. Here is an example:

Boys advancing to confront the girls:

> "Here comes a duke a-roaming, roaming.
> Here comes a duke a-roaming,
> Ratsa tatsa tee."

Girls advancing to meet the boys:

> "What are you roaming here for, here for,
> What are you roaming here for.
> Ratsa tatsa tee?"

And the following queries and responses:

> "I'm roaming here to get married, married,
> I'm roaming here to get married,
> Ratsa tatsa tee."

> "Why don't you choose of us, sir, us sir,
> Why don't you choose of us, sir,
> Ratsa tatsa tee?"

> "You're all too black and dirty, dirty,
> You're all too black and dirty,
> Ratsa tatsa tee."

> "We're just as clean as you are, you are,
> We're just as clean as you are,
> Ratsa tatsa tee."

"London Bridge Is Falling Down" was a favorite, and this song was often heard without an accompanying game:

> "Don't want none of your weevly wheat
> Nor none of your wormy barley,
> You can keep your moldy corn,
> I'm savin' my love for Charlie.
> Oh, Charlie is my darlin'
> The young cavalier."

Our green and gold Summers all too soon came to husk. Boys usually went into the mines with their fathers when they were fourteen or so, sometimes younger than that. Before the frost was out of the ground in March, we were "turning out barefoot" and remained unshod until the ground began freezing about the first of November. The mantle of responsibility was already descending on Joe when Mother called him in from playing in the pasture and showed him the heavy miner's shoes he was to wear when he started in the Monkey Nest the next morning. She loved poetry, and seldom was at a loss for an apt quotation. This time it was from Whittier. She sadly mused:

> "All too soon these feet must hide
> In the prison cells of pride,
> Lose the freedom of the sod,
> Like a colt's for work be shod."

Across the road the golden glow petals were closed for the night and the lambent light from the yellow bells no longer hovered over the Tramway. Darkness was closing in.

Jack Conroy (left) in Moberly, Mo. *Leland Payton*

Entering Time in a House
Photographed By Walker Evans

ROBERT GIBB

There is still something
Of November
1935 in Bethlehem—

The way the houses crowd
Shoulder to shoulder
In various degrees of grey,
And steel burns like hatred
Of living in shifts.

The faces on 4th Street
Are filled with gestures
From old snapshots.

They inhabit doorways
Like drawers, decades
Of light in their eyes,
Their heads in their hands.

The light tired as clapboard,

So that standing here
In the dog-eared window
I enter a frame Evans saw
Over forty years ago,

Feel the shadow of his shutter
Pass across my face.

Down below the streets unwind
Like faded rolls of film.

Up the hill the cross
That caught his eye
Is still standing,
Encrusted with roses
Of miraculous stone,

Perennial bloom of the dead.

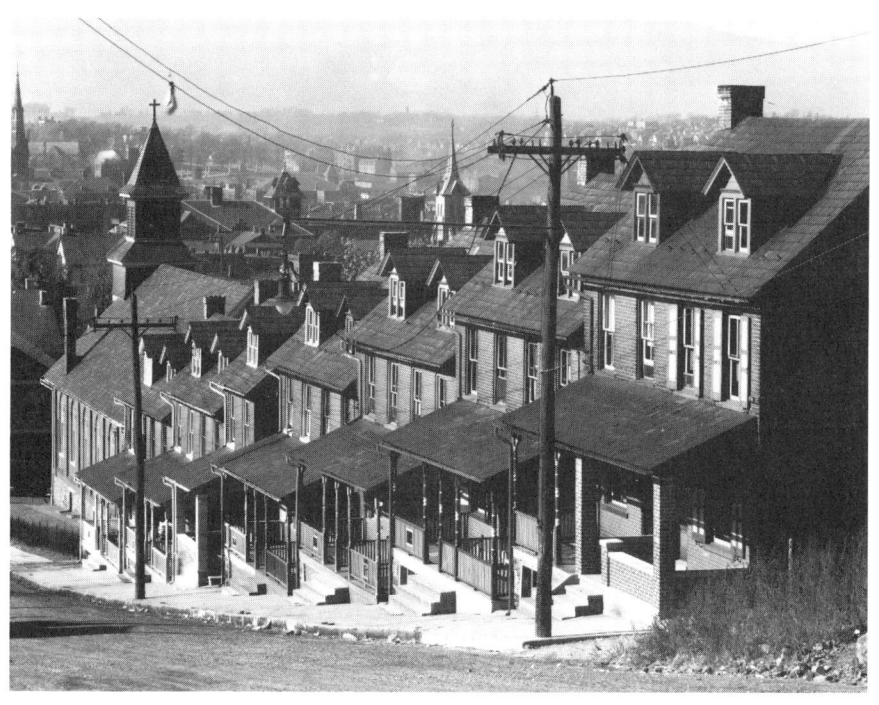

Walker Evans

John Vachon

Bambi

Henrietta Weigel

A Monday of gloomy rain envelops the city. To the too many —men and women: young, old, white, black, parents, children, drug addicts, drunks—on Relief, it is truly "blue Monday." Their bi-monthly checks are six days late. Rent is unpaid; children and adults are hungry. From experience, they have learned it is useless to phone. This branch—among others in Manhattan —either does not answer, or a weary voice repeats that checks have been mailed and advises patience or a visit to the Relief office.

Though it does not open until nine A.M., by eight thirty, a crowd has already jammed the building's lobby. Faces are all turned towards the two large elevators, gated and empty. The people at first seem like members of an audience waiting for the curtain to rise, or sports' fans in the bleachers. Tots are hoisted to parents' shoulders. A young woman who has her baby strapped to her body so it faces her, circles her infant protectively with her arms. Some have brought cardboard containers of coffee; those who've had no breakfast watch enviously.

At first, there is a feeling of camaraderie—those having cigarettes or matches toss them to others. The fog of smoke swells the stench—many look as if they've had no sleep or wash for a long time.

As minutes then hours pass, more and more people come. They spill over to the rainy streets, even turning the corner until they throng Park Avenue.

Those of us surrounded by the taller feel trapped, unable to see. A young pregnant woman, accompanied by her boyish, bearded husband, begins to wilt. Her husband helps her to squat, her back against the lobby wall. Though gentle, he now flails his arms, shouting, "Stop pushing!" as he attempts to create a small area of space for his pale wife.

"Who's pushing!" An angry chorus retorts. Each is prisoned by the involuntary pressure of others. We all might be in the subway during rush hour, except this train does not budge.

Suddenly one of the elevator's gates opens. There's a stampede to get inside. The elevator's safety capacity is threatened by being overloaded, but people refuse to leave though the elevator does not move. A man in the crowd tries to take charge. "Stupid bastards," he cajoles, then screams.

One man, his eyes seeming blind with dope, cries: "Let's tear up the joint, at least have fun...."

Finally, some of the elevator's occupants get out. The elevator moves, only to return almost immediately. The buttons have been fixed so that the elevator doesn't stop on the usual floor. Doors on the other floors have been locked, too, and Relief cops chase those who had somehow reached stairways.

It is now after twelve. A thin young man, wearing a *yamalka* (he is not a Jew, I learn, but this gesture is part of his rebellion against his Gentile family who have disowned him), and striped overalls (over a bulging torn sweater) snakes his way through the crowd. After each trip, he shares information he's gathered. He announces, too, that his name is Bambi. He informs us, in a lisp, that the Relief staff is on strike. His final report says that the Union has forbidden its members to work until more cops are available. Relief employees had been assaulted recently by Relief clients, and by applicants.

The pasty-faced man who had attempted to control the elevator situation sneers everytime his fellow-in-misery speaks. "Mr. Newspaper's here again..."

A wave of laughter washes over the crowd, as some yell in disbelief... "They're afraid of us!"

One lame old woman, carrying a battered cane, begins to fight her way out. "My daughter's in the hospital. They need her bed. I must go take her home. Can't wait no more..."

A neatly dressed — no longer young — Puerto Rican, follows her. "Terrible," he mutters... "I was poor in Puerto Rico, but felt like a man ... here ... "

He fades from sight, not hearing an old man—who looks like a cross between an elephant and an Irishman—say, "Let 'im go back where he came from..."

Stubbornly, I stay. A friend would lend me money . . . I could return another day. Whether it is masochism or curiosity that paralyzes me, I do not know. I endure being there, as if I were held captive by a bad dream I cannot escape.

Finally, my aching body propels me to action. I struggle through the lobby crowd, find a phone booth on Lexington Avenue. I call the Relief branch, amazed when someone answers. I give my name, and other relevant data. After checking records, she returns to the phone. Since I am in what they call the disabled category, she suggests I come up through the Park Avenue entrance (which I never knew existed). The elevators there are running. I'm to give my name to a cop—whom she'll alert to let me in.

The few of us who have been granted this privilege — despite a twinge of guilt I experience, thinking of the waiting crowds — follow instructions. A cop stationed at the door, after checking our names, lets us in. What joy the act of sitting down brings. I am pleased to see the young pregnant woman and her husband. I share the lifesavers found in a torn pocket.

Our reprieve is short-lived. A hatchet-faced white Relief worker asks a woman, rather demands, that she roll up a trouser, so she can confirm that the woman's not malingering. We, the audience, protest . . . but the sick woman puts her fingers to her lips in a gesture begging silence. The young bearded husband of the pregnant woman grumbles: "On whose side is she anyway, theirs or her own?" The social worker threatens to throw us all out if we make trouble. The worker, seeing the wound is authentic, gets ready to go out to lunch, saying acidly, "THESE days, you can't believe your own mother."

The hallway outside is now crowded with people. Their faces press against the soiled glass windows, that are part of the locked doors.

An elderly black woman sits down beside me. I take it for granted she is a client. I ask her whether she knows anything about what's happening. She jumps up from her seat. Her hatred is a wall, separating her even from the black clients.

"I'm a blue-eyed blonde today (I am neither—rage has taken away her sight), and jus' feel like taking the day off. I'm tayhed, oh Lord I'm tayhed . . . if you're expecting pap from this old mammy, I'se all dried up. Forget it! You're pretty, and younger, and healthier I bet. Get off that white ass and work. . . "

The black as well as the white clients are astonished. The old woman quickly summons three cops. They finger their guns, their clubs. "Out!" they order us. We ask that the pregnant young woman be allowed to stay, and have a seat.

"This ain't the Ritz," the tall skinny cop tells us. "Out!" he repeats, and we are once again lost in the milling crowd. "Favor one," his voice rises above the din, "and everybody gets in the act."

He pinches the cheek of a beautiful black girl. "Take your paws off me," she screams. He grins. Somehow, looking at her, I think of rain bronzing leaves on which it falls. Her head has fleetingly been resting on my shoulder. She lifts her head. "I'm just out of a nuthouse. Seems this one is, too. I shoulda stayed there," she sighs.

The woman with the wounded leg—on the other side—suddenly pants. She is having difficulty breathing. Her face turns pale, and wet. The black girl and I push through others, to reach her. She grasps our hands. Somehow, her touch comforts me, too. I also begin to have trouble breathing . . . trying to hold back hysterical laughter. We seem phantoms, dependent upon each other.

Bambi, accompanied by a neatly dressed youth I'd not noticed before—who has a worn sensitive face—fight their way through to the woman.

"Don't be afraid . . . " Bambi's companion speaks soothingly. "I've been a male nurse." He and Bambi lead her through the crowd. Gently, Ricky—who tells us his name—seats the woman on the floor, her back resting against the wall. He instructs her to thrust her head between her knees. Creating a small area of space around her, Ricky and Bambi squat beside her. Ricky carries a notebook. The crowd looks at him and Bambi hostilely.

"I'm taking courses," he tells the woman. "I'll get you up, don't you worry."

"As soon as I get my check," Bambi proclaims, "I'm buying me a puppy . . . My bitch of a mother had my dog put to sleep.

And it didn't even bite her . . . the sweetest husky in this stinking world . . . always smiling . . . "

"Where do you live?" Someone asks. He laughs and laughs. "Nowhere."

"We feel like a sister to you, if you know what I mean," Ricky winks at his female charge. He is skillfully helping her to rise, as doors begin to open.

"Can't wait," he guides her back to the others. "Got a class; don't want to miss it, or they'll think guys being nurses are kidding. Next thing you know, we'll be giving birth." He laughs, but his eyes stay anxious. "I'll come back tomorrow. Monday's rotten for coming here . . . wish it'd stop raining." He glances at his tired shoes, his shabby, neat suit.

The ailing woman peers into her purse, pulls out a dollar bill, folding it deftly and slips it into his pocket. Ricky protests, tries to return it.

She insists he use it for fares and coffee or something.

Bambi's eyes are blank; I project upon him the hurt I imagine he feels. He is going to leave, too. The woman takes out a silver half dollar, after digging into the depths of her frayed purse. "Means good luck," she says. "Was gonna keep it . . . maybe it'll bring YOU luck . . . " She holds it out to Bambi, who is eyeing a lithe black boy. Ricky shakes his head vehemently at the woman. "I'll split this with him," he pats his pocket nervously. "Better not let THEM see you tossing bread around . . . He'll," nods in the direction of Bambi, "buy you-know-what." Bambi lets himself be led towards the stairs by his friend, after Ricky has written down the woman's address, swearing he'll return the dollar.

The day's almost gone; the waiting has seemed endless. Fury and bewilderment seem to split faces. We might be cattle in a stockyard not knowing what to expect. At last, a Relief worker squeezes through the doors. "Probably going to the can," somebody shrugs hopelessly. He announces that we all have to return downstairs, and wait our turn with the others. In unison, we protest. Many of us had been there before nine; it is now after two. He avoids focusing on us, says, Wait. He comes back, saying we can come in, provided there's no stampede.

There's a great rush; people shove and push. Someone steps on a child's foot. She screams in pain, and is carried away by her mother.

The whole place is pervaded by fear—Relief workers are equally nervous. The cops, too, are tense. They play with their weapons, suddenly tune in on sounds we cannot hear. They seem to be seeking a victim or victims to absorb their restlessness.

The white plump interviewer tells how she cut her lunch hour by five minutes, because of so many clients. When I tell her of the long wait, she looks frightened, and makes a speech about no one being special. I shout, I want no special anything; I want ALL people treated humanly. She sweats with uneasiness, and hurriedly processes my papers.

After more waiting, my check comes through. It is four o'clock and still raining . . . the winter day dying even earlier because of the anemic sky.

I want to get drunk; to tear up the check; to squander it on a Siamese kitten, far more necessary at this moment to a feeling that I MUST LOVE SOMETHING, ANYTHING, if I'm not to break into pieces. I feel a kinship with Bambi.

From habit, alas (habit become home, refuses entrance to the unknown, I scribbled on a little pad I carry), I go to the familiar dreary check-cashing place, and then rush home.

My hunger, which I refuse to satisfy, as if by this self-punishment, I am punishing the Anonymous THEM, sharpens my fury. I phone someone whose name was given to me, at the Mayor's office. She is kind, but her voice seems disembodied, a tranquilizer that fleetingly masks my anger. "There wasn't really a riot," she points out, "nearly is as good as not . . . " I marvel, listening, at such logic, such health. "And Monday," she continues, "is ALWAYS an awful day, at any Relief office. Never go on Monday . . . ."

"Never on Monday," "never on Sunday," my mind makes jingles for the days of the week, as I no longer listen to her. I fall asleep, too tired to remove my wet clothes, no longer caring about food. I dream of cops.

Fayetteville Dawn

JOHN CLELLON HOLMES

Now cocks crow coop to coop
    over cicada-buzz
    bird-cheep
    and katydid
across the ragged pastures
    still noon-warm
this hour before dawn.

Without the sounds of our machinery
    air-conditioners off
    radios asleep
    no snores
here in an apartment complex
    on the edge of town
you hear this hubbub going on

of things with wings
recharging for the day

preparing to wait out our noise again.
                      —1975

Two Poems

DAVID PERKINS

A 1946 Nickel

How I envy you all the fingers
that have oiled your politics,
all the small pink palms
that have taken you like sleep,
all the change you have
made right,
all the cool black purses you have
dropped into
dumb with comfort,
all the great stories you know,
all the great stories you could tell
if your tongue were not
dead as your sentiments, dead
as latin.

Doing Time

she went through me
like a window through a house
                             yet
as I approach her now I seem entire,
a certain kind of flower
that closes up as it nears evening,
my wishes for more falling quietly
to zero

doing time in my own body things
are definitely getting better
the muscles in my face
have forgotten Charles Bronson
no words were spoken on either side,
but I have the feeling my nerve endings
are my friends again

    three times a day I settle down
    with all of me
    feeding the engine that hums and hums,
    spreading me everywhere smooth
    as a new runway

    things are getting better now
                          yes
    at four in the morning
    the touch of my own white shoulder
    gives me a hardon
    my great name goes out ahead of me
    through the city turning on
    bedlamps
    and when I stretch and murmur tomorrow
    tomorrow
    the sheets purr,
    and calendars everywhere suddenly
    love their jobs

"R.S.V.P."

G. N. GABBARD

The snowy egret
                regrets
that it will be unable
     to attend your function next decade
owing to a death
                    of the species.

Chickens in San Francisco

William Dickey

San Francisco. You can have four animals total. If you have a dog and a cat, you could only have two chickens.
—*Sunset* magazine, March 1974.

In aerobatics, white, red, speckled & spectacular
as if any spot on earth were the pin's bottom
of an enormous cage opening up to chicken heaven,
in a blur of parts, the eyes fringed and knowing,
the oviducts popping white eggs, brown, an eternal Easter,
hens running flat-footed, hysterical, the roosters up
in a little air, down, the scream, contentment,
chickens frying omelets, stuffing feather pillows, whirling
into feather fights, a believable feather winter . . .

If I kept chickens, that is how I would keep chickens.

Deduct the cat and the dog, which are imaginary,
and you have two chickens, a male chicken and a female chicken
(chicken sexing is high paid work, but you have to travel).
They are walking around the deck. They are Plymouth Rocks.
The male chicken wears a buckled hat and carries a shotgun
and the female chicken has the New England ABC:
A is for Abstinence, B is for Boils, C is for Colonel Sanders.
The chickens look terribly sparse on the windy deck,
as if born plucked. They look at each other,
conscious of a hidden camera. They approach a cabbage
and under it they discover Shirley Temple.
They register the salvation of the race.
Shirley clucks a little, she is well into
what they call the skin of the part . . .

Oh cut, cut, cut, cut, cut. I feel about chickens
the opposite of the way San Francisco feels.
I feel about chickens, I feel about other animals
the way Colette felt about truffles. It is no good having any
unless you can have too much.

Upon the Bible Belt

JOHN CAIN

Driving past narrow sidestreets
and solitary from my
sleeplessness I flick radio

channels; in Albuquerque
a very Reverend Jones rants
homosexuality

is much more than just a quirk;
from Fort Worth and from Dallas
I learn if I were only

driving a fast Ryder Truck
I too, indeed, could have lots
of fun, and luck, and women.

Throughout this Texas frontier
there is a solemn darkness
of a flat terrain. The stray

dogs near deserted derricks,
even they seem more concerned
about their spirits than food.

For a moment I agree;
my life is not fulfilled,
complete, or even factual.

Farmer

LUCIEN STRYK

Seasons waiting the miracle,
dawn after dawn framing
the landscape in his eyes:

bound tight as wheat, packed
hard as dirt. Made shrewd
by soil and weather, through

the channel of his bones
shift ways of animals,
their matings twist his dreams.

While night-fields quicken,
shadows slanting right, then left
across the moonlit furrows,

he shelters in the farmhouse
merged with trees, a skin of wood,
as much the earth's as his.

Mary Wilson

A Dead Woman's Eyes
Jules Supervielle
Translated from the French by Geoffrey Gardner

That dead woman I know
Who was so misunderstood
Still keeps watch deep in the sky
On a glance that wears her down,

On a faded linen rose
On top of an iron stem
And on some pearls of which one
Always returns to the sea.

On the far side of Altair
She smooths back her tresses
Not knowing if her eyes
Are to be opened or closed.

Judy Ray

My Moon Girl

Toby Olson

I took a lady out
into the breath of her own desire,
the obvious melody
of an amusement park, when I was 15 years old.

She had more
craters in her face than I had that year;
she sat near me
in the back seat of the car,
but was hiding her face.

How have we learned to trust, love
be gentle, give out
more than we take back,
treat things other than economic?

She was a blind date, wanted only
a little blindness from me.
          I remember I loved
the ancient
moon-scape of her face
she turned toward me
only in the dark tunnel of love;

I kissed
the unblemished
liver of her soft lips, but I wanted
to touch my moon girl's face.

Introduction

Heather Wilde

Our party.
Our quasi-quarrel with life.
You and me sipping tea
Wearing headbands of ten-thousand volts.
You and me passing plates
Of anti-psychotic barbiturates

It's too old.
A melodrama, a madness song.
We've all been in, we've all been out
And we're all back in again.

Everyone's been through THAT looking glass.
That's how it was and that's how it wasn't.
Whatever you said was a lie.

The nurses don't care,
They water the plants.
Talk to the plants,
Move the plants into sunlight.
"Look!" they say, "See how they grow!"
Not us.
Not like plants and not like plants.
It's all very elemental.
Ellie L. E. Mental.

Of course, I remember,
You aren't here at all.

Three Poems

John Knoepfle

a table here
and some empty
chairs

when you left
you did not tell me
how it would be

how I would lose
my place

---

house wind sleep

we do not
raise our voices
you hand me down
my body

---

some old plains drifter
his tongue slurred with bravado
nobody cares about him now
moth on a windshield
but you held up his head
drew his eyelids shut
set a spider mending his heart

he erased his own time
a ruined child in love with the hours
he was like a deer
ambushed no way to turn
and you cried seeing him fall

St. Louis Woman

ISHMAEL REED

I love to see that orbed heat collapse behind the white Jefferson arc as the downtown St. Louis sun temples burst

Orange as the inside of a Balaban's lobster they cater in the room of Renoirish Third Reich Speer-room nude portraits where Wash. U. grad student waiters resemble the t.v. crew filming a restaurant scene in "As The World Turns." On a stool outside a black man in little boy's cap and white butcher's coat attracts customers with the gleaming stars of his gold teeth.

For four days a storebought apricotheaded St. Louis woman in poor white powder and tobacco-road mascaraed eyelashes told the other waitresses in the Forest Park Hotel to quit putting cream and sugar in my coffee because "He looks spoiled. Big and spoiled."

Daughters of Davy Crockett and Dan Boone with high-Cherokee cheekbones, St. Louis women call closeted plantations with monopoly-board street names, "home" behind fake second empire gates which are locked at night to keep out the townies, Riding bicycles, their eyes buried in the streets, the only blacks wear supermarket names on their t-shirts

They stand on the street's dividing line selling rush hour copies of the St. Louis Post Dispatch like the apple-capped Irish lads in a book about the life and times of Jacob Reiss

They are the last people in the nation who take out their billfolds to show you their relatives and their *girlfriends'* and *boyfriends'* relatives and that time they went to Atlantic City

St. Louis is surrounded by ninety municipalities. Only a Filipino with a Harvard M.A. in business can untangle the town, Emile said. Emile said that St. Louis women are dumb blondes who stand you up. Equal rights to them means the right to tantalize but not to put out, Emile said.

"Are you Bruce Lee?" they asked Emile when he landed in Harlem.

Feeling tomorrow and twenty-two, a St. Louis woman told me she could run a whole radio station. She knew where you could fetch a Gucci raincoat for one hundred dollars. In her poetry she is "a black rose." I told her that if her skin really needed a flower why not an African violet to go with her yellow eyes. I told her that her eyes were all the evidence we needed to prove that ancient Asiatics reached Madagascar. I told her that a black rose was common and that she was anything but common and that she was as rare as a white tiger rarely seen in the jungles of India or rare as the image of a white owl carrying off a white ermine in the Bird Book we saw in the museum off Big Bend where we learned that the first words said on the telephone constituted a cry for help.

In the Steinberg auditorium I asked the Dalai Llama's stand in why there were black gods with nigger minstrel white lips and great Nigerian mound noses in Nepalese paintings dated 3,000 B.C.

Before rushing to the next question he said they represented Time. I told the "black rose" that she was as rare as Time hung on a monastery wall, while outside buddhists blow conch horns and chant like a chorus of frogs.

St. Louis women are rabbit-furred hookers who hustle to star wars in the steeple chase room of the chase park hotel where gorgeous george dressed in sequined Evel Knieval jumpsuit discos Elvis Presley and the hogged-necked bouncers in blazers threaten to break your arm. There are portraits in that room of horses, skins shining like chestnuts, life-sized statues of jockeys in polka-dotted blouses. The lamps are shaped like racing horns.

St. Louis women write body poetry, play the harp for the symphony and take up archery.

St. Louis women wash cook and clean for St. Louis women who write body poetry, play the harp for the symphony, and take up archery

A St. Louis woman is the automatic writing hand for a spirit named Ida Mae of the red dress cult who rises from the Mississippi each night to check out the saloons before last call.

She rises from the big river G. Redmond calls Black River, Mike Castro's River Styx, and every body knows about Muddy

Waters; St. Louis women are daughters of Episcopalian ministers who couldn't sit still for Grant Wood
Sternly scarfed they stare straight ahead inside Doberman Pinscher station wagons. Their husbands work for McDonnell Douglass, Ralston-Purina, and Anheuser Busch,
(They still talk about how old man Busch was so rich that when his son killed a man it was the trial judge who served time)
The great grandfather of a St. Louis woman appears in the 100 years of lynching horror book because he owned 300 acres and white men wanted those acres
The grandmother of a St. Louis woman told her that no man can say "I Love You" like a black man. "Velvet be dripping from his lips," a unique experience like the one recounted by a man in the bar of the St. Louis airport about the time when Nanette Fabray came into the audience and sat on his lap, New Year's Eve, The Mark Hopkins Hotel, San Francisco
On Sunday he stuffed the frig with dungeness crabs
You can find the quilts of St. Louis women patched with real chipmunks and birds in the Jefferson museum next to the Lindbergh collection "Nothing like flying across the Atlantic in a one-seater" he said, "When she rocks, you rock, when you thrust so does she, and when she dives it's as if your soul bought the circus and you owned all the ferris wheels, *The Spirit of St. Louis!*"
A black man wrote a song about a St. Louis Woman that go Hello Central, give me five o' nine, hello central give me five o' nine, the St. Louis woman said she liked my line about a man entering a woman's love pond, she thought i said love mine
like a Mississippi school boy loves his mint and rye i love to see that evening sun go down when the St. Louis women come calling around
Many St. Louis women are from Kansas City

The year was 1914
W. C. Handy wrote a ragtime march with a blues
tango introduction. (The Tango, derived from

the African Tangenda, was once banned all the
way down to the Argentinian South Pole)
but there was something missing.
"What this music needs is a Vamp," the trombonist
said, and that's how "St. Louis Woman" came into
being
The big publishers wouldn't chance her
They were only interested in Whiteman's blues
and so, at the age of 40, W. C. Handy went to
bat for his Vamp, publishing 10,000
copies of "St. Louis Blues" at his own expense

Handy flew up the Fatty Grimes diamond
from Memphis and presented it to her
(Hippolite's "Mystical Marriage")
He chauffered her across the nation in
a whale-length white cadillac like the
one i once saw Bob Hope get out of
He introduced her to a Carnegie Hall
sell-out audience which she delighted
with her shanty-town ways
Sometimes she was as icy as the Portage glacier
in Portage, Alaska,
At other times she was tropical as the
Miami airport at 5:30 when the Santeria
jets sweep in

Resting under that mellow creole
river in a silver satin slip
the color of an enshrined coronet
mooning on the silky meat of a giant
clam
guarded by chocolate dandies
Irises on their creamy waistcoats
and a Tennessee billygoat covered with
cowrie shells
St. Louis Woman

The Penny

Paul Goodman

> The privilege of coining has in all ages and countries belonged to the sovereign. —Britannica, 9th Ed.

The matter of the Coin is valuable: rare, got by labor. Densely valuable, so the coin may be small, to be carried and given and taken, fitting the fingers and the palm. It is durable, hard, able to go thru many exchanges. It is measurable, shaped in a regular geometrical figure. The coin and its value are identifiable, the auspices and value are stamped on it.

This is cold metal, warm in the palm because warmed by the palm. How do the *giving* fingers tend a coin? It may be pinched, held onto even while given; or as if disdainfully held away from the self; or flipped away, or rung down on the table, cast away. A coin is not given with a full-handed giving—the acts are sado-masochistic. How does one *take* a coin? Tentatively feeling, suspicious of counterfeit; or the palm and fingers fold tight around it; snatched, grasped, held onto. A coin is not easily received—acts of anxiety. The coin slips to rest, as foreign matter, in tiny crevices of the body, in purses and pockets.

The coin has a Head and a Tail, and we say, tossing it up, "Heads or Tails?" Coins and dice decide among alternatives by chance. The two-sided coin decides a conflict. This motion of the coin, to toss it up spinning, seems to me to be the original and natural one: the coins were first used to invoke Chance (I have no evidence for this). To find a way to proceed in a dubious crisis, rather than pause too long. One spins oneself around, to vertigo: one loses one's head and falls, with no more doubts. Then one has the God's head, or else the back of his head. In a conflict, the God faces toward A or toward B.

It is the decision of doubt that underlies exchanges: either of the exchanged goods is dubiously preferable. One risks and loses a part of himself, hoping it is for the best. Originally a sacred business of life and death.

The metal was at first a sacred metal. Perhaps this is why these metals have persisted as the media of money, tho they are no longer technically efficient. The labor-value is a rationalization of the inherent value. The unmixed, the unoxidized gold and silver, are reminders, as Plato would say, of the courts of Jove.

And it is primarily a God's Head, and the Back of his Head. Usurping the sacred right, the King or the State tries to assert that itself is the immortal thing among these changes and exchanges: the immortal stabilty of the world, the durable metal. The back of the God's head is darkness, night and death. The back of the King's head is a definite evaluation, 1 penny, a judgment that limits, not without humiliating, the infinite free giving and taking. "The King says that your love is worth a penny." The disfavor of the God is death (rejection).

But the counterface is also a Tail: that is, the coin is a little animal or homunculus. The tail with its grasped number is the anal holding and hoarding. The coin is a little idol: this is the grip of the ego to itself in the flow of the instincts. The Head is my public face of myself, exchangeable for other public things. The Tail is my saying to myself: "My love and anger are worth a penny."

The money is always alien to me. What is exchanged is not essential.

To put something up to chance, tossing the coin, is an imitation of spontaneity, after frustration and crisis, as the tragic hero who has lost his bearings cries out, "Come what may!"

The metal is not digestible, assimilable, but remains in the crevices of the body as foreign matter.

Yet the coin is our justice, such as it is: it is our medium of safe communication (calculated risk). Once we have admitted that we are isolated individuals and the continuity of love is lost, still we must somehow safely deal with one another, with a trust in the limits of the dealing: "I give you a penny's worth of myself." But this is *too* calculating: so we justify the justice of it by symbolically recalling the condition of unity underlying our isolations, and we embellish the piece with slogans and prayers: "In God we trust!" — "Liberty!" And with the faces and symbols of Gods and Heroes, eagles, crowns, owls, branched-candlesticks.

The coin was an Idol. An idol is the illusion of a permanent good dreamed up by sorry creatures of loss and mourning. Handling money is idol-worship. They brought the idols to the Temple, and there also goods were exchanged, consulting the idols; eventually they exchanged the idols for the goods. Historically, the early media of exchange were such things as cattle and salt, consumptible, digestible, assimilable. This was technical exchange. It is not the same as the deathly exchange that occurs by means of the coins, the idols, the fatal lots.

And now—is my offering worth anything? What is it worth? The Head says, "It is worth what is back of the head" (rejected), or even "what is behind" (a lot of shit).

The sovereign ego says, "*I* have the right of seignorage" (anal retention).

But also, instead of reading the coin I can carelessly toss it up and clap it on the back of my hand: devoting myself to chance; and this too is economic history:

> When any person undertakes to work a new mine in Peru he is universally looked upon as a man destined to bankruptcy and ruin, and is upon that account shunned and avoided by everybody. Mining is considered as a lottery . . .
> —*The Wealth of Nations*

One does not mine gold, or hoard gold, as a calculated risk.

Gambling: the impossible attempt to stake oneself (adult masturbation).

Let us distinguish *secular alienation* and *sacred alienation*. Alienation is the isolation of the ego from the soul and the world: secular alienation is the calculated acts of the isolated ego; sacred alienation is the desperate act of the isolated ego. (Relation between Marx and Kierkegaard.)

July 1948

The Psychiatrist

DAVID RAY

I admire the manliness with which Sam deals with me, approaches me to tell me of his anxieties. After all, I am his father, the proper person to tell them to. He's my little man and he comes to climb up onto my lap. "Daddy, I want to tell you a secret," he whispers.

"What is it?" I say, and there are some interruptions. Supper's making its slow, difficult way to the table.

"I want to tell you my dreams."

"What did you dream about?" He's up. I settle him on my knee, on my upper leg. He's still small enough that he can crouch there, his legs folded under him like a little idol.

"I dreamed about . . . piggies."

I knew right away, of course, what was coming. When Adelina had fed her pigs, beating at them with a stick as she let the slop roll into their trough, Sam had been right behind her. He'd watched her beating at their bars with a stick and kicking away at the pigs. As soon as she'd leave he'd throw anything he could at them, or run up and beat the bars with a stick of his own, and then run to me or his mother, screaming that they were going to eat him, if they grunted in his direction.

"They were eating," he said.

"Oh, and what were they eating?"

"Grass."

"They were eating grass, were they? And what else?"

"And books."

"What else?"

"And weeds."

"Grass and books and weeds, and what else?"
"Lips."
"What?"
"Lips, and faces."
"Well, aren't we lucky they don't eat lips and faces in real life?"
"Yes. What do piggies eat?"
"They eat slop, don't they? Orange peels and potato peels, remember?"
"Yes, that's what they eat. Isn't it?"
"That's right."
"And their own caca," he says, a free man again.

He unfolds himself and crawls down off my knee. Somewhere, in a psychology book, I read that a man hits his peak at three and a half, and it is all downhill after that.

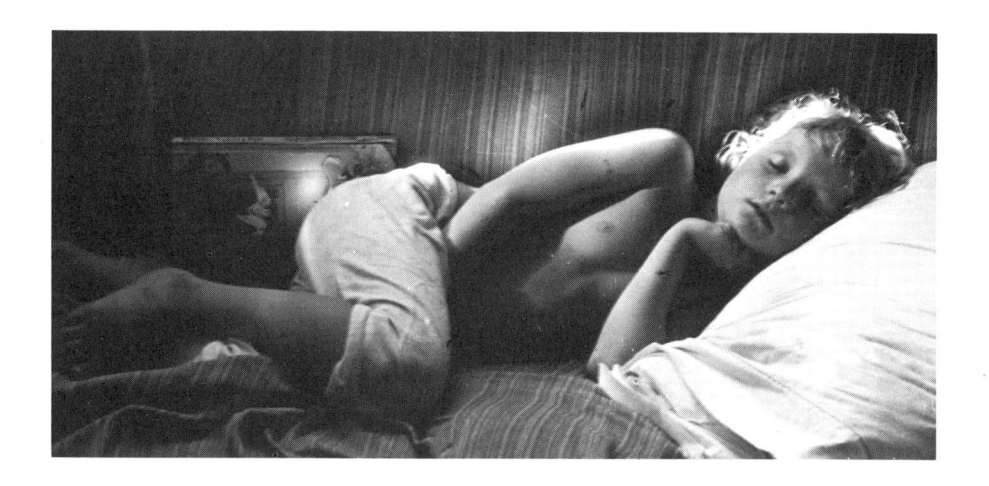

Alice Braxton Johnson

for KJH

Michael S. Harper

—the ritual of the golden stool is the telling of grandmother—

We lift your weight from chair
to bed to bedpan to chair to windowsill
as you stroke your way
from third floor infirmary windows
of our home;
I walk tearless to school
forgetting your name.

When you sit up all night
in your chair waiting for your children
to come holding their ginwheel caravan
of parties, roughnecks following to beat
your son: trumpet-playing playboy Barrett
would call to the window in hazy
first light: 'you there, Mom?'
and you always were.

So my mother nursed you over
years heart-stroked to the coalcar
of cemetery unnamed in my memory
but for the large kitchen where you reigned
hovering children, grandchildren plucked.
Your son, Barrett, would hold me loosening
in the '46 Ford from Rome to Brooklyn
breaking the limit—
as he was to die leaving Rome
in the hazy morning ride
driven off the road
in a favor for a friend.

Did you save these roughnecks
who hated his laugh
when they rode him into the marked tree;
did you know he was to follow
you in his coalcar of our family?

I watch his black sole plant
his size twelve foot jamming
the gas, my eight-year-old hands
at his wheel, his fight with my mother
in mortgages, my mother's weight
on the seasoned floor of the moon,
the moon bleeding onto linoleum,
my father's face in the transom
where I was born, your house
torpedoed on my tearless walk to school,
and this empty chair.

November

Jonathan Holden

There's little fanfare when the circus leaves,
it exits secretly. But one warm afternoon
there is more sky than there should be;
you can see all the weathered scaffolding
that kept the show afloat:
the sycamore's threadbare, the big top gone,
crews of blackbirds have moved in,
above you squirrels are taking measurements.
Even the sky is under construction.

Three Poems

CHARLES G. BELL

To Galway

I dreamed of you tonight, your liver
Doubling you up like a shrimp in bed.
I waked, the Yaddo scritch-owl
At it on the sill. Death-devoted
Singer — you, not that damned bird —
Something more than poet, a man:
For God's sake, mind yourself.
You are too sole to leave us here
Among so many cruds, the worse alone.

Weed Farm

Take a truck-jack after rain,
Wrap the corded stalk around,
Heave back, levering to a ton;
As if a devil groaned
    "Karrunk" —
Feet of dark bull pizzle jimmies out.

Green Vermont. Kinnell from Plaquemine:
Clubbed and jailed. I fling
The burdock, twist the next, heaving
For the death-groan — Ah —
    "Karrunk" —
As mad as wrong or right to purge the earth.

Sursum Corda

In cold night
The crooked log
Spouts fire.
No more asked
Of death-loves than this:
That punk at midnight
Bleed like stars in space —
How fiercely vindicated
The earth that wrings our hearts.

The Marble Distances
Byron Vazakas

The naked statues at Palais Chaillot,
erect, or bent to discus, empty-eyed,

as sailors staring into vacancy,
hurdle the marble of their nudity.

It is as if a sculptor, in himself,
had chipped from rumored Elysée the shapes

of sensual Eden, polished promises
of perfect forms, an alien Genesis

of exiled lovers, as a foreigner
imagines Paris he has never seen.

A Day in the Sun

for Stephen Logan

JOHN LOGAN

The magnolias merge each to each
with unearthly ease in a dance
of riotous flower among
other gnarled, leafless trunks. My son
takes a picture as I posture
in the bar open to the air.
We have had a drink or two there
where trees loom up over the walls
and ferns tumble from their tops
like waterfalls. He talks to me.
My son talks to me. He explains
the awfully intricate way
the camera works, tells its quirks,
how you focus the lens and how
for light you align the needle
in the multi-shaded circle.
Master now, I take a picture
of him, of my beautiful son.
We get in the car and make shots
all the way to Sausalito.
We park and go down to the shore.
We sit on a log together
and set it to take a picture
by delay on this sunbright day.
There is a background focused too:
Eucalyptus trees just for us
and (lower) the blue flowering
iceplant. And then we smile and hug
each other for the last picture.
We hear the snap of the shutter.
We grin and he winds up the roll.
Then Stephen frowns and mutters, "Shit.
Something wrong with it!" And we find

the damn thing didn't work quite right.
None of the photos will come out.
We pause for half a minute and
then we laugh: all that instruction,
posing at elaborate ease,
and "Cheese." We turn toward the car
Our thoughts a bit complex and far.

Shelby County, Indiana. February, 1977

G. E. MURRAY

My horses are dead,
but the hail has gone.

Three hundred miles south
the ground stands fit to plant.

I rinse out in a wind,
dreaming hard of lumber.

Logs and failed crops
appear in my songs.

In this looseleaf country
I can bury and build.

Rightly, it is winter.
I won't need more horses.

Photocopied Garments

PATI HILL

Riding pants, circa 1940 or 50.
I found them in the local thrift shop and have hung them on the wall like a landscape full of highways and byways of tiny stitches, irregular suede and cotton fields, ravines, plowings, etc.

On second thought, maybe they are more like an airplane, so beautifully tacked together with flaps for folding up or down and stress-points reinforced.

I don't know why the vision of a straight jacket has come into my head.
I saw one once, but it was a sleazy thing.
Clean and white. Pressed as if it had been run over by a van.
You felt you could easily find your way out of it if you really tried, whereas a garment like this seems so reassuring you'd hardly bother.

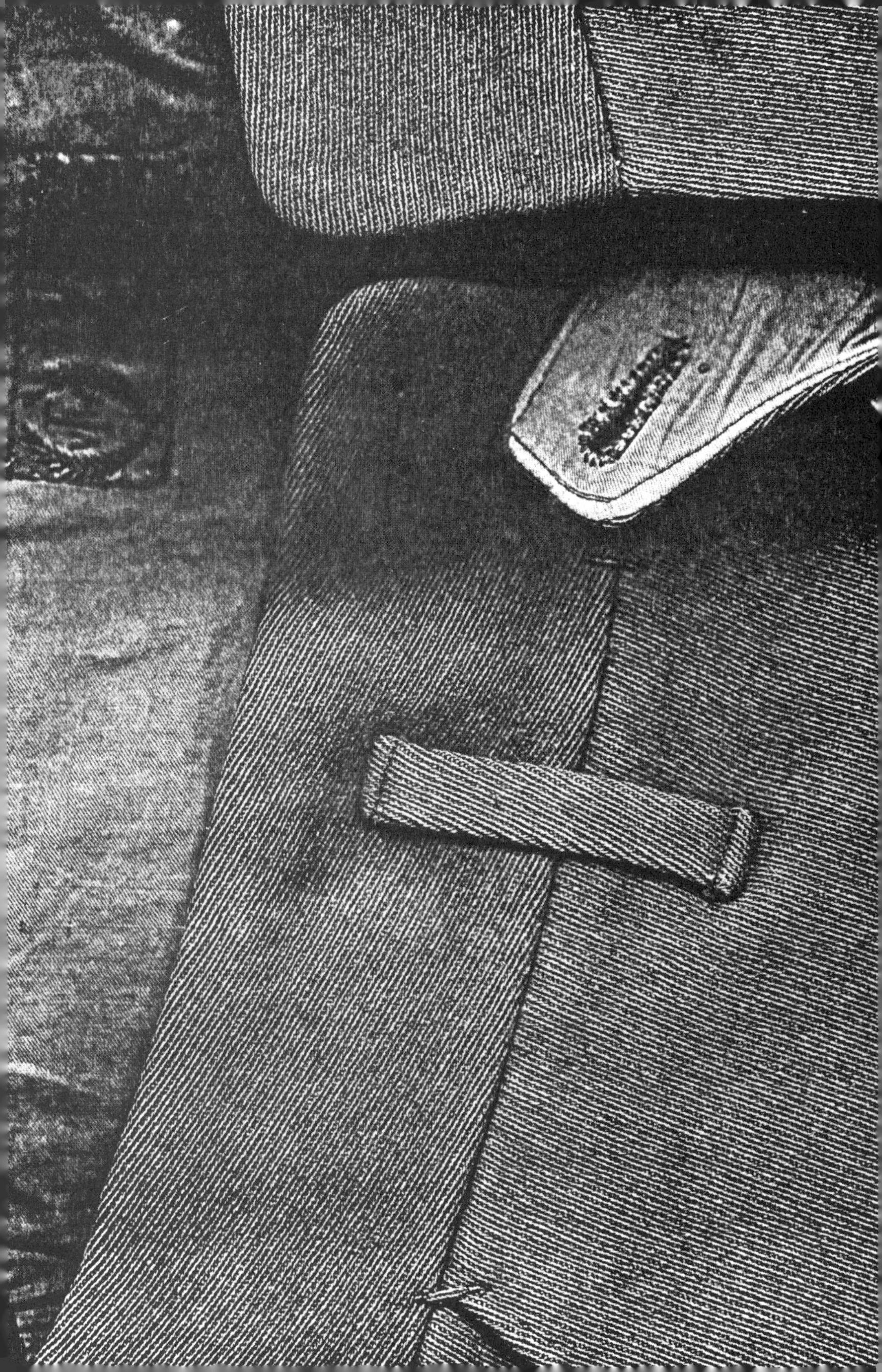

My old fur coat doesn't know me.
It lies on my back, a few limp cousins stitched together in my shape.

What a rush of grateful recognition I feel as I make my way toward it across a crowded room or in a restaurant.

Moths like it, too.

There's no saying you can't be well off in another's skin!

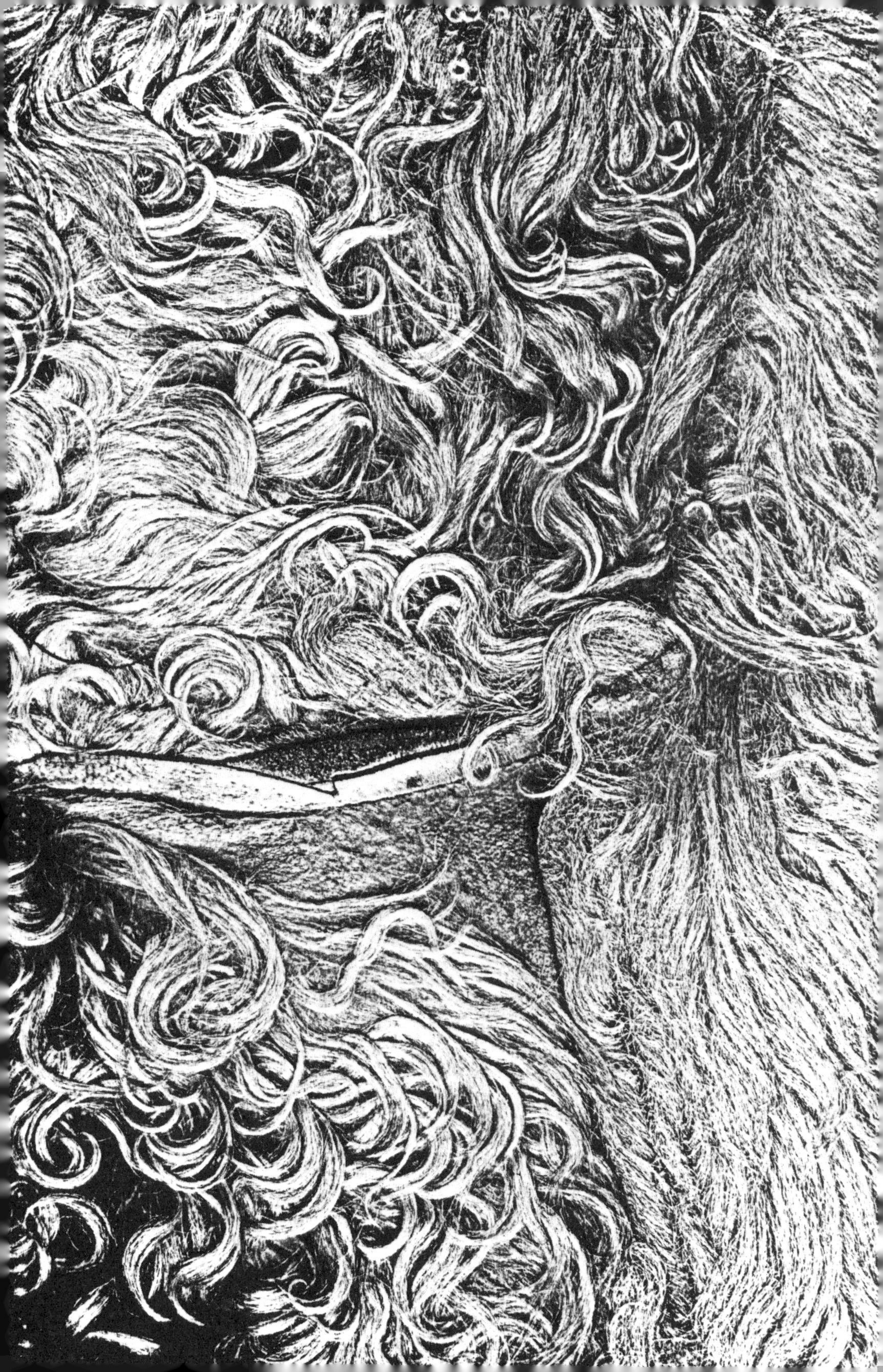

Missing Now 5 Days

Geof Hewitt

Our neighbor lives a mile from here by car,
but I can see her horses easily.
Her pasture and her mobile home
are on a hill that faces ours.
As the crow flies we're very close.

And we've had meals together,
maybe half a dozen since they moved here
three years ago. The paper says
that she's been missing now 5 days.
Bloodhounds and local rumor haven't come up

with any of the terrible evidence
needed to pin her to a particular spot.
Local rumor is so frightening
we haven't joined the search, even though
as the crow flies we're very close.

And as I watch the horses move across her pasture
from this distance I often mistake them for her
or her husband or some other human form
that moves smoothly against the whitened grass
stealing down to the fence for a nuzzle or some sugar

secret—from her hand—she holds

This

H. E. Francis

"So you're disbanding the house, Emma." Mrs. Bentley stirred, to go.

Disbanding?

"Yes. Time comes, you can't keep up. And prices." Out the window the frail wicker chair wobbled in spurts of summer wind. Creeper roses swayed the loose fence.

In the kitchen Don's chair was still empty.

"Your maple casts such tempting shade," Mrs. Bentley said. Meaning: I long to sit and visit. But she really couldn't; Reverend Bentley kept her going in the parish.

"My brother, the one who drowned, planted it—twenty-five years." When Sam died. "A blessing in the heat. We could sit out there if you like." Sometimes tiny caterpillars lowered themselves on individual webs. Strange: she saw Dan there in the blue sky, floating forever. Never found.

"Not with all you've got to do." Mrs. Bentley wound through cartons. "No goodbyes. You'll be visiting. I'll look up one day and you'll be back in the congregation." Her back went. Down the street was old Mrs. Rackham on her stoop, sitting it out with her daughter, Monica, hair a fallen white rose. Monica herself stood on the walk, rounded as a hook. Because she humped. She had always dragged a leg.

A minute she stood at the door, watching the Rackhams. The air filled with a great breath. In the heat the street moved. "Move yourself." Still, she stood leaning into it. What was she waiting for? "Fool!" Her throat laughed. But the empty street spilled up, two blocks, a dead end at the hospital on the edge of the crick, and all the ocean somewhere beyond. All her family had passed through. In the air sea lay against her skin. A thing rounded the corner as if a spider'd crawled over her sight: a man on a wheel. "Albert!" The sight disoriented: not in the *morning*. Was her head going too? All his life Albert had sailed up and down the street 7:45 and 5:15, a perfect clock, riding the years between the skimmer shop and home. She drew back. Years he'd never spoken. The silence proved she was inside him, or forgotten. But they'd been young together: he courted her. They sat on the back stoop in the dark, whispering. Her father would have none of it. He beat her. She was too young. So they'd taken to the graveyard, behind the stones, where crick water glittered below the bank. But it was Albert's mother, alone in her house—husband and the other sons gone—who waited under her dim kitchen bulb for Albert. Sometimes out of a night sleep his mother came down the slope to the back door and pounded. "Walt," she said to Dad, "I want my Albert." She wore slippers and a coat, but she was naked under. Nobody could look. Dad, his eyes blind to her flesh, put his arm about her. "Come, Carrie. Albert must be there now." He'd guide her back.

I didn't take him, Mrs. Dalton, she confessed.

But she had him now, in the yard.

She would never have believed! Albert posted his bike and knocked.

"Come." She was standing in the maze of boxes. The windows were naked.

"Your boxes have to be moved—and the shed emptied." She was appalled by that voice too far gone for memory.

"Yes." She was too stumped to say more. She could not of course resist.

He went at once to it—box after box. He was a man of no words. He'd always swallowed his voice. Speaking, he faltered, but how he once sang! Birds did no better in the church ivy. She watched him pile cartons at the curb for Derek's pickup. He was pure wire. His permanent cap shielded his face, but the edges said he'd gone white. He'd always kept his eyes to himself.

In the kitchen she packed the last rags for her scatter rugs.

But her eyes fell on Albert's moving back. Why today? Love? Not for a shapeless heap. She *was*. No. Love all closed up like his turns sour. But he *had* loved Dad. Or had it been a favor to her? Whether she was around or not, Albert always looked out for him, cared for Dad's dog when he was away or sick, wouldn't even let *her* take it; and over Dad's grave had been a gardenia blanket, FOR MY PAL. Funny: young, Dad hated him. Or could you know?

They'd said Albert crumpled at the news of Dad's death. Couldn't get his breath. She understood that. The night Sam went, she woke and her own breath was terrible against the walls. After, her lungs never felt the same: like he took some of her breath with him. Nights were worst. She couldn't comfort her body; it was slow forgetting. But now and again she'd cry because she couldn't remember the feel of him inside her. Now, she no longer knew that woman she remembered. Slow, you settled. The house got to be a new thing you learned. You moved different in it with no body to nudge. Her things got alive after Sam—her mother's crystal vase, blued from sun; the shiny faucet; an old green tie she couldn't discard; the waterfall plate from their night in Tiverton.

Over the fence the Vinsons' dog shot for the postman and struck the boards, fierce. In Wickhams' the Persian, sure of safety, tongued herself indifferently.

Her own grass was empty.

Hoisting herself up the stairs, over the red carpet—from the old church aisle—she prepared to lug the last down, but couldn't refrain from a look: over the empty lot on the rise, past swamps of cat-o-nine-tails and trees, to the Protestant cemetery and Gull Pond. There! She knew she'd see *one* gull anyway. Her own throat startled her. The bay beyond settled serene and blue in her head: the Plum Island light beckoned. Dan. But she'd have no more of drowning; that tree was enough. Her brother had plastered these walls too.

Suddenly a curtain flapped over the attic opening.

"Birdie! Birrrr-die?" She saw her gray tail asway, her head questioning. "Ha-ha-ha! *An*—gel!" Birdie braced against her, the tail thrilling her leg. She knocked the register put in—half a century now—to catch heat when Mama'd go down early to rage the kindling fire up to them, her and the boys. In San Diego her brother Jordan was staring out at an ocean they said he didn't even see. Down, she carried Birdie against her neck and carried all three of her brothers shouting and laughing in her morning head—but to no black stove, no mother. Her own kitchen was empty, walls stood, but her floor gleamed, ready for the Balders.

Windows open, from here in still moments she'd hear the tinkle on the door of Mott's Delicatessen on the corner. The blue MOTT'S and red MICHELOB signs were a comfort at night, but they were sores on the day. She held a breath now: no sound.

But a flick of gravel and then another silence harried: Albert—off without a word! And she denied the grace of thanks. But he did come. Once, as a girl, she was silent with him.

The boxes made a neat wall along the curb. Who'd end up with all their stuffings?

She walked through the empty rooms smitten with cruel sunlight. She stood clear. There was nothing to touch.

She was waiting for something to fill it.

The church chimes came, rushes of leaves, the pantry door creaked, upstairs a wall ached, and in the front room Jennie was suddenly standing there.

"Jennie! I didn't hear you. And the boys!" Adolph, Ted, Stanley. She tousled heads.

"Jees, you're getting bad, kid," Jennie said.

She laughed. Jennie's heart was right. "I get these spells. My eyes cut off. The world goes inside."

"You kids sit and shut up now." The three found empty crates and sat, pods about to burst. "You tell your son you black out? Now listen here, Adolph, I'll swat you 'f-you don't leave Ted alone." Adolph recovered his hand.

"Joel?" she said.

"Now who in hell you think I mean, kid?"

"I've written. Joel's got his own problems. You have to pay your own responsibilities."

"A rotten shame, this house. They let me see you up there when I want?"

"All you want, Jennie. It's a rest home, not a jail."

"Then what'm I bitchin' about? I brung you this—I know you ain't Catholic, only it been layin' there since my old lady died. Fourteen karat!"

The cross swam in her head. Jennie's warm flesh was still in it.

Jennie was up. She wiped her mouth and her lips made a wet swab against her cheek. Jennie never kissed. "Okay, kids!"

"O Jennie, don't forget the lamps." Two from her mother, one from her father's mother: wedding gifts.

"Wait up, you kids! Take them lamps and haul ass home, then you get down to the crick till supper." They went, shouting. "Christ, whatta ya do with'm?"

She could hear the kicked-up gravel.

Do?

In the kitchen his chair was still empty. She was afraid if she moved it, he wouldn't stay. In all the years—thirty-one!—he hadn't missed a morning. She would walk in and he'd be sitting there—in overalls, his cap on his knee, hands under his thighs, waiting. He would be fifty or so now, but his face was constant —flat; the lower lip hung, wet and idiotic. They kept his reddish hair short. When he was grown, he made gestures and blasphemies, scaring girls, so they'd castrated him. Even when his body got flabby and his breath panted, his face kept smooth. Her own men came and went. But he was like a beginning in her, and an end, all at once. She thought about the others, but he grew, silent as a child in her.

Motionless, she stood, hearing the house. Wind ran along the wallpaper. She loved listening: sounds never stopped. Only once in all her years had she heard stillness. It was the clearest moment in her life:

That morning Don was sitting in the chair.

"Why, Donnie . . . slipping in that way. Always surprising me." The words were constant as church. His eyes rotated. "A haircut! My!" Sweat shone on his new scalp, his neck ribbed wet, the clothes clung. July wet. "Come. Come *on*."

She pumped. Water sucked and wrenched in cool spurts. She thrust his head and arms under—"There!"—and left him drenched and unwiped, looking, with the sun, deep into his eyes —and gasped: for his hand went under her dress; it touched her thigh. It was cold. She could not breathe. She could not move. For a long time they stood, staring into each other. The blue in him was deep and clear, but splintered like ice, with no bottom. And such stillness. Death must be like this. But when he moved—bolted out the door with a curse word, as usual—she was afraid: where he touched burned and she felt weak.

That night she did not sleep downstairs with Sam. She went up to her brother's room. She sat on the edge of the bed. It was then she noticed the fine purple tree on her thigh. And remembering that locked and frozen sea in Donnie's eyes, she caught her eyes and cried. The tree grew. Years it fed on her blood and spread over her leg and deep into the other new ones.

Outside, her father, Bible in hand, was by the apple tree, his sandy hair looped by wind, white blossoms all over his black shoulders—come from prayer meeting, preaching this day, up the north fork of Long Island, his territory.

Fool! That tree was gone. Her father'd said, "Chester, be sure'n pull hard or it'll fall on the ell and Mary'll kill us sure!" His brother pulled just right. Uncle Chester.

She closed her eyes and clutched the sink. Spells will be more frequent, Dr. Sterling had said, and you simply must expect them; it's part of all this. But faces crowded her lids, trying to get in. If her eyes went, they would all come inside. She was glad there was another sight. Still, she couldn't bear them all at once. Someone called, "Emma?" and she opened her eyes. "You, Emma? You here?"

The others went. Catalina stood peering under cupped hand through the screen.

"Cat! For heaven's sake, come in."

Cat embraced her—always, the only woman. Latin blood had to touch.

"I bring *manzanas—por el bus*," she said, "so you no be hungry."

"Apples! We'll have to sit outside. The furniture's about gone."

Catalina was smaller now. From modesty she'd always worn long skirts, a swaying shadow on her property, which she seldom left. Bent over, she made a strange lopped stump in her garden. But how beautiful she'd been: a Puerto Rican girl marrying with great tribal ceremony the son of an Indian chief and a black woman. Coming into town, she'd sat colorful and high on the wagon beside her man, not knowing then the thorns she'd bear for that blood. When Geebo died, all the tribe buried him. The governor came.

"You know Catalina never go on bus? On train, *si*, *y* automobile, but never bus." She slapped her sides, laughed *He-he-he-he* softly, and opened her eyes wide; they were half milked over. Almost no one visited her—the house was a burial ground of objects, mounds she burrowed through—because she always fed you and she couldn't see mould or dirt or insects and she was accustomed to her odors.

"Then you'll have another reason to visit me!"

"Not in bus. Danny, *he* bring me—in *coche*." Danny's second wife had run away to her family in Brooklyn, so he drank. "Gottee good job, Danny—telephones company. Good boy, my Danny." But he'd fallen from a pole. They kept him on, but he was seldom sober. Her jaw chafed; the teeth clacked. "Gottee go. Danny come lunchtime." She'd stayed her minute, never more. In the dark face her eyes blanked, white as the rim of skin edging the dust cap she never removed. She headed back, swaying across the road.

The apples were warm with sun.

When she opened the screen door, the sight shocked: "Don!" He sat, rigid in his chair. She dared not blink, eyes and head betrayed so. But he fell into place. "How'd *you* slip in?" A tide filled the room. A painful joy pressed at her temples; her fingertips throbbed, but she held them back. "You'd think it was the Fourth, Don, the parade of people I've had through this house today." He was hunched on his hands, his eyes up, and his wet lip hung. He was her years of talk. *He* seldom spoke. Did words lie in heaps in his vacant head?

Once, she would like to sit in his head and look out.

She wanted to warn him all her words would stop. Tomorrow there would be silence here.

"First thing this morning it was the Bukowskis, asking could they take me there, then Laura Zettle, then Boots, Wilma—they offered too—but No I said." Clean. You must leave no tatters, her mother'd say, teaching her sewing. Briskly she rubbed the sink clear. "There's a time you take things in hand. Thank God for Sam, or I'd not have had the house or freedom, enough to live on and see my way clear to make arrangements without burdening . . ."

Don scratched his ear, penetrated it with his finger, shook his head vigorously. "Did it pop?" She laughed. One eye rolled. "God a winker, Don?" She squeezed the rag and hung it on the faucet.

But her feet scrunched. "Don! You've been on the beach." Glits of sand like seeds littered the linoleum. "You'll be bringing in sand fleas first thing." Down on her knees with that damp rag, she dizzied a bit, with weight on her head. Don's legs swayed her eyes. She pressed up, the room wheeling, and the sink rose into the willow, the window cocked, flowers melted into one another, then settled, neat again. The Balders would pick them.

"I saved the last piece of cake for you, Don, but no plate—just a napkin."

His mouth ate. His eyes never shifted from her. He never blinked.

Did it matter to him that the room was empty? Or was the place where she was?

What would happen tomorrow when he looked into the empty room? The sight was strange even to her: whichever way she turned, windows gaped, she saw the whole world, clear to the Sound, saw the hospital full, saw the road down to the cemeteries and Gull Pond—all bared too full. She'd never walked in so much empty space and light. You had to have *things*—to know where you were. When Sam's things were all around her, she never thought of him. Or Joel. Or Dad. Now, they crowded in, making a room of her head.

But could she hold them all?

Don's hands went under him again. Frosting rimmed his wet mouth, crumbs like snow on his thighs. Was she a thing to him?

Next door a howl went up. "Loretta's going to work. Lash'll moan till she comes home." His eyes stared.

"I'm taking a trip, Don. There'll be lots of people, and I'll be right on the Sound." Like Jordan, in San Diego. "The place is clean and bright, and I won't want for anything I need, and it's not really far from here. If Joel comes, he'll be satisfied I did the right thing, though his wife'd like this house; but she'd just turn it to money because they're always owing. I don't see why. All his life Sam never got near as much salary, and look what he did with it. *Look*, Don—there's Mrs. Doyle, still on her way to the deli." The old woman inched her feet, a snail; stopped; called to Eddie and Joe, the Polack boys sitting with their beer behind Hinkelman's, in a thin flutey voice, "Hey, boys! I'm eighty-five today! What-ya think of it?" They whooped. Proud, she went on.

"Imagine! Eighty-five. And Ed and the kids watch her like a hawk. A good old soul. I thought seventy's a long time to be till *I* got there. Ha! Ha! You're just a boy, Don. Got the world ahead." Since a boy he'd come to that chair. He was longer than marriage. Dad—though she'd run off as a girl—had come when Ma died and lived out the years. You were the men you cared for. Was that it? "You, Don! Stop picking your nose." He wiped it on his pants. "Never learn, do you?" She smiled. "I'll dump this last grease. Never pour it down the trap. If you get a wife, teach her that." She swooshed it into the dead spot behind the Eisenhowers—the pretty things! Her eyes longed after them. The pan slipped and conked against the ground.

"Oh-oh!" A voice crossed the lawn.

Sam. There was a quick blot of dark, then sun blazed in again. Her breath quickened into laughter. "Amiel!" Wearing Sam's clothes. One by one she'd given him everything, just Sam's size. Amiel wore clothes into the ground, maybe even slept in them. "Whee! You gave me a turn."

"You got a nice day." Was he wobbly? From early morning —since the time he'd stopped digging graves—he'd guzzle beer with the boys, all bachelors. Her joke when Sam went, whenever she'd take them the now and again rice pudding or casserole: "We bachelors have to stick together." With beer, Amiel traveled back. Hours he'd play his accordion under that apple tree—polkas summoning up Momma, too big to move from her rocker, and Poppa, "what left me my house," a rugged old German with a fist. "I seen Albert workin' here. I said Emma coulda called *me*." He favored a foot, hospitalized for it once from one of Sam's mouldy shoes. She'd felt mortified.

"I didn't expect him. *You* know Albert. Are you going to keep those blossoms to yourself?" For he'd borne a white apple twig.

"You seen dot tree?" An umbrella of soft snow.

"What happened to your *buttons?*" He was so big, enormous rough hands that dug, crabbed, fished and a barrel chest that wanted to break through. "Take that vest off. I kept my kit. You sit on that bench." In no time flat she'd finished, a near match. "Figured," she said, "I'd while away time with it, though it'll be good to *have* time for a change." She laughed. The neighborhood milked over, but settled back around him. A throb came behind her eyes.

He stood, too big on the lawn, and still. "Your fodder—" It heralded a sentimental journey.

"You go to the shed," she said. "Take the box of tools I've saved. They'll come in handy. And tell the boys hello." The sun was high. It clutched her head. She'd deliberately chosen this time of day, the hour she usually withdrew into her cool house. Amiel headed for the shed.

"That poor man," she said, going in.

The chair was empty.

"Don! *Don?*" Space cried out.

He was playing with her: she went from the pantry to the living room closet to the bedroom closet. "I know you're up there, Don. You come down here." And she laughed in pursuit up the old church carpet. Too fast. There was a churning, and far waves in her head; in Amiel's yard the boys bobbed. She held to the window. "Don?"

No, he was not here.

Far, past Albert's, down the road, streaks of blue water glittered. On the pane her fingers touched it. It was never more clear.

Downstairs the chair was still as an island. Gone, he was terribly clear. She hadn't known: why was he the hardest to leave? Because she had never gone? *They* had gone, leaving great spaces inside her.

Amiel was crossing the lawn with Sam's toolbox. "What-ya got there, Amiel?" That was Eddie. One by one they'd steal his tools, or he'd trade for a beer; at least somebody'd use them. Suddenly Amiel halted and cocked his head and at the same instant she heard the sharp shriek, "Aaaaagggggggggg!" The cry ran up her leg. A thunderous pummeling came from the shed. Something inside her leaped and seemed to hurtle her out the screen.

"Don, Don, Don!" Trapped in that dark.

Her hand raged toward the shed. "Help him!" The kicking was furious.

"I hooked dot." Amiel unlatched it. The door bolted free.

"Goddamn fool dope!" Amiel said to Don.

But she could hardly speak, her breath tore, and she leaned so close to the casing she saw Don's black pupils shrink, his eyes grow too wide and clear and empty and fill with sky: there was a long space and she saw perilously down.

But she said, "You all right, Don?"

His mouth churned a furious spasm of curse words. His eyes rimmed with furious tears.

She turned to go, but he screamed, "Aaaaggggggg!" He clutched his finger up: blood. His eyes froze there.

"Now, Don." He was so taut she dared not pull the finger. "It's just a small cut," she murmured. She touched the blood to her lips. "There!"

He stared. The clean finger stilled him. Then he put his mouth to it and marched across the lawn.

Over the fence the Vinsons—she waved—withdrew. She heard laughs from the boys in Amiel's yard.

Deep, her blood was reeling. There was the taste on her lips. She had never put her hand on him all those years since the stillness. He was in the purple tree in her body.

126

She locked the back door. The front would lock when she slammed it. The two suitcases? Yes, on the stoop.

"Birdie?" Nowhere. Well, she would soon be at home with the Balders.

She sat on an empty crate. The heat was rising; it chafed thick.

Her eyes would not stop exploring. Each space was so filled. Her sight hoarded.

There were moments you did not want to leave behind.

From the corner the horn sounded. *Derek*. Gravel rushed under the wheels.

"Right on time, Mrs. Windham."

He set the suitcases in the trunk and waited by the car door. Always polite, that man.

"You'll be on time at the very last, Derek."

Before she stepped off the stoop, she heard a catch of breath and halted for a quick glance back. But the breath was her own.

Judy Ray

Four Poems
ETHERIDGE KNIGHT

Three Songs

"I was so in love I was miserable" —Guitar Slim

I. Slim's Song

I knew something was wrong
when he said
I want this whiskey tested
and my money invested
'cause times are bad
just lost the best girl
I ever had.

Of course it didn't last long.
Not after the coconut was opened.
No milk. No milk.
Just bubble, bubble.
Toil and trouble.

We call and call:
it wasn't me.
Me neither—
It wasn't me neither,
neither neighbor.

II. Song of the Reverend Gatemouth Moore

Gatemouth Moore
became a preacher.
Now it's *The Reverend*
Gatemouth Moore.
This is where the wind
begins to stretch
and cling to solids:
like a rock is a rock
a bird in the sky
is a bird in the sky.

A tornado warning is something else.
Teach them to run
from the enormous funnel.
Sometimes the retarded children
come to play and are ushered
about like lepers.
Teach them to avoid the sickness
that waits in the well.

Bwana this is your game
(bwana mean *friend*:).
Because we have the music—
So, please, come dance—
come dance with me.

III. Healing Song

The power returns. We remember.
The night of the tennis shoes.
The eyes in your garage.
These twins. These twos
glare at you
in and out, up and down.
But it all
comes out the same place
and fails to convince.

(Meanwhile in the heart of the city
the night is long and moonless
but the fire is bright
in the hearts of the people.)

It all seems so simple
so I'll tell you where to look
not what to see. "Dr. i-john
the Conquerer" has roots.
He sees. Sometimes the music
makes you want to boogie.

And always the white streets
and ladies departing. Ladies
departing.

Indianapolis War Memorial

Young boys play in pairs,
Touch the war weapons: Tanks, guns,
Dreaming blood and death.

Crown Hill Cemetery

A black and white dog
sniffs gravestone to gravestone;
pees on Hoosier Poet.

Riverside Park

A brown oak tree leans
in the arms of his brother.
Squirrels leap, limb to limb.

Duchamp's Nude

Crystal MacLean Field

All those gold brown oiled bones
coming down the staircase
where the eye waits
for the smooth sureness of the limbs
the round sharp of that hip bone
the one my friend has
a good wild bone

Card Island or Cod Island?

ISABELLA GARDNER

I did not know then and I do not know now.
The child I was went there nearly every night for a winter
or more, half a century ago. My younger brother George
slept in the same room. The muttering embers
in the grate spoke quivering pictures to the ceiling.
What a viewing! From these slipping shapes I construed
a hill-side coastal village and staring hard I was transported
to that primal coast I stood on the pier I climbed the steep street.
All the cobblestoned way up that hilly street every single
tiny house was full of light. The little houses all alight
by the light of whale oil lamps. All doors ajar. HERE you are
All the people in their houses shouted here you ARE
Here's cookies, ginger people baked for you Here's a
     BOTTOMLESS
pitcher of milk for you. From each glowing little house
they beckoned me and they welcomed me and they hugged me.
I was theirs. They were mine. Such Love!
     Wolves bared their teeth at my little brother in his dark.
Only to my father each bedtime, and to our Irish laundress
those mornings she was there, did I recount the serial tales
of where I'd been and gone. George, two years littler than I
cried, "Take ME Take ME why can't I go too?"
How could I answer him? The laundress, crisp
and tactful Celt, asked me "and who was it then that
you saw *last* night, dear?" I'd tell her. She would nod.
It was understood between us that she'd been there too and knew
the Island and each Islander. "Give my love to all,"
she'd bid me. If I missed a night of going there
she'd say "Well now dear I couldn't make it myself last night.
They'll know we both had other fish to fry."
    Cod Halibut Haddock Scrod
    In the afternoons my mother played Cards
    Scrod Haddock Halibut Cod
    At my bedtime my father played God

The King the Queen the Ace the Jack
I was the joker in the pack
Island Island Cod or Card
Once your coast was my backyard.

Liv

Philip Booth

Not to dream her to bed, not to drink
in mid-age to the shapes of her body an old hand
might cup, nor to sleep in her own dream,

but to wake in some change of one's life
beside her: to measure dayrise in her steeped eye;
first, if ever, now to belong to how her face

assumes morning, and crinkles against
an old anguish into her dearest smile:
now to wake with her: to give prime love

to how her eyes admit of self-possession,
yet yearn, like children strayed to nightmare ice,
for loving and forgiving; forgiven now,

being so enabled by her being: to touch
the day's contingency: to face
with how she looks her ways of seeing.

Two Poems

WILLIS BARNSTONE

God

They made me.
Gave me a white hippy beard
and my throat sang
a loud cuckoo and the godly nightingale
and they heard.

I was a star
in the morning of their book,
a fly at noon,
a beast in their chest, angel in their ribs,
a purple hat.

I was king,
sun, frog, a lily that lived
in the winter.
They wouldn't let me die amid the murder
from the clocks.

I was a bell,
a cowbell and clavier. At dawn
my whole light
woke the bubble of the earth, burned its edge,
blew me inside!

They made me
and unmade me. My best friends
left. I hang
around the old neighborhoods, lonely man
behind the times.

My good friends
suffer for truth. I was
their joyful lie.
They need me. I make their day ridiculous
and cast them

alone in dark.
I was a morning star. Now
Im nothing. Zero.
Theyve got nothing like me. Before I left
I made Hell.

The Angel

Is a boy with wings.
Like folk rock in the black air
he spins his gold
net above a dark girl who hides so he can find
her bed.

Is a girl with dreams.
A surgeon gave her a heart. He
lights up and sits
in her angel legs. They glide to the earth moon
and back.

Is a man and girl.
When the dam broke they ran from
the killing mud.
They soar. Fire. Strong as butchered bulls. They float
on sheets.

Is a man and woman.
Armies clash on Asian hills.
They want to help
so they kiss candidly and float in the perfect
night air.

Rain

Jorge Luis Borges
Translated from the Spanish by Willis Barnstone

Suddenly the afternoon is clear and spread
With light, for now a fine rain is falling.
Is falling or fell. The rain is a thing
That surely happens in the past measured

Now. Whoever hears it has recovered
The time in which chance fate is wakening
A flower called a *rose*, and more, revealing
The curious pigment of the color red.

This shower steaming blind the windowpanes
Will brighten some lost neighborhoods with rain
On black grapes of an arbor that divides

A certain back yard that is gone. The moist
Evening brings the voice to me, the wanted voice,
Of my father coming back—who has not died.

Widow

Felix Pollak

"Our life together," she says,
and her voice breaks.
All around, a desert of stones,
grey sarcophagi for the living
reaching into a smoky sky. Her voice,
a tremolo of retrospective visions,
transforms the stonescape into a
flowering garden, leading to the beach.

"Our life together," she says,
her voice breaking into song.

His sardonic counterpoint is not
in earshot now, his half-smile
out of sight. A pun, incognito,
dies on the carpet. His silence
is audible only to few. She covers it,
quoting him freely — a filter-tipped
replay that bears her out.
"Our life together," she trills.

Her words, endowed by faith, move
mountains and mausoleums. She is not choosy
as to her confidants — any pair of
willing ears will do. Naturally, there were
grievances, he was not easy. Of course
there were spats. But even Adam and Eve,
she suspects, had those. Yet would you
denigrate the sun because of sunspots?
"Oh, our life together," she sighs.

If there are whisperings of guilt,
they're drowned in the song of the brook
that winds its way through evergreens.
And nightmares? Lightning flashes in the wee
hours illuminating the barren structures that
contained her bed and a cold grave? If so,
they have no witnesses — not even herself
the morning after. Nor will her dreams
have witnesses again, she vows, for quite some time
to come. "Remember our life together," she whispers,
as she falls asleep.

Two Poems

Tom Hanna

Sues Seas

The old hag down the street
with no children
dried up.

where does she walk?
out of what part of the universe did she come?
out of what sky did you hate her?
out of what dryness of your own?
out of what light

where did she learn to open the earth?
where did she learn to bother you?
where did she learn to stay so dry and bitter?

try making it easier for her
try telling her what you know
try seeing what's inside her and what
juices she knows how to make flow
the sea   and the sound of the sea
and the shape of the sea
and the way the sea talks to us
and makes us know its forms

look for the old lady down in the tricky desert
watch her go, burn, burn away.

I did not know this was her land.
I didn't know we were supposed to look for her land.
I didn't even hear the wind when it did come up
or the lights when they blew our way
or the lady's open window shade

or friend
or sky
or sea
or life
or tree
or shape
or edges
or creepy dream.

Businessmen's Lunch

What Happens when poets
get together to discuss business?
We decided that the broken angels
were more viable than tethered goats.

Nothing to Remember You By
Jan Gauger

You'll be leaving. The days ahead
are edged with light.

Lloyd Reynolds, Calligrapher

Albert Bellg

in memoriam

It's not so much
        what exists.
                Names
are easy words
        answers.
                In between
is the pause
        the white space
                the inhalation
that presumes
        what we mean
                beyond words
the force
        behind words
                like a blizzard
white
        between the snowflakes.

Late
February
snowfall—
—the violets
are almost
hidden

Haiku from the Japanese Masters translated
by Lucien Stryk and Takashi Ikemoto

Fish shop—
   how cold the lips
of the salted bream.
           BASHO

Moor:
      point my horse
   where birds sing.
           BASHO

Plum-viewing:
   in the gay quarter
sashes are chosen.
           BUSON

     No need to cling
        to things
   floating frog.
           JOSO

Calligraphy by Lloyd J. Reynolds

Father's Day

Harry Roskolenko

My father, who had died in 1937, suddenly phoned me. If I was shocked, I did not let on. It was too unusual to get such a phone call. After all, he had been a kind man . . . and I remember the jokes he used to tell me in Russian, Yiddish, Japanese—and the walks he took me on when I was old enough to walk; the clothes that he bought me—and the way he argued with the clothing storekeepers about their prices. They gave him a schnapps first; then a second when they were reaching the closing price for a blue suit. It had started at thirty dollars. But an hour later and four schnapps later—when the sale and the drinking was completed—my father got the suit for eleven dollars. And he would laugh softly, kiss me, let me hold the box with the suit and as we walked home he told me Japanese jokes he had learned when he had lived for five years in Osaka, after running away from the Czarist army in 1889.

"Well, son," he said over the phone, "how do you feel? Did you ever marry? Did you travel a lot? Did you become a learned man? Do you still write stories? If so, tell me a story and I'll tell you a story."

How do you tell a story to your father over the telephone, especially a sad story? Should I talk about the wealth of one of my rich brothers? Would that be important now to my father? He seldom thought much about money, though he had worked very hard as a cloak-presser on Greene Street to keep his large family in shoes and bread. No, I would not talk about money. Nor about greediness, indifference, brother against brother—not that. But I was thinking it. I was trying to comprehend the power of my father's unique telephone call. How had he managed? Did he know God? Had he become a physicist in the 41 years since he died? Everything was probable in America, which my mother had called, in some humorous anger, *"America goneff*—America the thief."

"Are you a learned man? Did you become a scholar?" my father asked again. "What kind of books do you read, son?"

"I've just read a remarkable book by Isaiah Berlin. It is called *Russian Thinkers*, father. Have you read the men Berlin writes about?"

"Whom does he write about? You always read, read, read—and I had to carry you to bed when you were a boy—because your head was asleep over a book on the kitchen table. So who does Mr. Berlin write about?"

"About the Russian intelligentsia. About anarchists and socialists, people like Herzen and Bakunin . . . and about Vissarion Belinsky, Gogol, Tolstoy, Turgenev . . . and one time when we were walking in Jackson Park, you told me that you had read all of them, father. You read them so long ago. I think it must have been in the 1880's, before you were a soldier in Siberia. It was very cold there, wasn't it, father? And wolves? And the *nagaika*—the whip across your back? Do you still have the scars?"

"I don't see myself so well, son. But scars are scars, son. Tell me, little-boy-big-boy, are you happy? Are you well? Do you still dance the *Kazatzka*? I liked to watch you when you made those big jumps, son. Tell me, tell me—son, do you pray? Do you go to synagogue? Do you still believe like I taught you to?"

Should I tell him that I was very ill? No, not that. I wanted to make my father happy or he might not call me back. Should I lie? I had, at times, when I was a boy, especially about attending Hebrew school. I used to skip classes, go to the East River in the summer time, take off my clothes—and along with my kid friends—we jumped in. Swimming was better than becoming a *melamed*. I could always become a learned man. Scholarship in America? Money in America? Welfare, ethnics—all the changes that had taken place on Cherry Street—should I tell him that Cherry Street had gone away? Impossible! How does a street go away? Does it walk like a man? Do builders rebuild and a street vanishes?

"Have you called your other sons, father? They would be very happy to hear from you. Will you call them?"

"What will we talk about? They never read books—and they never understood the heart. You did, son. I saw that when you were a child. You took care of other children, saw that they were not hurt—and dogs and cats and roaches—everything. No, I will not call them. And, please, do not tell them I phoned you. They would be jealous . . . and they would not believe it. You know, you always made up stories, son . . . once that you had sailed to the Statue of Liberty on a raft, all the way from South Street. Did you really do it, son?"

"Yes, yes, father—I did. And did five wolves really try to attack you in that sentry box? And what was the name of that army post in Siberia?"

"I forgot the name—but they were all shot. I was a good soldier. We learn from the dead. I heard, where I'm really at, that there was a Second World War. Is it true?"

"Yes—and millions were killed . . . and there was a man named Hitler?"

"I knew about him, too, before I left in 1937. Did you go and fight against him?"

I had fought against the Japanese in the South Pacific, but I might have hurt his feelings. After all, he had lived in Osaka for five years. He spoke Japanese; but then, too, he also spoke German. My mother was part German. We were part everything, it seemed. We looked like Russians, Germans, Irish—and Jewish. We had very strange faces in our internationalism.

"Did you get hurt, son? Oh, malaria! Oh, your back was broken! Does it still hurt? Is there some aftermath in your bones? I too had injuries, son. A bullet went into my right thigh but I managed to come through. Hospitalized? At least, son. You too, for six months? Nothing else? No terrible diseases? There are so many still around, I learned when I called the wrong number. I got a hospital and they asked me what was wrong with me, so what should I have said? That I was dead, not dead? Alive, not dead? I just wanted to talk to my youngest son—nothing else, and we are talking."

"Can I see you soon father? I would like you to kiss me like you did when I was a boy. Can I see you father—please!"

"Now, now—don't cry, son. I have gone away and I have only made a phone call. You were always running away on ships, on freight trains. You were wild, wild—like a wild body. Don't cry, son. It hurts too much to remember too much. But it would be nice to see you, to walk with you, to hold you, to talk about books—especially about all those Russians. Don't cry, son."

But I was crying. I was overwhelmed with his memory, those terrible jobs, our poverty, his strange courage, and he always dressed as if he was a doctor or a professor. Professor Father. Doctor Father. Loving Father. A great and noble man to have been so patient with my wild ways, my angers, and the time we had struck each other when I was thirteen. How could I have done it? It was right for him to strike me for what I had done—when his patience was no more. But it only happened once, not every day, not every year—just once. Father! Father! Please knock on my door. Please come to my dreams. Please awake me and take me for a walk. Father! Father!

My tears and my memory were interrupting bits of our common history. So many veins of memory per fraction of a tear. More for salted tears. Less for laughing tears and nothing for numbness. Go numb, I thought.

Will I always cry when I hear the phone? It might be my mother next time, who had gone the year of 1949 when I was working in Paris. Ah, the tears of Paris! Just like the high sky and the artists painting along the Seine. Just like the tears of Osaka when my father went to a Japanese bath and the Japanese men asked him about the cruel scars across his back. My father would smile, he said—and in his Russian and Japanese he would tell them about the seven-thonged belled whip, the *nagaika*. Why? What had he done wrong? Had the Tsar ordered it? Had some officer or a sergeant ordered it? But my father took his bath, went home, had some saki to keep warm—and then he told my mother . . .

And she had said, "This is a public display. You must go to the private rooms like when I go with you . . . "

"It costs too much," he answered.

"It costs more to talk about it. You were almost killed, remember?"

They remembered. I remembered—for I had lived in Japan for six months during the occupation. I used to get drunk with Japanese artists and writers—and they got drunk easily. A half a dozen sakis and they were on the moon. They were on Mt. Fuji telling the emperor where to go. Go jump! Cut your throat, you imperialist emperor! They used to talk like that and laugh with some minor hysteria . . . and they said, so often, "If you did not have blue eyes you would look like one of us . . . and you remember everything your father told you about Osaka . . . " Then another hot or cold saki . . . and all the baths I took and the massages I got from the little women and girls—and the baths had not cost that much.

I said something in my badly remembered Japanese—1947 learned; my father's was about 1890 or some such year. Yes, but what was my father saying to me? That he had lied about loving me? Then why had he phoned me so many years later?

I tried again, in Japanese: *"Watashi aishite musuka, otosan?* Do you love me, father?"

He sounded nervous on the phone . . . and then he said slowly: *"Omaega chilsakatta tokiniwa omae o sukanaki. Omae wa sorewa ranbo datta shisokeni omae no kyodai mo onaji yoni aisanakereba naranakattanda. Socchoku ni itte lika?"* And he repeated it in English: "I never liked you when you were a child. You were so wild—and I had to share my love with all of your brothers and sisters. Can I be honest?"

"We are, father. I am, at least. *Iitomo, otosan. Sukunakutomo watashi . . wa sono tsumoridesu."*

Now my father cursed me in a little affectionate curse. *"Bakamono!* You silly boy."

I cursed back and laughed into the telephone warmingly—*"Bakataro!* You silly old man."

Then I laughed like I was his son and he was my father. He spoke in Russian but my Russian had gone. We spoke in Yiddish and I answered. We were saying the same things all the time to assure ourselves of our affection. It was a telephone game making me a boy and my father then about 40 years old . . . and suddenly I said, remembering one of his great adventures: "Tell me a story! Tell me a story! How did you run away from Siberia? How did you escape the Tsar's army where you were beaten on your back? Tell me a story!"

It had been my favorite as a child. He described the heavy uniform, the fur hat, the fur gloves, the thick boots, his rifle, his bayonet, his knapsack—and I was seeing him soldiering.

"Son, son, it was very hard. No one else would run away with me. I went alone. We were at Yakutsk. We had built a winter road near there. There must have been two hundred soldiers—and I went with the wagons to the port at Okhotsk —on the Sea of Okhotsk, to get supplies. There were so many wagons, so many sergeants, captains and soldiers. It was the Spring and the rivers and lakes were overflowing. After many days we were there. We were loading up at the small port. I think the supplies came to Vladivostok by railroad; then by ship up the Sea of Japan to Okhotsk. Do you want to hear more? It is such a long story, son. Oh, the operator wants another ten cents—so please wait, son. Do I have it? You want to call me back? You want to know what my number is? My number?"

"Yes father, from the phone booth. The number is on the top of the coin box. Please give me your number—please! I'll call you right back."

"But there is no number, son. Please, operator, do not hang up on me. I have not finished telling my son a story. Thank you, operator. Thank you very much, operator. *Ziy gizint*, operator. Yes, my son will pay for this part of the call. His number is 212-243-4211."

"Thank you operator," I also said. "Father! Father! Are you there, father? I never heard of a telephone without a number? Does it have a dial?"

"It has a black dial and little numbers. I can hardly see them, son. Imagine my getting a hospital first—but I'm glad you were not in the hospital. I was in a hospital, son. Where is there? Where is here? Anyway, the story. I am in Okhotsk. I find a Jewish fur dealer. I tell him that I want to run away from the army. I show him the scars—and he is sympathetic. The fur dealer says that a ship is going to Japan, to China—and he can get me simple clothes for my soldier clothes. There were no passports then."

"No passports? What a wonderful world you lived in then, father. Where did you go? Where did you go? How did you go? Did the Tsar chase you with horses, dogs, soldiers, wolves—how?"

"There was no chasing, son. The fur dealer gave me a working-man's clothes, took me down to a small ship, got me a job on the ship—he was sending furs to Japan—and then, so many days later, I saw the most wonderful places. The names? I am sure that you were there in the war you were in. Seoul, Pusan, Kyushu—you were there? How nice that we had both been to the same place. And what were you doing there, son?"

"Talking to people, mostly; about that war, mostly. I made up stories about what the Americans and the Australian soldiers were doing while they occupied Japan. You know, father, Japan lost a war in 1945. Against who? Against everybody, father. But please, finish your story—and then come over and and we'll have a glass of tea. Do you know where I live? No, not in a hospital. No, not in a graveyard—father. I am still alive. Where did you get those silly thoughts you silly old man? *Bakataro! Bakataro!*"

"Bakamono! Bakamono!" he answered and we both laughed —and he went on . . . "And the small ship, stinking from furs and hides dropped part of its cargo at Kyushu. Do you know that small cove where the dock is, son?

"Of course, father. I used to fish there during the occupation. It's near Shikoku—and I met a rich Japanese girl there who wanted to marry me? Should I have done that, father—out of my religion?"

"Oh, that—well, would she have converted and gone to the *mikva?*"

"Perhaps? Her father made a lot of money on the black market. Do you know what the black market is?"

"Where I'm at we know everything, especially black things. Yes, Shikoku—and that's not too far from Osaka. Maybe a few hundred miles. Oh, I smelled worse then from the furs and hides than I smell right now."

"Then, please—come over and have a bath, father. Tea, schnapps, sponge-cake—whatever you want. I've got everything, father."

"Everything? Like your other brothers? What do they have, son?"

"Not my kind of a telephone, father. It comes from God directly and God is the OPERATOR, father. But what am I talking nonsense for? Come over for a bath, please. Do you remember on Fridays before it was time for *schule* you took me to the Rutgers Street Baths—do you remember?

"*Ich gedenk! Ich gedenk!* Please operator—not another ten cents? No! No! Don't cut me off, please. Son, tell the operator that you'll pay—please! Please, son—hurry! Where am I? This dark black telephone. This infinity. This dread. That life. That *nagaika*. That last day in 1937—and was it my heart alone, son? You silly boy—*Bakamono! Bakamono!* Yes, yes, I love you, son. This infinity, this dread, this telephone. You were so wild, so wild, so wild—*Bakamono.*"

NEW LETTERS

A magazine of fine writing   Edited by David Ray

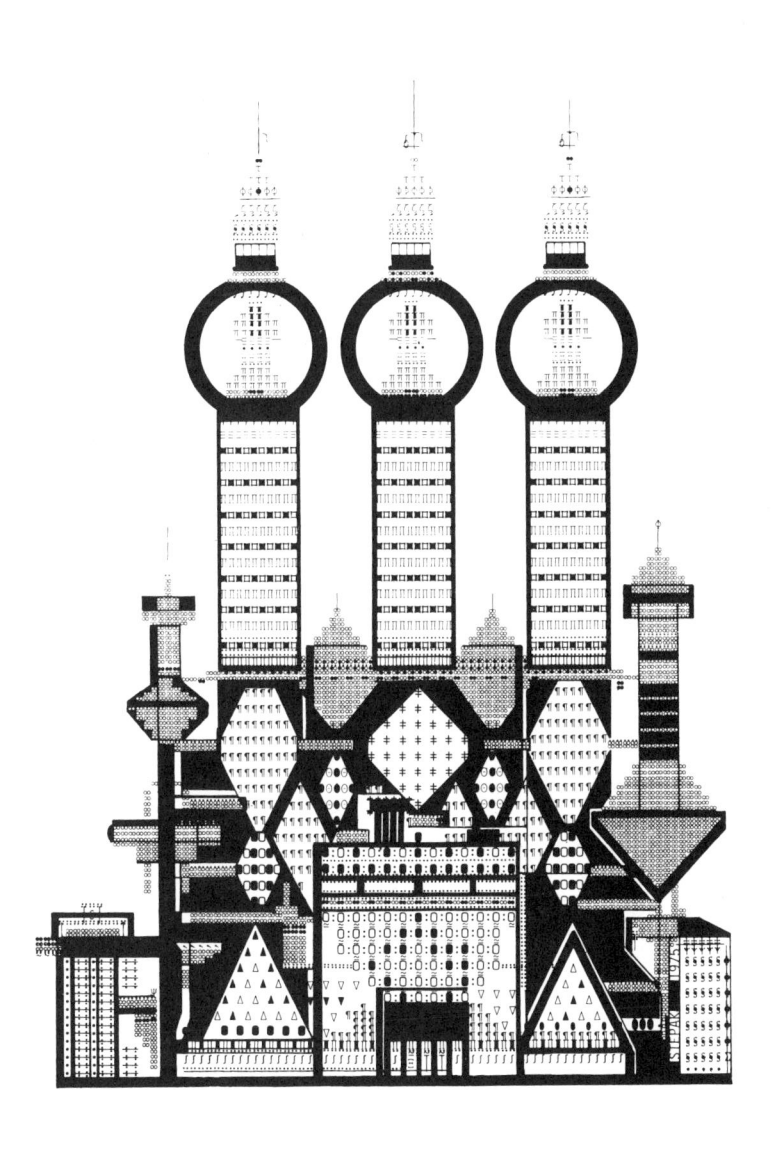

The Latest Fiction by Willard Manus, Robert Taylor, Jr.
Essays by Elizabeth Von Vogt and Wang Hiu-Ming
Five Texas Poets * Reviews

NEW LETTERS
A magazine of fine writing

Since Feeling
Is First

An Anthology of
New
American Poetry

Edited by
David Ray
and Gary Gildner

NEW LETTERS

A magazine of fine writing

The Writings of Paul Goodman

Edited by David Ray
Guest Co-Editor: Taylor Stoehr

$5.00

NEW LETTERS

A magazine of fine writing   *Edited by David Ray*

A Sonnet Sequence by Marya Mannes

New Fiction by David Madden

Poetry by George P. Elliott * Joyce Carol Oates

Photographs by Judy Ray

$2.50

Recycle

Thomas Zigal

What Johnny liked most about Tidy Town was the constant hum. The washers gushed, they agitated feverish water in their round bellies, they clicked on and off and at times pulsed steadily, monotonously, like a drum beat. Dryers rumbled; wads of wet clothing churned round and round behind glass faces, and now and then he would find himself dozing to the rhythmical metallic pinging of a button or a zipper scraping against the dark hot insides: snapping, snapping, snapping in perfect cadence. The laundromat was a comfortable place to be. There was no silence. Never.

From a pink plastic chair, contoured smoothly to fit hips and lower back, he watched a very tall, casually dressed young woman push through the doors carrying an unwieldy bundle of laundry tied into a sheet. At her side, struggling to support part of this enormous bulk, was the woman's small daughter, her face half enveloped in the massive whiteness. The two of them groped the last few feet to washers numbers seven and eight and dumped the dirty clothes on the floor, dust balls scurrying in all directions from the heavy thud against the tile.

He lifted himself from the contour chair and wandered over. "I can help you with your laundry," he said.

"Pardon?" The young woman was breathing heavily. She bent down to untie the knot corked on top of the lump, and her peasant blouse fluffed outward, revealing soft white skin from her thin neck down to her cleavage.

He swallowed. "I can help you put it in."

She looked up, smiled, then glanced at her cotton-haired daughter standing silently by the machine, staring at nothing in particular. "We do fine," she said, nodding toward the girl.

"No, really, I'm very good at it. Quick too."

She brushed back a strand of blonde hair that had escaped her flowery scarf. "No problem. We can take care of it." She broke open the package of soiled laundry. Nylon panties, t-shirts, and socks spilled out.

"I just came back from overseas," he said. "I was in the war."

"Oh?" she said, sorting through the clothes.

"I guess you realized that. You probably noticed. But everything's going to be okay," he said. "I'm lucky, I suppose."

"You know, we appreciate it," she said, standing, azure eyes warming him, "but we can do this ourselves. Thanks, anyway."

"It's no worry. I want to help you," he said, bending to examine the coloreds and whites.

"We don't . . . need your help." She turned her back and plunked open the lids of the machines.

"I—I think you should at least give me a chance."

Adjusting the chrome selectors, her back to him, she said "*Please.*" Then, turning: "If you don't mind."

He shrugged and returned to his chair, scrutinizing her work with the Speed Queen washers. The outline of firm buttocks shifted under her jeans as she strained to empty her laundry into the gaping machines. Not enough powder, he thought. She hadn't measured the white crystals carefully before dumping them in. The yellow stains would remain, the dark smudges and ground-in grime. No cleaner clean, no brighter bright, no freshness you could smell. He knew. He had become an expert.

She slammed the lids and shoved in the coin slots, the Speed Queens swallowing the quarters and dimes with a rattle. Small red lights flipped on, then water began rushing, hissing like a broken steam pipe. As she turned to gather up the clothes hangers on the floor, she noticed him staring at her. Her unsettling blue eyes glanced at the wire hangers, up to the wall clock near the money changers, then back to him again. They lingered on his face a touch too long—studying the scar on his head near his hairline, he imagined. She couldn't hold back her disgust for him any longer. With a flip of her head, as if to toss off those pesky strings of hair loose on her forehead, she took her daughter's hand and walked quickly out into the afternoon.

Lying face down in that sopping rice paddy, an awful silence beating all around him, jungle silence, he had sensed somehow, in the flickering dimness of what had happened to him—the coldness, the wetness seeping into his flesh, into the raw stinging in his scalp—that he'd deserved what he got: he had expected it every time he patrolled, every time he trotted out with his platoon those last . . . it seemed an entire lifetime. But he could deal with that. It was since he'd come home, since his mother had granted permission for surgery, that he had not quite been himself. He suspected the doctors lacked sympathy. They were not careful. They carved more out of him than was necessary; while incising his skull they tried to fix him so he would hear the silence, that awful jungle silence.

His mother and the doctors were foolish to think something so crude would work on him. That was why, he suspected, they kept him as an outpatient in the hospital—to observe him, to figure out what they had done wrong. His only complaint, and it was one of the few things he discussed openly with anyone, was that they had not confined him to a Veteran's Hospital but to some private medical conglomerate that treated men like stockyard animals.

"I didn't think you were a soldier, son," the old man had told him yesterday on the hospital bus carrying the group of regulars downtown, those patients who could get about the streets and spend their money in bars and cafes, watch the young ladies play tennis at the girls' school. "You had to be in the service before they'll let you in the V. A."

"Excuse me, sir," he'd said, coldness in his voice, holding back the impulse to strike the old man, to drag him into the aisle and kick him, "but I was over there for god knows how long. All my friends were there. Practically everyone I know."

"Beats me, then," the old man had said. He shook his sunken-eyed face, rested his hands on his cane. "Seems like they probably have some good reason."

The buzzer sounded on an overloaded washer, a gnawing *yaaaannh!* that turned everyone from old magazines and the bulletin board announcing massage and yoga and pups for sale. Young mothers folding handkerchiefs stared at the guilty party—a college student fumbling with the lid, trying to quiet the ugly commotion and put everything straight again. But to Johnny the noise held a certain hypnotic magic all its own. As harsh as the sound was, he missed it once the student had righted the machine.

Tidy Town was the only place he felt at home, the only place he frequented when the bus dropped off the outpatients for the afternoon. He would sit for hours, basking in stark fluorescence, the roaring and shishing and chugging like an industrial orchestra playing his favorite tunes. Washers were juke boxes—a few coins, a dial selection, and the music would wing him away. Often, if business was slow and the thrumming threatened to cease, he would spend his own money, pocket change the hospital allowed him. He had his pick of the machines.

As he sat there, it still disturbed him that the woman and her daughter hadn't used enough detergent in numbers seven and eight; he couldn't neglect it. They were gone now, probably returned to their apartment nearby for a few minutes or out to buy chocolate for the child. Too bad, he thought, how poor the wash would turn out. He felt somehow denied that she and her daughter would move about in less-than-spotless garments: it ruined the delight he enjoyed around clean, sweet-smelling girls. As a man, as much a man as he could be since the operation, he felt obliged to see that their charm was not sullied by a mother's carelessness. Especially since he'd been *over there* and knew the disgrace women and little girls could fall into so easily.

The vending machine for detergents hunkered in the rear, near a door marked PRIVATE where the Oriental owner constantly darted in and out. Johnny fished for the change in his pockets and produced enough to buy several tiny boxes of Cheer. When he thought no one would notice, not in the hubbub of people stirring around—rolling the squeaky baskets full of wet clothing to the dryers, measuring exact amounts of bleach for diapers—he uncovered the lids and began seeding the steamy wash, green panties and twisted, bubbling bra cups tangled around the gray middle prong. Two boxes, three, four. That would do it. He eased down the metal tops and stepped back—smiling, relaxed, spent from the accomplishment.

"What did you do?" The voice was behind him, female, urgent. "Those are *my* things. What was that you were doing?" The woman was back, her daughter staring up at him innocent-eyed and blank. The mother peeked into the washers one at a time, dropping each lid with a bang. "You were fooling around in my machines, mister."

The evidence, the small square boxes empty of all powder, were lodged three across in each hand as if magnetized to his skin. In his excitement his fingers closed around them, crumpling the cardboard like tissue. He tried to fold his arms but realized how silly he looked holding crushed boxes under his pits.

"I told you we didn't need your help!" Her watery blue eyes were livid.

"Uh, well, no, see . . . You didn't put in enough . . . I thought I might . . . ."

"What's your problem, anyway?" She was staring at his forehead, at the hairline scar. He dropped his eyes, his face tingling.

Foamy white suds boiled up through the cracks in the tops of the machines and spilled down the sleek beige sides, leaving long wet trails to the floor. "Look what you've done!" Tossing open the lids, peering down into the lathery tub, her soft lips parted in disbelief, she lifted a dripping, soapy, unrecognizable snarl of garments from the fuming mash and held it up in the light. "Look!" she said. "You've ruined it! Now what am I going to do?"

The sight of the frothy, carcasslike mass revolted him. The gruesomeness, the deformity of the unnamed bundle—the spite and ridicule in eyes once so fine, so perfect. Even the little girl was mocking him, a wicked, knowing smile faintly mussing her tight lips. He dropped the boxes and ran outside.

The scrap of sheet he found in the laundromat's outside dumpster was perfect for the note. In the too quiet emptiness of a neighborhood afternoon he sat on a bench across the street from Tidy Town, under magnolia trees, white flowers in full blossom, their fragrance drifting down toward him as he fashioned his message, careful not to form the letters too close together. He didn't want the ink to blotch and run words into one another. He was taking a chance, anyway, that the note would remain readable after a half hour in a dryer—her dryer.

There was a tap-tapping against the sidewalk. He looked up to see the old man approaching slowly, his cane rapping firmly with each step. The old man hobbled to the bench and without a word plopped down, raising the brim of his hat off his forehead and letting out a weary breath. He remained silent for some time, his old eyes transfixed on the building across from them. Then, his face still solidified in that gaze like an arthritic joint gone stiff, he spoke sadly: "I saw your mother last night, son. She said you were never in the army." His bottom lip began to quiver. "That's the reason you're not with the V. A."

Johnny finished his message and capped the pen. "She would like everyone to believe that," he said, struggling to his feet. Without regarding the old man further, he started off across the street.

"You've got to stop telling yourself those things," the old man's voice behind him, a dying voice that secretly said he could not move from that bench until energy again restored his limbs.

But he had the overriding proof, he told himself as he neared the laundromat's glass front, the strip of cloth clutched in his hand—undeniable proof etched across the top of his forehead in a nasty arc toward his ear. What could the old man say to that? And his mother and the doctors—how did they explain it? No matter now, he thought, there were more immediate things to consider.

The woman stuffed the last of her wash into the dryer and clanged the door closed. Choosing coins from her upturned palm like a little girl picking out candy, she fed the machine, turned the knob, and started the tumbling. Her daughter watched all this awestruck, her little fingers playing with soft white locks of hair. Shortly the mother took her by the hand and came toward the door.

He skirted the front of the laundromat to the other entrance: waiting until the perfect moment, the slightest movement of the door at the far end, watching closely for the second it would swing outward. It creaked, and he pushed inside, escaping their sight, hearing only merry laughter—mother and child—as if running out to play in the spring sunshine.

The clientele had thinned out considerably, and the few patrons paid him no attention, an innocuous figure marching boldly to a random machine. Before opening the door and tossing his message into the hot cauldron of spinning, jumbling clothes, he read his print once over: "You didn't give me enough time. Let me make it right. Please just try me. I can help."

He retreated to a row of washers at some distance to await her return. She would not notice him, he figured, but would withdraw the crackling cotton socks and nylon wear, her dungarees and wash'n'wear shirts, and place them on a table; then she would fold everything neatly, precisely, creasing the towels and wash cloths deeply. . . .

Warmth from a nearby washer spread through him, a pleasing sensation like stepping into a hot bath: a rush up the spine. He pushed himself against the machine and let the humming cut through his trousers, vibrating into his crotch.

. . . Tangled with a dainty handkerchief, static popping, tickling the hair on her arms as she freed the strip of sheet, she would find his faded note and begin to read.

Strange that nothing was happening—flesh unaroused, even with the warm throb of the washer in its cycle. He thought of her, clean and white and naked, lying in torrid bundles of freshly dried laundry, laughing, rolling in it, covering her naked little girl with sheets and dish towels until snowy skin glowed pink with heat. Yet he was unmoved, his lower parts soft and faint. It was the operation; they had robbed him of everything he once was. He tried again, pressing himself harder and harder into the fervid metal.

. . . Scrubbing themselves clean in a scalding tub, the two

of them, whisps of hair curling from the steam, swirling each other in bubble bath—mother and daughter—laughing, showing the little girl soft mountains she would grow in time, mountains that would fill with milk and feed other little girls.

It didn't work. Something was dreadfully wrong. All he had left was the sound, the washer's heavy murmur against his stomach.

"Prease, you must go now." Someone had slipped up beside him and was talking. "Must leave immedia'ly." Nudging him with a small sharp finger, his dark eyes showing signs of shame, the Oriental proprietor studied him cautiously. Then he shook his head disapprovingly. "Not good for custamuhs. Must prease go."

Jerking spasmodically, as if shaken by some unrestrained impulse, he pushed off the rattling washing machine, his movement sudden and violent, sending the little Oriental back a step. "I wasn't doing anything," he stammered, the rushing blood burning his face. "Honest, I wasn't."

"No. Must leave or I call porice."

"Police?" The idea seemed perfectly all right. "Go ahead. I . . . I don't mind. They're my friends. Most of them spent time with me overseas," he said. "I was there, you know. That's where . . . " He lowered his eyes. "That's where I got the wound."

"Prease. Not to make trouble."

"I know you already noticed it. You shouldn't pretend it's not there," he said. "I can't stand it when people just pretend I'm perfectly fine."

The man took him by the sleeve. "Must go," he said in a low voice, kindly, as though he understood some carefully guarded secret.

Quickly Johnny snapped his arm free from the little man's grip. And as the Oriental reached for him again he flung himself backward, flinching, withdrawing his hands against his chest. "Leave me alone," he said.

The clicking and buzzing of the machines was growing weak. A familiar, painful silence was swallowing everything in its stillness. He knew he was in trouble.

"You can't do this. I . . . I'm a veteran," he said. "You can't just order me around."

Where had he seen those cold, unblinking eyes before, coming toward him so ruthlessly, undaunted by his size and strength? The little man approached him steadily, slowly, a beast stalking in the jungle . . . that awful silence brewing all around him.

"I have the scar to prove it," he said, inching backwards. "Here, look, you want to see?" He swooped back a tuft of hair to show the Oriental. "There, have a look. What do you say now? You can't throw me out of here." But the little man moved toward him unfalteringly.

Then he noticed the girl, the same child with white hair and pink glowing skin, standing so quiet and prim by the last washer. She was gazing up at him as she had from the very first, her wide eyes as blue and curious as her mother's. Her tiny mouth was slightly agape.

"You can see it, can't you, honey?" he asked her, squatting, trying desperately to hear what he knew was true, to have the proprietor hear it too. "Look," he said, forcing his hair aside. "It's nasty, isn't it? A big ol' nasty scar."

The little girl looked at him, then craned her neck toward his forehead, examining him as if she had never seen skin and skull before.

"Melissa, come here!" her mother shouted, but the little girl's eyes were fixed on his head.

"Well?" he said. "What do you think of my scar, sweetheart?"

She turned up her nose. "There's no scar," she said. "Mommy, he's teasing me!"

He stood up suddenly and backed into the tepid metal door of a dryer. All at once it seemed they were upon him—the child's mother, the Oriental, even the old man with the cane had materialized from somewhere. They were all talking in different pitches, voices rising like the notes of a wind chime. But the cacophony was gradually being smothered by another sound, a sound like gentle dew dripping in a forest. Fading, dimming.

In the dryer's glass he could see his reflection. He lifted the wave of his hair, and for a second he almost believed the little girl. But it was there, the indelible mark no one could take from him, the scar that distinguished him for life. And behind that face, that glossy image of himself, was a place dark and perfect and filled with warmth. Its roundness, its heat would save him. He opened the door and began to crawl in.

Someone was tugging at his legs—the little Oriental. Johnny planted a foot hard against something solid and bonelike and shoved the rest of his body into the unlighted pouch of the machine, the porous metal still ardent and smelling of scorched cotton. Voices were hysterical in the brightness outside. He reached out and swung the door closed.

Now he could see their faces peering in at him through the glass—panic stricken, horrified. They were people in his own private screening, his very own t.v. show: the mother grasping her innocent child, the old man near death, the Oriental trying to unfasten the door. But he held the burning latch as tightly as he could, his fingers aching from the strain. They would never get him out. Never.

"Turn it on," he yelled, listening to the echo of his own words. "Please turn it on!" The silence was beginning to affect him. He needed the rumbling roar that accompanied the dryer's motion. "Turn it on!" he shouted again, feeling sweat ooze from every pore—hair, face, arms.

Eyes studied him nervously. He thought he saw the eyes of his mother and the doctors there, observing his every twitch. But no one seemed able to move. They were frozen on that screen before him . . . still pictures in a slide show. That was why they couldn't turn on the noise. Do him just one last favor.

Two Poems

A. R. AMMONS

Spring Tornado

The trees warp:
the low-down
comes over the hills and
falls valley-deep
through here:
terror pops out
like shoots:
just the sky will be
left whole.

Certainty

I have certainly felt a documentation of terror:
I have certainly known my
insides to turn all hands
and rush to the surface for help
and felt all the hands go loose:
I certainly have come to believe in death:
my head rustles with footnotes and
quotation marks
that pinpoint beyond doubt
places where my blood
has certainly stopped cold and certainly raced.

Four Poems

E. L. Mayo

A Fair Warning

Practically everyone goes to the Petrified Forest
As visitor or tourist,
Staying no longer than permits of the barest
"We drove through Saturday. Every contortion
Of those grim trunks staggers imagination."

But once in a great while among these strong
Motionless boughs and leaves unwhispering
One stands as if he heard
A petrified bird
And stays long.

Serpent

The serpent said: Forgive me, being serpent,
I always have possessed the power of speech
But since the Fall have grown more taciturn
And seldom bother with words except as now
For critical instruction. Did you know
That Kingston, New Jersey was the capital
Of the United States for several months
During General Washington's last campaign?
And may be so again if what goes on in Washington
Goes on. But I'm not here
To talk politics. I mean, damn it,
Look about you. What do you think
Of this lovely tree with all the apples on it?

The Shift

I stood in a room I knew, a beautiful room
Where on bright rugs and furniture a-gleam
The sun shone, but now it was time to go.
I passed the door and entered the dark hall
But half way down turned and peered back and knew
That what I saw was not the room at all
But a flat picture seen as under glass.
I shrugged and sauntered on. What good does it do
To caterwaul? This alteration
Is instantaneous and will go on
Till memory is the only thing in the world.

House

House
Vast and ambiguous
Which was before we were

Did you
Build yourself and then grow populous
By taking thought, or

Did someone leave a tap on long ago
In you
Which with its spatter

Affirms at the very least a householder
Who will return at last if only to
Turn off the water.

The Best Dance Hall in Iuka, Mississippi

THOMAS JOHNSON

Nothing's too good for the women
Of the Klan.
One by one
The records slot and spin

As they fan out over the dance floor
Like flies
On a bull pile,

Unaware that cut three to one
With the sawdust
Under their heels

Is that disappearance in shantytown
Of a young girl

From which their husbands
Have ground
Their complicity

To a fine, squaredance grit
Of powdered tooth
And bonemeal.

Morning Raga

ROBERT SLATER

Listen. I'm ringing
The bell to heaven.
Jump. Push. Ring.

The cycle remains
The same. Processions
Of gods mingle

With the women
In the old section
Of the city.

Only seldom do they
Carry water. The
Drone always brings

Us back. Keeps
Reminding us
Of important constants.

The temples relate
Still more variations.
These monoliths

Were carved with bronze
And reveal what
We always suspected.

The frailty of granite.

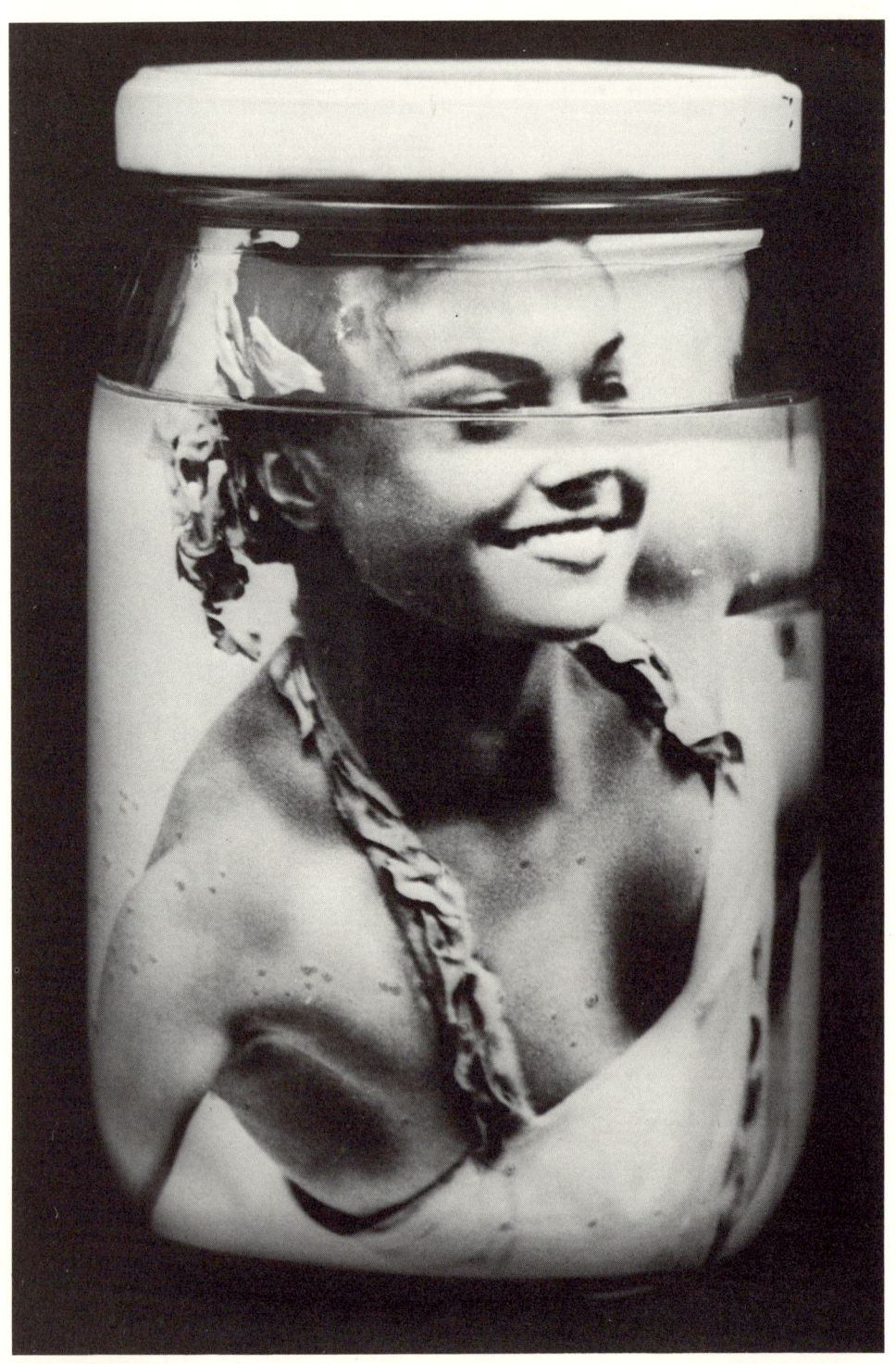

From "Esther/30 Disintegrations" — *Elizabeth Boettger*

End of the War in Merida

ANTHONY OSTROFF

Furnace for a life that's done,
this wet, tropical place
dries in the sun of Cancer,
& the scorched cells of my soul,
wet from their red bath, dry
& swell with dryness, mad
to natural law, & run
from burning red coal to coal,
& swoon for joy in their own char
here in the courtyard garden of our
Colonial Hotel. O Beautiful,
so foreign, flowering, aflame!
We're here for this, & kiss
amid the garden's blaze.
Though Penance play with Pride
& all that grows decay
in the ripe, unholy sun,
we are innocent.
This holiday, personal,
exotic, paid, is our last one.

Four Poems

MBEMBE (MILTON SMITH)

African Art

took one long look
at a common any ol' way
yeah man ain't nuttin' jim
African mask & cried for all
the years i was so dumb.

African Art No. 2

crackers were in a museum
walked by an African sculpture
said it was primitive,
piece stuck out its tongue.

Did They Help Me At The State Hospital For The Criminally Insane?

MBEMBE (MILTON SMITH)

For this one
You need a pocket dictionary
That enters biblical charity
As a synonym for atrocities
Committed in a silent
Partner's best interest.

Cleave end & mean,
Wall them, pin them
In antagonistic corners,
Departmentalize, dissect them
'Til the sense in such nonsense
Is twisted loose. Say "normal"
By all means, by any means
Is correct, justified.
Don't question this!
Declare a holy war on madness,
But stay unmoved by it all like god,
Keep the goal aloft.
& if the goal is missed,
A fraction too long
On the electroshock machine,
A little too much Haldol,
Be quick & resolute with disclaimer.

Then i suppose things could be compared.
Did Truman help the Japs?
By saving countless Kamikazes
From thoughtless death?
Did Hitler help the Jews?
With Jewish enterprise?
Sticktogetherness?
At least the bathwater
Finds its way home to sea.
So when the baby
Who was thrown out with it
Grows up despite all odds
Having drunk his fill
Of castor-oil reality
& held it on his stomach,
Commend the state's parental guidance,
Shake its rank statutory hand.
The state has made a man.

Yeah, they helped me.

Survival Poem

we can slide into sleep in dead winter
in front of the pool hall
or in the alley behind the record shop
denying that we are oppressed,
awaiting the arrival of our saviour
with trump cards like w.c. fields
drawing the fifth ace.
we can be corny,
relish in our own trips.
we can count the cracks in the sidewalk,
scratch our asses
smile hiply at sisters
wear dashikis and drive little cars.
we can watch the greenbay packers on t.v.
or airplanes in the sky.
we can be niggers
while every breeze whispers death
& finally perish like dinosaurs,
our skulls in showcases at the new york museum.
we can let our speech become air
& our fists soft clay

or we can rise
up thru these filthy towns
to rule our own space.

Macabre

Cyrus Colter

"Neat" and "unobtrusive" are the words, I guess, best to describe the new girl they had hired in our Chicago office. She was black (of race, not color—her color was sort of an unclear tan-ish brown) but the fact of her race caused not a ripple, for we already had four black girls out of twenty-five or so. Most everyone liked these girls and when Doris came she was well enough received. She seemed to take this for granted, as she should have, and went about her duties—mostly just typing, no dictation as yet—in, as I say, quite an unobtrusive way. I wasn't high enough in the company (wholesalers of art supplies) to have my own private secretary, so most of the time I used a couple of girls, white, who'd been made available to me for dictation, using one about as much as the other. One day Alicia, the Italian girl, took a sick day, and the other, Katie, was doing some work for Jack Broyles, my very competitive colleague, but sidekick. I wanted to dictate and was sent Doris.

When she entered my cramped, cluttered little office I was impressed, as I've also indicated, by her neatness. She was not a pretty girl, nor very shapely—rather straight slight legs, high *derrière*—but I could see she spent time and effort on her appearance, and to good effect. Her dress was short, as was the fashion, but when she sat down to the right of my desk she made no attempt to tug the dress toward her knees, as Katie and Alicia generally did, but merely pressed her knees together and placed her shorthand pad down on them. Her pencil ready, she exhaled (I thought) a little nervously. It could have been a sigh. I was a little ill at ease myself, in fact maybe irritated; for I had a lot of work to get out before catching a plane that evening for Denver on company business. I wasn't sure—because she was new—that she'd be able to turn out the amount of work either of the other girls, accustomed to our office's rather brisk routine, could have, so I too perhaps sighed as I began dictating a tardy, and somewhat lengthy memorandum to Gerald Lawler, the company officer to whom I reported. At this, my trace of a sigh, Doris seemed really to tense—she sat very stiffly, hunching, shrinking her shoulders as if the room were freezing. Finally after the memo I dictated three letters, then asked her to go type what I'd given her, by which time I'd have more. She said "Yes, sir" and went out—unobtrusively. Looking back on it, I perhaps should have taken time to be a little more pleasant with her, smiled occasionally, put her at ease, but I'd never done this with the other girls. Besides, I was very busy.

Considering the work I'd given her, she wasn't gone too long, and brought back the memo and letters well within the time Katie or Alicia might have, and placed them on my desk before me. Her face was still a vacant mask, and this, I must say, also irritated me a little, although I wasn't at all sure she was really being difficult. I told her I wasn't quite ready yet to continue but would call her in a few minutes. She left again. What I really wanted, of course, was an opportunity to see what kind of work she had done before I dictated more. I leafed through the typed pages. They were immaculate. And the typing was good indeed; the spacing, indentation, and paragraphing beyond any but the fussiest criticism. I began to read the first page of the memo then. The sixth word in the fifth line stopped me . . . "advertisement." I had not dictated that, but "divertissement." Three lines farther my eye collided with "descending." I had said "dissenting." In the very next line I saw "casual"—I had dictated "causal." The last line on the page had "stick" instead of "stitch" and "make-up" for "macabre." (!) I didn't even begin the next page, but picked up the phone and called Marge Beall, our office manager. Marge and I after work occasionally had several martinis together (and I do mean several) in our favorite lounge—mostly when her husband was out of town—but, so far, that had been all.

"When will Jack Broyles be through with Katie?" I said to

her—rather hotly, I'm afraid. "This girl you sent me either can't take dictation or she's hard of hearing, one. Or illiterate. She gets so many words wrong."

"Who'd I send you?"

"That new girl . . . Doris."

"Oh, Doris. . . . Why, you old confederate, you," Marge laughed. "Isn't her work okay?"

I'm from Georgia but took this sally, this playful gratuity, and its implication, at least without overt reaction. "Of course her work's not okay," I said. "Who tested *her?* . . . Send me someone else, Marge—quick. I've got a lot of work to do."

"I can't, Reggie—not right now. There is no one. Katie'll be tied up for another hour or more. Why don't you have Doris type the work over?—you write in the correct words and have her do it over. I won't send you her again if you don't like her."

"I don't care who you send me as long as she can take dictation."—I was slightly petulant now. I hung up and called Doris in again.

"Doris," I said, "pull up a chair and let's go over this stuff I gave you—you've got quite a few words wrong. What I'll do is write in the corrections and then you can re-type this work." She directed toward me what I thought at first was a wary look, but afterwards I concluded it was dry fear. She pulled up the chair beside mine and eased into it. "If I dictate too fast for you," I said—in the most agreeable, understanding, way I knew—"feel free to stop me and tell me. Or if I use a word you don't know, stop me and I'll spell it. Okay?" I looked at her.

"Yes, sir," she said, but almost inaudibly.

I pulled the memo over before us and picked up a pencil. "Now, this word here should be 'divertissement'—that's the word I used." I crossed out "advertisement" and wrote in "divertissement." "Are you familiar with the word?"

Looking blankly at the page, not the word, she exhaled heavily again. "No, sir," she said.

"And this word here," I said—"it's 'dissenting,' not 'descending.'" She watched me write in the correction. I next changed her "casual" and "stick," respectively, to my "causal" and "stitch." Then I came to her expression "make-up"—for my word "macabre." To be truthful, I was a little unhappy with myself, contrite, for not having originally spelled the word for her, without making her ask me. For I doubted very seriously if either Alicia or Katie knew the word. Yet they most assuredly would have stopped me and got it right. Instead Doris had used a word she very well knew was wrong, rather than ask me to spell the correct one. Brushing aside all my contrition now, I thought this not only stupid of her but a little devious. I was unhappy with *her* now. I crossed out "make-up" and brusquely wrote in "macabre." "How did you ever come to use 'make-up?'" I said, smiling testily—"The two words don't sound *anything at all* alike."

She looked at me for a moment, then glanced furtively away as she spoke. "The words I didn't know I tried to look up in the dictionary. . . . Some of them I couldn't find. . . ."

"Of course you couldn't—you can't locate words in the dictionary you can't spell. 'Macabre' is an unusual word anyhow—maybe I shouldn't have used it, because it's generally meant to describe something gruesome, perhaps some miserable, appalling, condition of life; while in this memo I was simply referring to the properties of certain paints—artists' paints and oils, etc.; not anything about real life. After this, Doris, just have me spell any word you're not sure about. I won't mind—it will save a lot of time."

She didn't look at me but gazed vaguely at the memo before us. "Yes, sir," she said.

I spent the next twenty minutes going through the rest of the memo and the three letters with her. There were so many inaccurate, bizarre, substitutions for the words I had dictated that I, besides being exasperated, was at a loss to understand how she could have tested well enough to be hired as a stenographer. As a typist, yes—a stenographer, no. For it was apparent her education was so deficient she had hardly any vocabulary at all. But really, at the moment, this fact was at best only dismaying to me—my job output was suffering. When I had finally finished with all the corrections, she took the corrected pages and re-did them, and had them back on my desk even before I went to lunch. The job was perfect—perfect. Nevertheless, I was much happier that afternoon when Katie returned to me and I was able to finish all the work I had to do before leaving for O'Hare Airport.

I was in Denver three days. I returned home Friday evening but of course wasn't back on the job until Monday morning. Almost at once Marge came to my little office and asked me, in a curious, a slightly concerned way, really, what had happened—between Doris and me. I told her. And in my innocence I was very accurate, very complete. Yet I was unable to figure out quite what she was driving at. Then she said Doris had not returned after that day of our encounter, and that the day following had phoned in that she was resigning. No more than that . . . just resigning. I was surprised to hear it, naturally; maybe disappointed, and gaped at Marge for a moment. But I knew I had not treated the girl any differently than I would have any girl in our office under similar circumstances. One thing, though, did upset me—definitely. Marge, only *half*-kidding this time, had called me a "confederate" again—"You unregenerate old confederate, you," she'd said. I didn't like it a bit this time and I know I showed it. Sure, I'm from the South and no doubt that's why I took such offense at the insinuation I had mistreated the girl in some way, and because of race. I'm an educated man. And a compassionate man. I *know* this. And I take the greatest pains to be correct, indeed meticulous, about these matters of . . . of race. Although I do admit I'm no fuzzy bleeding heart either. But somehow Marge's remark, under the circumstances, offended me terribly and I sulked the rest of the day.

Around four o'clock that afternoon she phoned me—although her office is only about seventy-five feet from mine—and asked me if I'd buy her a drink when we left the office. She meant at our favorite spot, Terry's Lounge. Although I was sore at her, I wanted, really, to do it. I wanted a drink. I needed to talk. I also knew her husband had probably left town that day—he worked for a city-based public utility company yet had to travel a lot—or else she wouldn't have been able to stop for several martinis on the way home. But I wasn't sure whether or not I would take her—I told her only that I'd let her know by five. I knew I wanted to do it, though, and finally called Carrie, my wife, and said I couldn't get home for dinner—which created no problems for Carrie, who had her super-pious mother (a real Christer) and our teen-age (flit-to-be) son, Armand, there to eat with. Thus the way was cleared.

Terry, the owner of this small lounge, was a great little Irishman (although cocky when drinking *calvados*) and greeted Marge and me with beaming, avuncular embraces—he thought himself all-wise in all matters clandestine. Because of its wierd lighting, the place was always in a kind of half-murky gloaming, and Terry practically had to lead us to a booth, where (outside it had been snowing) he insisted on helping Marge off with her boots.

Our first pair of martinis were always straight up, with a lemon twist. Thereafter we customarily ordered them on the rocks, with an anchovy olive. Terry's man, Joe, was on tonight. Joe made the drinks huge and dry. "Why do we keep coming here?" Marge said, then took a sip of the first drink and chased it with water. She smiled: "This is the first time I've been brazen enough to actually ask you to bring me here. But you've been peeved at me all day."

"Well . . . oh, well, forget it," I finally said, and lit her cigarette. She was a plump blonde of thirty-six or so, and too short, but her face was candid and attractive. "You *were* a little raw with me," I added, however.

"I was nothing of the kind, Reggie—I've called you all those names before . . . 'Reb' . . . 'Dixiecrat' . . . 'Red-neck' . . . 'Confederate.' And most of the time it's been when we were both drunk. . . . You only laughed. But, God, this morning you looked like you wanted to kill me. I know why, of course."

"Your saying that this morning, under the circumstances, was at least thoughtless. I'd told you what had happened between the girl and me, and I gave you a very truthful account. Tell me this, how would you have handled her any differently?—and do me the favor of being as truthful as I've been."

"I would have made the girl feel wanted," Marge said simply.

"I didn't make her feel *unwanted*."

"Not consciously, no. Yet you somehow really socked it to her. By the whole incident you told her she was practically illiterate but that because of your magnanimity she would be tolerated."

I was furious. I knew I'd better keep quiet now or be sorry

later. And I could think of so many telling, dispositive arguments —like: you can't run a business or a country on sentiment and with incompetents. I did say: "You're nuts . . . *nuts.*"

"Look, Reggie, the girl is a product of ghetto schools. Solid black. She's a high school graduate, sure, but from a *ghetto* high school—you've simply got to make allowances for that. Such a person has first got to be made to feel wanted—till she can be taught, taught *on the job.* Sure, it's hard. It's exasperating. I've already failed with four girls. But I've won with four others, too. A .500 batting average isn't so bad. Yes, it was *I* who tested her —*I* who hired her."

"I did make allowances," I said. "And deported myself as a gentleman—I treated her like the lady she is. Marge, I tell you, you're nuts."

"I hope you don't think *you're* the first to call me nuts." Her eyes flashed angrily—she had finished her second of Joe's martinis now and it was working; she was getting a little mean as she spoke—"A girl fresh out of the ghetto doesn't know the word 'macabre' and you make a big deal out of it. Jesus, Reggie."

I was determined now not to quarrel with her and later after ordering our third martini I somehow laughed, leaned across, and whispered to her: "Marge . . . *Marge* . . . let's not fight— let's make love." I surprised myself. It was the first time I'd made a real pass at her.

She looked at me, startled. But at last she smiled wearily. "No, so far, I've managed to be faithful to my husband," she said, ". . . whatever that is. God!—men are so insensitive . . . ha, so *'macabre.'* "

This plummeted me into a long, morose silence. I was truly hurt again, for this time I could feel her disappointment with me; really, her disdain—not about the pass I'd made, not that; but about what she construed as my bigotry. And I knew I was *not* a bigot. Besides, I thought her a starry-eyed, impractical visionary now—who had, moreover, been callously unfair to me. I regretted I hadn't gone straight home from the office. Neither of us talked now. That Doris! . . . Oh, that darned Doris, I thought. I *knew* I had done no wrong. She couldn't do the work . . . she was helpless. What was I to do?—compliment her for this? Yet, I was hurting. I felt a deep, knifing pain.

By the time we had finished three of Joe's martinis apiece, we were both a little woozy. I'd had enough and wanted some convenient way to break up this murderous tête-à-tête. Soon I said (lying): "You know what I'll do?—Tomorrow I'll go find that girl and bring her back." I grinned unsteadily at Marge.

"That would be the decent thing to do," she said without batting an eye. Yet I could tell she was half drunk. She reached down now and began putting on her boots. Then she got up and unsteadily put on her coat and in a moment strolled ahead of me toward the door, while I stopped and paid Terry and tipped Joe.

When we crossed the street in the snow and got in my car, she watched me with a strange, almost hysterical look. "Where are we going?" she said, now in a quavering, lachrymose voice I'd never heard before. . . . Yet it was essentially conciliatory, at least at the moment—or triumphant, or something . . . oh, it's impossible to describe it. I do believe she *felt* me changing—I had somehow become the object of a near instantaneous metamorphosis, and although I wasn't immediately conscious of it myself (it was subliminal, you see), she had sensed it at once. But perhaps it was both instantaneous and gradual—in a word, pervasive? . . . yes. I was in its throes for almost a week of tortured hell—a cruddy time I'll never forget. Yet sort of an immolation, I guess. Quite a period, to put it mildly. But isn't all this incidental? Or is it? It is too terrible to speak of—this metastasis, this five-day mutation. I can only compare it to King John rolling on the floor and chewing straw at Runnymede, or to Saul stricken down en route to Damascus. But in the car that night I did not deign to reply to her question, and started the motor and drove off in the general direction of her house.

A howling wind had come up. It got under the snowdrifts and, lifting them up, hurled them in great spiraling mini-cyclones that rocked my new Dodge on the Kennedy Expressway. Marge seemed to shiver now, and cuddled closer to me as I drove. "Take me to a motel, Reggie," she said—"now." Again, the eerie quaver.

Instead I took her home and let her out.

But within the week, by Friday, I had located the girl, Doris, and persuaded her to return to the office and work for me. Then one evening after work, soon — very soon — thereafter, I took Marge to Terry's Lounge again and later to the beautiful *Su Casa* motel. It had all turned out so exhilaratingly. I felt so whole—and after such a hairbreadth escape. The great British physiologist Sir Charles Sherrington has described pain as "the psychical adjunct of an imperative protective reflex." Ha, or more simply, pain is what the victim perceives in his mind after he has touched a hot stove.

Loving

Percival Goodman

A Short Novel

Peter Everwine

A woman took a man for her husband, but things did not go well for her.

She would come in from digging in the garden. "Worms in the cabbage," she'd say. "The bright horns of Moses," he'd reply.

She would be banging the pot in the kitchen. "The cracked dish," she'd say. "The princess is dancing in the ballroom," he'd reply.

She would be darning socks by the fireplace. "The rip in the seam," she'd say. "Two birds in the bush," he'd reply.

She would come back from speaking to the neighbors. "I'm leaving," she'd say. "The wind in the orchard," he'd reply.

So the woman packed her trunk, went off to the next village, and was courted by another man.

"Worms in the cabbage," she'd say. "No doubt," he replied.

"The cracked dish," she'd say. "Just as I've always thought," he replied.

"The rip in the seam," she'd say. "And not a moment later," he replied.

The woman took the man for her husband. They became prosperous, raised a family, and grew old in the even tenor of their days. The man died looking out the window. The woman died with her eyes tightly closed. Their children gave them a grand funeral and took a different name.

Two Poems

HUGH MACDIARMID

To Most Of My Contemporaries

I hate them because like animals
They have no comparisons to make,
Because they cannot see beyond their own lives.

They have no mental ability
To make any worth-while choices.
They know only what appears on the surface.

They can see the bees swarm, but
They do not know when the old queen dies.

The Unicorn

What matters most in the unicorn
Is unquestionably the horn.

What a pointer this is to the way
Man has evolved to the present day!

Just so the frontal lobes of his brain
Their salient significance gain.

Till cortical understanding stands out
Pre-eminent beyond a doubt.

But the unicorn's horn can only point
Pointlessly in a world that's out of joint

And what minds men yet have painfully won
Still point in all directions — and none!

The Day After The Election

DAN JAFFE

The agents
loosen their holsters,
unclasp the straps
from their tense thighs,
let their lingo go gutteral
as their collars crumble.
In and out
of the back bedroom
of their Shoreham Suite
they stumble, tilting
their glasses to
their campaign choice,
the cocktail waitress
from the Victory Lounge,
drugged and smiling
like Miss America.

Why the Eskimos Never Answer Their Letters

M T. BUCKLEY

Maybe the letters take too long
To get there: maybe they're
Frozen solid and very hard to
Open. Maybe the Eskimos
Eat them. Maybe they use them for
Bait. Perhaps to tile their bathrooms ...

I really don't know why.
I never write to them myself.

Some Modern Good Turns

(poem found in the 1936 Boy Scout Manual)

DENNIS DIBBEN

Helped the cook pick a chicken.
Cranked car for one-armed man.
Helped a paralyzed man fix his papers.
Took a small child across three streets.
Boy was sick, pulled him home on wheel.
Splinted and bandaged broken leg of dog.
Took chewing gum off the street-car seat.
Went to town to get husband for sick woman.
Removed slipknot from around cow's neck.
Attended to neighbor's baby while she went down town.
Made scrapbooks for the Home of the Friendless.
Climbed a tree at night to get a chicken for a lady.

On Being Native

DAVID BUDBILL

The Vermont Jewish mother says:
So who's native? Don't talk to me native.
Because you got here early makes you more?

Witch grass, zucchini, tomatoes, you and me—
all immigrants is what I'm talking.
Native is dirt and stones, mountains.
What else?

We, love, are water
Oi!
just passing through.

Ballet Under the Stars

ROBERT J. STEWART

Now, the people are getting their art
warming this park hillside,
behind a pine tree somewhere, Basho
mourns the rising souls of crickets

we could be in Athens now, trees
all we see—sirens coming through
the leaves and knot holes
squirrel nests flashing red

last week beside the swan lagoon
two girls danced beneath a knife
no one announced the event
or heard the quick crescendo

applause rises with the arabesque
silent drama edging us together
safe now: every bug that can fly
is down at the spotlight.

dazzled

ARTHUR SZE

reality
is like a contemporary string
quartet:

the 1st violinist puts on a crow's head.
& the cellist

soliloquizes on a white lotus
in the rain.

the violist discusses
love, rage, & terror.

& the 2nd violinist reports on the latest coup
in afghanistan

a gazelle leaps
in october light.

i am dazzled.

David Ray

Why Not?

LINDA PASTAN

Why not try again, although the past
in all its fine detail seems infinite?
I close my eyes and it's like putting on glasses.
The old landscapes jump into focus: grass
greener than grass; my surgeon father so anxious
to heal he drinks his coffee standing up;
my small bed angled into my small room
like a barge that might carry me into
my own dream of a future. Everything

I expected has long since happened.
Everything I wanted I took— but
always too early or too late.
Still there may be time. The old ladies
of Cambridge with bookbags and bicycles
laugh through faded teeth and beckon. To them
failure is just another rough cobblestone.
They say about loving, about riding
a bicycle: you never forget how.

Poem for My Wife

MICHAEL SHERIDAN

Last night you warned of grandfather,
how he napped through life
and woke to die. Listen.
This morning I hear your music,
faintly, from another room:
Mozart & the birth of D minor.
Our house smells of smoke & boiling tea.

Outside the sun moves
where it moves, killing dark places.
And our blond daughters call us to play.
"Easy out," they sing, "daddy's an easy out."
I've never felt more ambitious.
Be kind, Mamma. Come into my poem.

Root River

DAVID KHERDIAN

Drawn into inlets
by transparent minnows—
suddenly gone to myself
& following where they
lead,
I fall to my knees
to catch them,
though to catch them
is not what I want,
& they lead me to
underwater grasses,
razor sharp pebbles
& silt & mud hollows
of tadpoles & star-
flecked sun spotted falls,
into a home I can
never leave,
dreaming of fish,
breathing fish
swimming into
fish

My Mother

James T. McCartin

She has been dead so long that now
she exists for me not as a person
but in images—her freckled legs
in a swirl of grey receding waves
as she sat on a jetty at Rockaway,
her dress and slip timidly pulled
just slightly above her knees,
the legs scored by white ridges
from elastic bandages meant to control
the pain of varicose veins, arthritic joints.

A photograph—her pain-worn face
as she stood beside a country wall
that week in the Catskills,
one week out of fifty two
when we escaped our Brooklyn flat.

But then, beside the images, are whisperings,
like wind rustling through a ruined church,
that say, I'm always here, part
of your topography, and when you feel guilt
because you gave expecting gratitude, or
returned rudeness by being equally rude,
you are that church alive to what I loved,
sensitive to what made me turn pain
into compassion instead of hate, loneliness
into joy at the companionship I rarely shared
but did not begrudge.

And perhaps, like that ruined church
I too will leave a legacy
of decent whisperings.

Father and Daughter

WALTER LOWENFELS

Dante says you should always tell the reader what you're going to tell him before you tell him. That's O.K. if you are Dante. I have quit making that mistake. I no longer think I am Dante. This is real news for anyone interested in the Latest Word.

* * *

Man is a cellular pimple, sexually speaking — just an overgrown boil. How can you compare it to the really inborn, ingrown physiological female thing?

Man is a bridge, Nietzsche said, but I think he is a bottle-opener — doomed. I can see him in a museum, and the girl-boys will look at him the way we do at gorillas or lemurs. Pretty little thing. But so careless and sloppy.

* * *

When we were in Paris in the 20's and 30's, I got others to help in drawing up a long list of permanent objects that could always be relied on in poems for image communication — sun, sea, earth, trees, mountains. Now I believe that long after socialism has become the universal past, and discrimination, on account of poetry, has become an extinct fossil, the uneven level of the selves bound to inhabit the same stellar system simultaneously will doom some of us to be pushed around from our settled ways by others who bust in with their eternal youth and knock the brittle arrangement of our day to pieces.

* * *

A terrible tragedy hits most of us somewhere between seven and 12. We stop being children and become adult horrors. The exceptions are the poets, the lovers. It's different (I hope) under a social order where people aren't commodities. But I only know this place, and here we are varieties of Adenauer not Du Bois; Trumans and Hoovers, not Shaws and O'Caseys. Children are terrors in their own way, but they rarely kill you unless provoked beyond endurance like that one little boy who shot his mother because she wouldn't let him play with matches.

* * *

It's true (as Manna & Judy say) that in my books I am anti-infant and don't go for people until about age four. But there is a difference about what I say about infants and what I do about them. The twins are living proofs.

Nothing I ever saw was less human looking than the two of them as infants. They weighed less than three pounds each, and looked it: two tiny skulls peering out of an incubator where they stayed for three months. And for three months it was I who fed them. This was no easy trick (like you putting a bottle into your baby's face, or a nipple).

The incubator in the American Hospital, Neuilly, was at the other end of Paris from where we lived in the rue Val de Grace, (14th Arrondisement). After the first few weeks on this planet Lillian came home. But the twins still had to have mother's milk to keep alive. How?

I was the milkman. I rigged up a pump (using a bicycle hand pump) to get the milk from Lillian into bottles. (Sterilized by me, of course), then kept cool, which wasn't as simple as it is today. We had no electric refrigerator. I had a small window box which I filled with ice, and kept Lillian's milk in shape. Then every day I made the trip to the twin's hospital home, either by bicycle or bus. Either was a grind. At the end of the bus line in Neuilly it was a long walk to the hospital. Did I falter? Did I show my anti-infancy by neglecting their lifeline to Mother's milk?

Here they are today, living proof of my devotion to babies.

Furthermore, there are other former infants alive in Paris today because of my milk route. I delivered all the milk we could pump. The twins were so puny they couldn't drink it all. Other infants who needed more mother's milk got the extra supply and thrived.

I don't object to being scolded for what I write about the infant-parent syndrome in my books. At the same time I think the twins might give me a Milk Award for the way I overcame my intellectual anti-infancy to keep them alive. "By their milk ye shall know them."

* * *

All I have learned about children is to let them look at any TV program they want any time they want. The rest is socialism, and I don't expect to achieve it through teen-age Red Guards. My hope for the future is not in teen-agers per se, but in changing society so children will not continue forever to deteriorate into us.

Meanwhile, I say — forgive them for they know what they do (as far as our adultness is concerned). Look what we gave them: after 50 years of socialism in the USSR we have LBJ! And if we didn't we'd have someone worse. Our grown-ups have become personifications of the gold hoard in Ft. Knox.

"What have *you* done Granpa, to think you know better than me?" Tamsie and 100 million others.

Anyhow, between what I say on paper and what I achieve otherwise is approximately the distance between Jupiter and the constellation Scorpius.

So, I keep a supply of sugar-free gum in my pockets and on the shelves, and my grandchildren love me. I learned this from a dancing bear act I saw at the *Cirque d'Hiver* years ago. The beautiful big brown bear got on his hind legs and danced and never kept his eyes, or snout, away from the trainer's hand which kept feeding him sugar. And when the sugar was all gone the dance was over.

* * *

Lawrence used to say that in the USA people just can't stand each other, spend their lives hiding themselves behind perfumes, deodorants, bathrooms, cosmetics, and senseless rounds of work that leave them totally alienated.

And if I tell you there's no answer to this except a totally new way of living — to begin with, a different relation to work, a socialist framework for our lives — don't look scornful and say, "Look at that campaign to elect Judge Rainey to Congress, and what did he become? A radio announcer. Look at Khrushchev! Look at Stalin! You call that socialism!" The agony of being with the reverse of socialism here needs to get so awful that you have to find another way out, not the perfect way "come the revolution," but the only way it becomes possible to stay alive.

* * *

This supersonic Rehabilitation Hospital is the inverse of a mausoleum. I mean, here they send the paralytics out the other way, walking. (Lillian got carried in, feet first.)

Except for the palm-lined swimming pool where paraplegics don't swim, everybody is doing the same thing. Most of them are grandmothers and grandfathers but some are young with polio hangovers. All of them total only 19 in-patients against dozens of nurses, attendants, doctors, therapists, aides. Everybody gets taught how to wheel to The Place and transfer to The Seat and between times we eat at a high-class cafeteria and private tables and go to the Recreation Room afterwards where there are corners for those without legs looking at television and those without hands listen to the FM music or watch Lillian play chess and you wonder which of us is little two-eye because the normal here is not to be able to stand or sit or walk and even some of us don't talk so good.

In hospitals, even where they have PT (physical therapy to you) what counts is the people going into or out of death and operations, and not small things like just being paralyzed and unable to get out of the sideboards of the bed where the patient got stuck, because after all it won't kill her to lie with her neck in between the slats another hour but the Lady with a Cancer has to have it out right away or else, and the gall bladders are crying out for glucose, and even sometimes there are emergencies inside emergencies as when Lillian's hospital roommate in Cleveland — last month — Mrs. Haas, a few days out of a gall bladder removal, suddenly started to gurgle with a coronary.

I ran out to tell the nurse something was going on. She hurried in and slapped Mrs. Haas and the whole hospital began to converge — not walking, but hotfooting it with syringes and needles and plasmas and medicine kits on trays and three doctors and asking me please to leave the room. . . .

A few minutes later, an attendant wheeled Lillian into the parlor where guests sit. It was the only empty spot. She lay there a couple of hours, not even asking why only saying it was too hot.

She thinks to this day that Mrs. Haas got moved to a private room and just yesterday, talking of last month's Cleveland days, she said how Mrs. Sterner, her new neighbor with asthma, who had replaced Mrs. Haas in the next bed, didn't know she had been operated on for gall stones. . . .

Such a good grandmother, too, Mrs. Haas — told Lillian she ought to go on the Kosher Kitchen — the food there was better — so interested in others and to lose interest suddenly in everything was so unlike the little we knew of her kindness.

It makes you wonder with some of us when we are so close to the existence level whether all this therapy is changing the contour of the earth's orbit enough to throw it off balance.

And yet — we are all precious to someone, like old Mister Haas in Cleveland, leaning on his son's shoulder, and coming over to me in the hall, crying softly: "I wish you better luck, sir."

It might not be so bad if death ended it all, but there was Mister Haas having to come and take it away and arrange the funeral and how much the coffin would cost and what is it they bury anyway when Mrs. Haas left so much behind that nobody but Mister Haas will ever dream about?

* * *

I put my old shoes on top of the table yesterday. And I suddenly got a purely objective view of my shoeself. I slope like a hillside, right shoe to the right, left, to the left. So there I stood, in front of me, without the feet and legs, obviously a very lop-sided fellow.

Which reminds me of an Indian legend I have just been reading, about Utluntam, the "Spear-Finger," who seems to have been very strangely put together. She is described as a terrible enemy of the human race — a stone-armored ogress who fed on the livers of people whom she killed by stabbing them in the neck with her forefinger, which was hard as bone and sharp as a spear.

The warriors had a hard time killing her, because when they trapped her in a pit, their arrows could not penetrate her stone armor, and she was about to climb out and destroy them all. You see, they were aiming at her breast, where her heart should be, but the arrows just glanced off her rocky mail, and fell broken at her feet.

At last, when all seemed lost, a chickadee flew down into the pit and lit for a moment on Utluntam's right hand. The warriors were sure this must be a sign, so they aimed at the hand, and soon an arrow struck just where Utluntam's spear-like forefinger joined her hand, and she fell dead. It was there that her heart was.

I had better be careful when I say "the poet is the writing finger of the world."

* * *

You die only once says the Insurance Collector, whereas any voter knows each of us dies endless deaths, beginning with our diaper stage. The last death is the only one that really doesn't matter. The others are amply documented in poem after poem, each of which gives the reader the electric shock of not being dead.

Investigation shows there are lost poems always being written by someone who discovers surprises in match boxes or the footsteps of caterpillars or an unusual juxtaposition in making love.

Sometimes the surprise is that we don't know what the poem is talking about. And this makes us angrier than anything, even new music. For after all, we do know each word that is being used. It's only the way they are strung together that makes neither rhyme, rhythm nor sense, until maybe tomorrow softens us up and the new poem begins to soak into us a little, and so on, until the Researcher comes onto the scene with his army of ants and cleans up the whole affair and preserves somebody's first kiss in the formaldehyde of the library stacks.

* * *

Maybe we'd better buy you a river, and a stick, so you can go down to the water's edge with the women of Burgos, Delhi,

Leopoldville and Tierra del Fuego, and beat the dirt out of your clothes? But a stick like that is hard to find and even harder to learn to use at your stage of the game, softened up by detergents as you have been for so many generations.

* * *

We are so introspective, we wouldn't be at all surprised if the stairs remembered us for the way we clattered down them, and we expect gulls to know us for the way we leaped to feed them, but in human beings we expect gigantic illusions about our grandeur. It is only the painter we recognize as making eternal objects out of inconsequential details like the shadow on a glass of milk, or the angle of the spear in a Fra Angelico painting.

* * *

If I talk now and then about outer space, maybe it's because I'm skeptical about the earth future of our order of placentals. I can't help it — in fact, I fight against it, but science and something antenna-like inside my vertebrae assure me that the human race will never make it as is. We will do it better, as they are doing it better, Moscow, Budapest et al. And more people will have better lives, in bigger cities, with less pollution, but I'm obsessed with the future where they'll be a completely different set of air breathers and not even an old shoe left of you and me and all our billions who did it so sweetly in the Magellan Age.

Anyhow — it's assuring to have a framework in which to exercise our hands and typewriters. It leaves one really nothing to worry about except to make the present as bearable as can be and get to the next stage as quickly and painlessly as possible. And of course, get rid of the pterodactyl monsters among us as rapidly as can be.

* * *

I have been reading Gordon Childe, the archeologist, who says only two things last — poetry and pottery. Now Bertrand Russell calculates the mathematical possibility of erasing whole areas of the earth in five minutes of "nuclear exchange."

What happens then to the lasting qualities of pottery or poetry? I don't mean in the unknown future, but today as I write you on the hot line between hope and disaster?

What other age ever fired their pottery and poems from such launching pads?

So, don't call it "poetry" — call it "paper-pottery." Because in the Great Explosion, if it comes, nobody will know the difference. And if it doesn't come, all our cliff-hanging eternities will seem as old-fashioned as elegies by a dinosaur.

David Ray

NEW LETTERS

A magazine of fine writing   Edited by David Ray

Featuring **Spinning like the Rocking Horse Queen**
by Heather Wilde

&

Cherry Blossoms
by Taiko Hirabayashi

NEW LETTERS

$3.00

David Ray

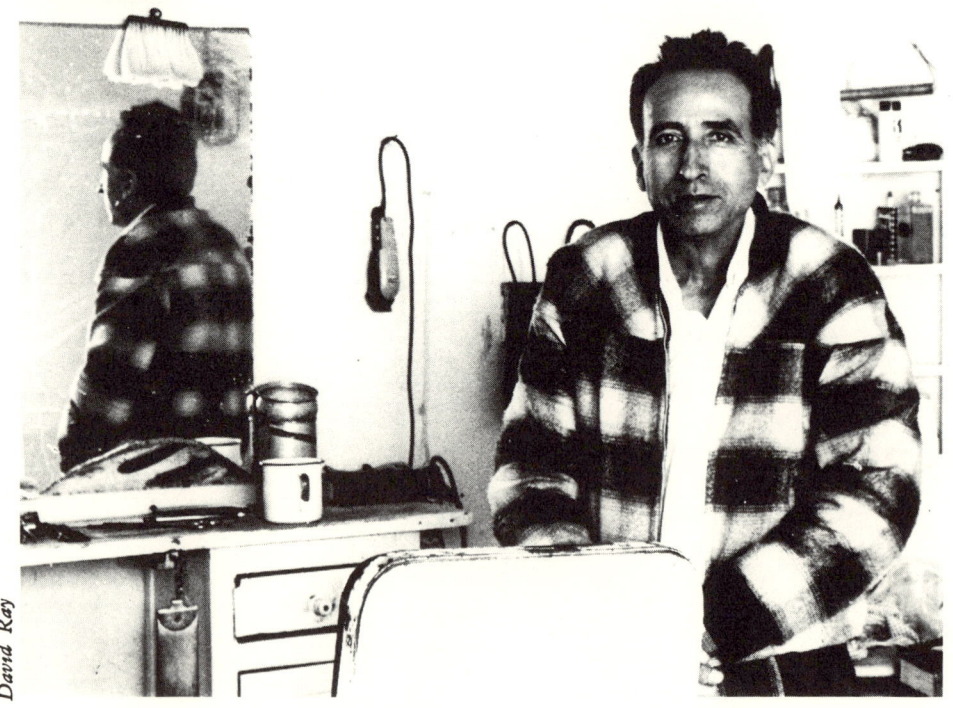

*A magazine of fine writing
Edited by David Ray*

Each New Springtime, Each New Summer

An excerpt from the novel by
JAMES McKINLEY

Atropos

Quite a ceremony, and you have noticed, I am sure, how ceremonies can sanctify, or satanify, people. A prostitute who attends a store-front church service, for whatever reason, is radiant for two or three hours after; similarly, we are told, murderers become through ceremony sacred in the eyes of God, at least in their last communion. And politicians become wise through the ceremony of office-taking, and tea parties significant with the ceremony of teaing and so on.

I mention this merely so that you will believe Sylvia's change after our marriage. True, her most personal characteristics didn't change. She was still lustful, spiteful, artful, material and shallow. Nevertheless, the ceremony—that ten-minute mumbling of meaningless words, accompanied by money-passing, feet shuffling, and insincerities—had changed her. It was as though that ceremony ripped from her a shell labeled single, promiscuous, teasing, goalless and flung upon her another marked married, ambitious, discreetly sexual, bitching.

In the weeks before my married mother returned, I was introduced to this new person. Sex became a favor. Sylvia took sudden interest in my career. Though she remained outwardly gay, after the parties she would begin carping about our future.

"What are you going to do? After the summer?"

"I don't know. Go to law school, maybe."

"School? Don't you know enough yet? You know you can't, well, get anyplace in school."

"Get someplace. Where? Where shall we get?"

"Don't be blasé. It only fits students. You've got to have money to live, you know. How long do you think my father will support us?"

"I don't know. How long?"

"Ass! You're so detached, aren't you, great Zen student. Couldn't care less about money. Of course, he likes to eat and drink and party and go places, but he really couldn't care less about the filthy thing of . . ."

"Shut up, Sylvia."

"You shut up! If you think I'm going to spend my life in

holes like this with you . . . what are you laughing at? Do you think I would have gone through with it if I hadn't been raped and shocked?" The poor dear, in the clutches of an apprentice Tarquin. What horseshit.

"I told you to shut up, Sylvia."

"I won't. Listen, sweet Gregory the Innocent, you're married now, like it or not. We've got to have money. When my father finds out, you know he'll cut me off. He's hopelessly old-fashioned."

"Yes, I know Sylvia. All right. We'll get some money someplace. I'll go to the placement bureau. Don't worry. And you'll always have a silken pillow for your precious little hips."

"Bastard."

"Nice talk for a lady. Let's have a drink."

The alcohol was our mediator. If we could both drink, the future receded to its normal miniature size. So we drank much too much that summer, and I passed my twentieth birthday with definite alcoholic tendencies. Sylvia didn't do better. I could drink more, but she could drink more often. Where I got lethargic, she got loose. The game of catching her in kitchens started again, though, as I said, she was more discreet. No more three-party bedroom conversations. Now, I only caught her kissing. And so it went. We were misbegotten twins, condemned to live together until some surgery severed the connection.

My mother returned from her wedding trip on Labor Day. Her wedding ceremony, or her trip, or her partner, had altered her, too. On the station platform I could see the change. She looked diminished. Frailer. Afraid. She had had a few drinks already. Fred looked the bulbous same, perhaps a trifle redder in the nose. He had the uncertainly triumphant air of a gladiator who had won when he thought he would lose.

"Son," he boomed, "glad you came to see us in. The old married folks return, eh?" I touched his bloated hand and kissed mother.

"Hello, Mother. You remember Sylvia, Fred's niece?"

"Yes, I remember, Hello, Sylvia."

"We're married, Mother. Sylvia and I. For six weeks now." Looking back, I am proud of my mother on that moment. Halfcrocked, weak, shocked, tired, she showed true gentility, a nobility born perhaps of drink and desperation, but I think of the arid reaches of Nebraska. She looked a moment at Sylvia, then at me, then, curiously, at Fred, as though looking in Fred's face for something she had seen in Sylvia's, cross-checking. In her eyes I saw she had seen it in both and I was senselessly, abruptly afraid. But mother carried on.

"How wonderful! A surprise, of course, but wonderful." She went up on unsteady tip-toes to kiss Sylvia.

"Well," she said, "we must all celebrate. So many marriages. So close. We must celebrate." Then we were all talking at once. Fred, smelling of bad bourbon, was clapping me on the back and calling me his son and nephew, while my mother prattled on to a whitened Sylvia about china and recipes and how they would get together and take care of me, etc. Mother put her arm on Sylvia's as we walked back to the station and I saw large bruises on her triceps. I was mumbling about our plans, what we would do, a silly defense I continued all the way through the hideous lunch together, until the four of us had had enough to drink and had relaxed into a mutual befuddlement. Parting, we vowed to keep in touch.

The next week, over Sylvia's furious objections, I registered for law school. I called my mother to ask for the tuition money. After several rings, her weak voice said hello.

"Mother? I need some money, for law school."

"Gregory, oh come and see me, please, Gregory, I need you." It was the plea of a stranger — perhaps that is why I responded to it.

The stranger said, "Please, come and see me, I need you. Please."

"Yes, Mother. I'll be right there."

"Oh, Gregory, thank you. I'll wait. Please hurry."

Sylvia, sulking in the living room, was startled at my uncharacteristic burst of energy. I brushed past her from the telephone, on my way out.

"What's the rush? Miss your first class?"

"I'm going to see my mother. She's sick or something." Sylvia turned her head back to her magazine. The movement gave life to her lovely blonde hair. Blonde. They haunt me still. Blonde hair and women.

"How sweet of you to visit her. Ask her for money. Next month dear Daddy's stops."

"I don't know when I'll be back."

"Don't worry. I'll amuse myself. Perhaps I'll go to the laundromat with some of the other too, too cunning and cute student wives. If I can afford it, that is."

"Goodbye, Sylvia."

I took a cab south. Again the streets and sounds and people had a heart-stopping similarity. I felt like the spirit of those streets, wafting back to see that nothing had changed, that whistles still called children home, that the Good Humor Man's bells still announced dusk, that parents sat on wooden backsteps, that Duncan yo-yo men gave exhibitions in the candy stores, that kids saved Popsicle bags for prizes. It all looked the same. For a moment I thought I could stop the cab, step out and melt into it, going to the prairies for ball and war games, to the alleys for tag and cycle races. Then with a sadness almost unbearable I knew my body had betrayed me, grown too big for that, had strange chemicals coursing through it which threw me into a world of Sylvias and Freds and mothers who were women, and missions like this that could never be joyous or innocent.

The stairway to the apartment was very cool. Unseasonably, like a cave. The hot air shocked me then, flowing from the apartment when mother opened the door.

"Oh, Gregory . . . Come in." She looked terrible. She was in her robe; it hung loosely on her. Her face so drawn that the skin seemed ready to burst, to reveal the yellowed skull beneath. Her hair was frizzed, crispy, as though touch would break it. She shuffled stooped to the living room, to the red chair and dropped into it.

"What did you want, Mother?"

She looked at me, without seeing. Then very slowly, like water oozing up from a pipe broken under ground, she started to cry. Soon sobs rolled from her, shook her thin body, shock waves going out from something fundamental that had ruptured in her. I sat on the arm of the chair, putting my sleeve around her.

"Don't cry, Mom. I'll help. What is it? Don't cry." I said it over and over until the sobbing eased and she rummaged in her robe pockets for one of the too-small handkerchiefs that women, the mourners, carry.

"I'm sorry. I'm so upset. Excuse me." She left to repair herself, walking more upright, cleansed for the moment. I looked around. The apartment was more a mess then before. My father's books were scattered on the shelves. Every ashtray was full, a mixture of cigar butts and lipsticked cigarette ends. A pair of man's shoes stuck out from under the desk. Glass rings formed surreal designs on the glass-topped coffee table. There were fuzz balls beneath the sofa. A new hole marred the upholstery of the red chair. Over all was the smell of used air, of decay, of neglect. I rose and opened a window.

Mother came back with fresh make-up violent against her chalky skin.

"That was quite a scene. I'm sorry."

"It's okay, you were upset. What did you want?"

She lit a cigarette and went unsteadily to the mantle. She leaned against it.

"It's about Fred and I." I waited.

"Well, it's not what we . . . I thought it would be." She took a long painful pull on the cigarette. The exhaled smoke obliterated her face for a moment.

"Fred is a bad drinker. I know it looks as if I drink more, but he drinks much more. Before work every morning he has a pint of vodka, then he drinks at lunch and comes home and drinks more vodka, sometimes a fifth at night." She went to the desk and rubbed her hand along the dusty surface.

"And he gets mean when he drinks, Greg. Very mean" She turned to me. "Oh, I get nasty, too. I mean, I have to drink with him. You can't live with someone who drinks like that and not drink. You know that? I suppose not. But it's true. If I don't drink with him, I can't stand it. I try to avoid him, I really do, but he paws me and wants me to drink too, and then I have to, to stay in the same house, and it's every night, you can't stay away every night." She paused to inhale. "So we both drink and he insults me, and insults your father and you, and I get mad and mean to him, and we fight. Look!" She threw open her robe. All over her body were bruises. Some large, like she'd fallen on furniture. Others small, finger sized. I looked away.

She gasped a small breath-seeking sob. "Honestly, I can't stand him, it, any longer." She put her face in her hands.

"Why don't you leave?" I said, "You don't have to take that. I told you that. Leave! C'mon. I'll help you."

She looked at me, stricken, like a doe caught by a poacher's flashlight. She raised her head, her eyes red and terrified.

"I can't now, Gregory," she said hoarsely. "That's why I called you. I can't."

"Why not? You can leave anytime you want."

"I can't, not now. I'm pregnant with that bastard's child."

It took a moment for that to penetrate my consciousness. And then there were no words ready as there usually were.

"What?"

"I'm pregnant. With Fred's child."

"You're sure? You can't be. I mean, aren't you . . . too old or something."

"I'm sure. I'm not too old."

She went and sat in a little imitation Chippendale against the window. The soft afternoon light made her look younger. Like Sylvia. Strange, I had never thought of my mother as young. Yet once she had been. When I was a little boy, she was very young. I'd seen pictures of her and my father. She had been thin, her hair long, her face unwrinkled, fresh. When she had been pregnant with me, I remember my father had said, she'd remained thin. Pregnant. Young. And now pregnant again. From Fred. Old.

"Are you going to have it?"

"I don't know."

"Do you want it?"

"I don't know that either."

"Does Fred know?"

"No. I don't want him to know. Not unless I decide to have it."

"Would he want it?"

"I suppose so. Men always do. They don't have much to do with it. Just wait." She gave a little laugh. "Funny, isn't it. When I found out I was pregnant with you, I rushed home, we had a little bungalow then, in Omaha, as fast as I could to tell your father. He was so happy. Picked me up and swirled me around, and we sat down and started to think of names and toys and schools and places to go with you. Everything. Then, when you came, we were so happy. You were beautiful, Gregory, you really were. So beautiful and happy."

She lit another cigarette.

"Gregory," she said at last, "I'm thinking of an abortion." She got a small, bitter smile. "Times do change, don't they?"

"You were young then. And not with Fred."

"Yes. Those are differences." She sat quiet again. The grandfather's clock ticked. I remembered my grandfather had really hauled it from Kentucky to Nebraska. Now it tolled in Chicago, in another time. What really was there to do? Have it, and the kid grows up with an old mother and a drunken father. Hell, when it was twenty, mother would be sixty. I'd be forty. I'd like you to meet my younger brother. Well, you see, my mother remarried this charming drunken chap and he knocked her up and this radiant cretin is the result. Christ!

"Do you think the baby would change Fred?" I asked.

"I don't know. Maybe, but I doubt it. He's such a souse. What am I going to do?"

Something called to me.

"Maybe . . . maybe the thing to do is get rid of it." She looked from me to her abdomen to me.

"Yes, maybe. It isn't much of anything yet."

"How long are you . . . how many months?"

"Two or so." Two. Before Minneapolis.

"That's not too late, is it?"

"I don't think so. Within three, I think, is all right."

"Do you know anybody who could do it?"

"No. I suppose I could find out." The talk about details made mother seem her old capable self.

"I mean, it's done all the time. Lois Reynolds, the lady who lived across the street, you remember, had two or three. And she loved her husband. Just didn't want any more kids. I could find out."

"Isn't it dangerous?"

"I don't think so. If somebody good does it. A doctor, not some old lady." She brightened as the talk drove away her fears. She even looked better, less tired.

"Yes, that's probably best, isn't it?" she was saying.

"I guess so, Mother. If it's safe."

"With a child, I'd really be tied to him. For good."

"Are you going to leave him now? You should. I'll help you."

"Yes, I'll leave him, unless he straightens out. I'll tell him that. I'll tell him unless he stops drinking I'm leaving. I bet he will. You know, Gregory, he really loves me. Honestly, he does."

"He shows it in funny ways."

"Oh, sometimes you do have to hurt things you love. Just like the song. You do. You and Sylvia don't know that yet. How is she?"

"She's fine, Mother."

"Why did you marry her, Greg?" The question came in the old sharp way I remembered when I was a child, when she was concerned about politics and argued them, that way, that sharp way.

"I guess I loved her, Mother. That's all." The lie felt bad, even to me.

"You must have decided that quickly. But I suppose you got to know one another living together."

"You knew about that?"

"Of course. I could tell you were living with someone. You had that co-habitation look. But even if I hadn't guessed, I'd have known."

"How?"

"From Fred."

"Fred?"

"His brother. Sylvia told her parents she was going to marry you. That's why they sent her money. They wanted her respectably married, so they sent her money."

Again, it took a moment. She'd told them she was going to marry me so it was all right, send money. The scheming bitch!

"She's very pretty, Gregory, anyway. Aren't you happy?"

"Happy? Yes, I mean, everything's fine. Don't worry."

"I can't help worrying. I wish . . . I wish you hadn't married so soon. I wish I knew her better. I feel as if I'd lost you to a stranger."

"You two should get together. Don't worry about me. It's you. You've got to get out of this thing. And you've got to quit drinking." She looked at me then, for a longish moment, as though memorizing my face to take with her on a long trip because she had no photographs. Then she stood up.

"Let's have lunch. I'll get dressed and we'll go. And then I'm going to clean this place up, before Fred comes home. I can't issue ultimatums in a dirty house." She walked, very briskly, into the bedroom.

It was the nicest time I ever had with my mother, at least as an adult. We taxied to our favorite Italian restaurant and ate just what we wanted, hang the cost, mother said, that's why she'd married the fatso. Antipasto, minestrone, two pastas, toasted ravioli, cheese, nuts, two wines, espresso. Through it all she was vivacious, so vital in word and gesture, a different being from the tired old woman who'd opened the door that afternoon. Her eyes shone, the gold was mysteriously back in her hair, her gestures were quick. She was full of resolve and purpose. I could see how my father loved her, even why Fred did. I loved her, too, was conscious of it for the first time in a long while. While I ate, she talked. Yes, she would find a doctor and have it done. In a week or so. She'd call me first. Fred would be straightened out or else. They'd quit drinking, start going to theaters. Living again. She wanted to live again. If it wasn't love, it was companionship at least. We could have dinner together occasionally, Sylvia and I, she and Fred. She must give Sylvia some recipes. Sylvia was probably a very nice girl. She just didn't know Sylvia, was all. And I must work hard now in law school. Law was my field, she knew, had always been in the family. I'd do fine. She paid the check finally, with a flurry and a charm that turned the heads of other diners and waiters. I felt proud again. She came into the street on my arm, and I put her in a taxi for home, where she was going to clean up.

Three days later the phone rang in our apartment. It was mother, I knew. I picked up the receiver and said the greeting. Fred's voice came to me, an awful, sick, frightened, drunken voice, saying, "Gregory, your mother's dead." He said more, too, about blood and liquor and pills, but I didn't actually hear any of them, only those words careening through the cavern of my mind, from wall to wall, seeking acknowledgement, meaning, from cells too stunned to do more than register their sound, "your mother's dead." I put down the phone and leaned against the wall.

"What's the matter?" Sylvia asked.

"My mother's dead."

"Dead drunk?" she smirked. I hit her once, and took a cab to our old apartment, where the undertaker was just taking her body out. I couldn't look at it. That would come later, in the beautiful memory picture they promised you, compounded of wax and cosmetics and other phony items, like grief. My father had not looked beautiful, just dead.

The police were in the apartment. A sergeant told me that my father had called them. My father had found her, they said, dead in bed. She had aborted herself apparently, with a long-handled chrome drink stirrer. Then taken a bunch of sleeping pills, to kill the pain probably. They knocked her out and she just bled to death. Ruptured something with the drink stirrer, they guessed. Besides, she was drunk, it looked like. Bottle of whisky next to the bed, almost empty. Too bad, the sergeant said, nice-looking woman. Shame somebody wasn't here sooner, he said. Your father just got here himself, the cop added, then whispered that I'd better look after him, looked like he'd been boozing for a week.

I walked into the living room, past the bedroom where one bed was made in red linen. Fred was sitting in my father's red chair, his head bobbing on his fat, pocked neck. His face was slick with sweat. His nose was hamburger. He saw me and tears sluiced to his eyes.

"Gregory, my god, how terrible, Dee-dee, my sweetheart, the poor little thing, what will I do?" He had a bottle of cherry-flavored vodka beside the chair.

"Where were you?" I asked. The sweating head swiveled to me. The pig-eyes focused for a moment on me.

"I was on business, Greg. On business. We fought and I went on business. A coupla days, is all. I didn't know she wanted the money for that. Christ, no. I didn't know. Who'd a known she'd do a thing like that herself. I mean, I didn't even know about the kid, you know?" He took a swallow from the pint. The cherry vodka streaming into his gulping mouth was the blood on the sheets. I knew he had refused her the money, had gone drinking, and I saw in my mind the fight and the fear and the blows and her degradation and her anger at her body, at his penury, and then, hideously, the gleaming drink stirrer, a gift of mine from my thirteenth year, coming toward me, filling my eyes, turning red like the vodka. I felt the scream building in my belly, erupting through me, spilling out my mouth, as my hands reached, slowly it seemed, for the red, red nose and my teeth for his pocked throat, and he sat there, smiling.

I am told the cops pulled me off in a few seconds, but not before I had torn part of his nose and left his throat with some curious marks. They put me in a hospital for rest and observation. So I missed the funeral and beautiful memory picture. Fred, after treatment, flew to the safety of some aunts and cousins someplace West. Sylvia went to visit her folks. Mother went to her grave unescorted, though my father met her there. That was something.

When they had determined I was calm enough to re-enter society, they let me go. I went downtown to my father's lawyer and was paid the balance of his life insurance, which was passed to me on the occurrence of my mother's death. Then I went to our apartment and packed a few things I wanted. In a day I was on an airplane to New York, thirteen thousand dollars in my pocket, and my mind running in odd circles, starting from a point that was neither beginning nor end, and returning to it.

Things To Do Around Taos

KEN MCCULLOUGH

Get up after a nightmare in which some dead men have your house surrounded
Wash thoroughly, chant, meditate, do yoga
Eat a lot of yogurt and bananas
Write twelve letters and look over the rough draft of the short story you're working on
Put a little cognac in your coffee and pretend you're an aristocrat
Walk into town and go stand around the plaza in your black hat pretending you are Billy Jack
Hope that Dennis Hopper sees you and puts you in his next paranoid movie
Pay a dollar at the La Fonda Hotel to see D. H. Lawrence's dirty paintings, or think about it, anyway
Pay fifty cents to go through the Kit Carson House
Be amazed when you find room after room having nothing to do with Kit Carson
Read about what Kit Carson did to the Navajos' peach orchards;
Plan to desecrate his grave
Plan to do Sufi dancing some Sunday out at the Lama Foundation
Plan to make pilgrimmages to Mesa Verde, Canyon de Chelly, Chaco Canyon and Oraibi
Plan to do sSufi dancing some sSunday out at the Lama Foundation
Go into the shop next to the Kit Carson House
Have the woman who runs it follow you around to make sure you don't rip anything off
Go to the bookstore across the street run by a woman with cruel eyes
Buy one book, rip off two
Go to the Harwood Library and look at the death carts upstairs
Walk to the Post Office in the late afternoon to get your mail
Drop in at Dori's Bakery
Curse Dori's jovial face as you sit there eating pastry after pastry

Start home, get splattered with mud by some redneck in a pickup just as you're admiring your picture on a poster of a contest you've just won
Get home and do some more chanting, some more yoga
Read THE PENITENTES OF THE SOUTHWEST
Sit in the yard with your shirt off feeding crackers to the sparrows
Watch a magpie beat up on a solitary sparrow
Go to the laundromat and do clothes
Forget to turn the knob from "cold" to "hot"
Be the last one out as the lovely senoritas sweep up
Have fantasies about them as they lean over in their tight jeans
Go home and dress up entirely in black
Go to La Cocina and drink brandy, hoping a rich young widow will see you, be impressed, and say let me take you home with me and be your Sugar Mom
Make eyes at the cocktail waitress
Check out her profile against the fluorescent lights
Imagine skinny-dipping with her on a moonlit night out at the hot springs in The Gorge
Give a skier hard looks when he catches you perusing his bunny
Be awkward when some lady asks you if you've found Zoot Finley yet.
Be embarrassed when a member of the group playing nods a friendly hello
Wish it was summer
Hear from everybody that D. H. Lawrence was the biggest fascist that ever lived
Go across the street and hear Antonio entertain the turista
Stand next to a couple from Denver and develop instant rapport
Dance a flamenco with Benjamin, drunk simpatico from the pueblo
Tell the couple your life story
Bid goodbye to Benjamin in his blanket as he is being tossed out
Go to Los Compadres and be the only Anglo there,
Finish your beer and leave in a hurry
Go to a dance at Casa Loma,
Feel like a child molester

Go back to La Cocina and ask the cocktail waitress if she'd like
    to go for a drink at Antonio's
She says yes, you go, she finishes half the drink and leaves in a
    hurry
Talk to the guy you're left standing next to about Ireland
Go to the Men's Room and notice you still have a big glop of
    mud in your left ear
Make a date with the barmaid with no intention of keeping it
Sneak out and get splattered by some mestizo high school kids
Get in your mud-splattered battered car, drive home, find the
    phone number of a friend in New Orleans, drive to a freezing
    phone booth
Punch the phone when it eats your only dime
Drive home again in a swoon and go off the road into a snow-
    bank
Leave the car and walk home to leftover black-eyed peas, a
    cold bed, and the dead men surrounding your house

The Artist's Intention

A. G. SOBIN

Regarding the yellowed photograph
dated "1868:" Whether the two anonymous
men, alive in this blurry photograph
(but by now, of course, long dead)
and standing far in front of a wheelbarrow
had perfectly usual bodies in real life
or whether this is a perfectly sharp
photographic portrayal of otherwise
unrecorded 19th Century freaks—A Pair
of Blurred Men—is so open to question
that you could live forever.

Characters in Motion

Josephine Jacobsen

Working on two stories, I leave them arrested this morning.
Let *them* take over.
Look at the expression on those faces...

It's the scent of possibility.
The children, a little frightened,
watch each others' eyes.

The ghost on the tractor, the ghost
from the beach, nod,
a little shyly, to each other.

Sometimes, observers get the illusion they are keepers:
one I never had. But I didn't know
they were actually

this free. Under the sun—or is it moon?—the girl
turns from her lover, toward
an empty street.

The Lifting

Ralph J. Mills, Jr.

Long after you died
I felt you were really going
not that I wished for it
or could even now
after more than a decade
but in one moment
as if the wind had shifted
unpredictably

or the sun and clouds
altered pattern
something rose up through me
swiftly lifting along my body
a light curtain, a veil of fine silk
that a woman draws over her head
in the length of an airy gown
and I knew you'd gone
I was alone
and still listening as tonight
to the whisper and soft surge
of your gathering wing

Two Poems

Victoria McCabe

Running Head American Heritage Dictionary

Yearning/You

On His Low Self-Esteem:

Dismiss given abilities, would you?
Refuse to shake hands with yourself?

Don't you see the dozens of bastards
who'd give a limb for your intelligence,
an eye for your profile, several teeth
for your natural wit? Look around: hey:
use those pretty blues.

Now: get out of your own way.

Wind

John W. Moser

The wind snaps
around the corner and snarls along
the building wall.

A newspaper flails
about a telephone pole.

An old woman inches
along the wall, her body contorted
her fingers gripping the face-work.

At this moment
the contest is undecided.

Rain For Two Days

Roberta Paley

    from the mountains
    fog rises
    in shapes of woodsmoke

    at night
    water on this copper roof
    is a milk song of spring

Two Poems

Elliott Coleman

Late Words

Late words
may not be the
best words
but they are the
last words
one would have thought of
uttering

First words
bespeak middle words but
late words
say everything or
nothing

Holy Communion

whatever is whole
and shared in common
is holy communion

After Our War

John Balaban

After our war, the dismembered bits
—all those pierced eyes, ear slivers, jaw splinters,
gouged lips, odd tibias, skin flaps, and toes—
came squinting, wobbling, jabbering back.
The genitals, of course, were the most bizarre,
inching along roads like glowworms and slugs.
The living wanted them back, but good as new.
The dead, of course, had no use for them.
And the ghosts, the tens of thousands of abandoned souls
who had appeared like swamp fog in the city streets,
on the evening altars, and on doorsills of cratered homes,
also had no use for the scraps and bits
because, in their opinion, they looked good without them.
Since all things naturally return to their source,
these snags and tatters arrived, with immigrant uncertainty,
in the United States. It was almost home.
So, now, one can sometimes see a friend or a famous man talking
with an extra pair of lips glued and yammering on his cheek,
and this is why handshakes are often unpleasant,
why it is better, sometimes, not to look another in the eye,
why, at your daughter's breast thickens a hard keloidal scar.
After the war, with such Cheshire cats grinning in our trees,
will the ancient tales still tell us new truths?
Will the myriad world surrender new metaphor?
After our war, how will love speak?

Holiday Inn, Oklahoma City
August, 1973

White the Bones of Men: Asian Poets React to War

BEN W. FUSON

Disturbed by TV portrayals of the ominous "Tet" offensives of 1968, I happened to come across the following poem. It's translated from the Vietnamese-language original by Thich Nhat Hanh, dedicated Buddhist monk, scholar, and nonviolent opponent of both the Thieu regime and the Viet Cong: a young man who is marked for execution if he dares return from exile to Saigon. The poem's English title is "Condemnation" (*The Cry of Vietnam*, p. 14):

> Listen to this:
> yesterday six Vietcong came through my village.
> Because of this my village was bombed—completely destroyed.
> Every soul was killed.
> When I come back to the village now, the day after,
> there is nothing but clouds of dust and the river,
>   still flowing.
> The pagoda has neither roof nor altar.
> Only the foundations of houses are left.
> The bamboo thickets have been burned away.
>
> Here in the presence of the undisturbed stars,
> in the invisible presence of all the people still alive
>   on earth,
> let me raise my voice to denounce this filthy war,
> this murder of brothers by brothers!
> I have a question: Who pushed us into this killing of
>   one another?
>
> Whoever is listening, be my witness!
> I cannot accept this war.
> I never could, I never shall.
> I must say this a thousand times before I am killed.

> I feel I am like that bird which dies for the sake of
>   its mate,
> dripping blood from its broken beak and crying out:
> Beware! Turn around to face your real enemies—
> ambition, violence, hatred, greed.
>
> Men cannot be our enemies—even men called 'Vietcong!'
> If we kill men, what brothers will we have left?
> With whom shall we live then?

Already in agony about American policies in Indo-China, I found this poem poignant and powerful: as an authentic native protest, more significant than most similar poems by Western authors repelled by the Vietnam war. I began to wonder—what other Asian poets, either recently or during past centuries, have expressed their reactions to armed conflict? How have they done so: by revulsion, or stoic resignation, or lachrymal description, or flag-waving celebration, or creative coping with the cruxes of war versus peace?

I found no "anthology of war poetry" limited to Asian poets, and most editors of broader collections included none or very few such poems. Yet initial explorations did yield some 200 titles focused upon this somber topic and available in English translations. This article presents some highlights, limited to citations from China, Japan, and Vietnam.

Perhaps the oldest Chinese poem extant is "Paak Sing" (as my childhood Cantonese reminds me to pronounce the two characters meaning "Hundred Names"); the title symbolizes the common Chinese surnames, like our Smith, Jones, and Brown, and the poem's speaker is thus "Joe Wong" (Hart, p. 37):

> From break of day
> Till sunset glow
> I toil.
> I dig my well,
> I plow my field,
> And earn my food
> And drink.
> What care I
> Who rules the land
> If I
> Am left in peace?

From the *Shih Ching* or "Book of Songs," China's seminal collection of anonymous ballads and folk poems of the 11th to 7th century before Christ, several anti-war poems have survived; for example, in this first of three stanzas, the grumble of a conscript to "The Minister of War" (Payne, p. 46):

> O minister of war,
> We are the king's fangs and claws.
> Why have you piled on us this misery?
> We have no place in which to rest.

Lao Tsze, the "Old Boy" philosopher of around 600 B.C. (if he really did live then), left the notable *Tao Te Ching* or "Book of the Way," which includes several quietistic—if not doctrinally pacifist—injunctions among its eighty poems (No. 68, Bates, p. 7):

> The best captain does not plunge headlong,
> Nor is the best soldier a fellow hot to fight.
> The greatest victory wins without a battle . . .

And his warning (No. 57, Yohannan, p. 348), "The more weapons the people have,/The more troubled is the state," might be passed on the National Rifle Association!

As Robert Payne (in *The White Pony*, p. ix) writes, "For 4000 years the Chinese peasants . . . have hated the arts of war" and yet "seem to have seen war in a spirit of fatal expectancy, as though they knew it would always recur." This grumble of a Chinese conscript in 400 B.C. (Bates, p. 92) could easily be echoed by a G.I. in Vietnam in 1972:

> Grass withers and likewise we,
> Marching incessantly, also
> lose our strength, yet always
> new marches are planned . . .

Chu Yuan, who drowned himself in 295 B.C. because he could not influence the bad conduct of his prince (his suicide is yet commemorated annually by the Dragon Boat festivals), wrote these elegiac lines (Waley, pp. 39-40):

The warriors are all dead: they lie on the moorfield.
They issued but shall not enter: they went but shall not return.
The plains are flat and wide; the way home is long.
Their swords lie beside them: their black bows, in their hands.

Several poems from the hectic Han Dynasty echo these grim sentiments: this excerpt (Bates, p. 41) is from "War in Chang-An City" by Wang Tsan, who died in A.D. 217:

>   everywhere
> the white bones of the dead were
> scattered and on the roads were starving women
> putting children they could not feed
> into the grass to die . . .

Similar in grimness, but translated in a version which more ruggedly communicates the laconic directness of the original, is this old Han folk-song, "Fighting City South" (Sackheim, p. 41), the first part of which follows:

> Fighting city south
> Dying wall north
> Field dead unburied, the crows can eat
> For us to tell the crows
> Now, for aliens weep
> Field dead surely unburied
> Rotten meat: how can it leave you, escaping?
>
> Waters deep clear clear
> Rushes/reeds dark dark
> War horses—fighting/struggling/dying
> Old nags—back and forth/crying

From the 5th century A.D. comes this restrained plaint by Pao Chao (Frodsham, p. 151), that begins

> Have you not see the young men
> Marching off to the wars?
> They have turned into white-haired exiles
> Because they can never return

and ends with a sigh—"what is there to say?"

The T'ang Dynasty, allegedly the Golden Age of Chinese

poetry, was far from an era of peace. Tu Fu, greatest of all Asian poets on the war/peace theme, belonged as a minor official to the Establishment; yet he reacted in agony toward the byproducts of battle. As Robert Payne asserts: "No one else would have dared to sum up all human history, as he saw it, in six Chinese characters so charged with meaning that they burst out of the page with the effect of an explosion":

> *Blue* is the *smoke* of *war*, *white* the *bones* of men.

From Tu Fu's widely-anthologized "Song of the War Chariots" comes this quiet but deeply-felt indictment (Miller, pp. 31-32):

> . . . We have learned that to have a son is bad luck—
> It is very much better to rear a daughter
> Who can marry and live in the house of a neighbor,
> While under the sun we bury our boys . . .

More intimately confessional is Tu Fu's "Look at Spring!" (No. 72, Hung, p. 105), with verse paragraphs blocked into prose form:

> The nation is shattered. Only the landscape remains. Spring in the city? Yes, unpruned trees and overgrown weeds. Flowers are watered with tears of discouragement, Birds sing heartbreaking songs of separation.

> Beacon fires of battle have been burning for months. A letter from home would be worth a fabulous fortune! As I scratch my scanty white hair, more falls; it is almost too thin to hold a hairpin.

Many other poems by Tu Fu could be cited, but none more poignant than this monolog by an absent soldier's wife (Wells, p. 45), its first stanza as follows:

> I know that you will not come back from war.
> Still, on this stone
> I pound your cloak while you must die afar
> And I alone . . .

Tu Fu's friend and Byronic fellow-poet Li Po dwelt less often on the war theme, but one of his longer poems (Cromie, p. 14) limns harsh details of battle:

> In the battlefield men grapple each other and die;
> The horses of the vanquished scream lamentable cries to heaven,
> While ravens and kites peck at human entrails,
> Carry them up in their flight, and hang them on the branches
>   of dead trees.
> So, men are scattered and smeared over the desert grass,
> And the generals have accomplished nothing!

Other poets of the T'ang and succeeding dynasties left somber poems about war, including the 9th century Po Chu-I whose "The Old Man with the Broken Arm" (Anderson, pp. 228-9) is a reminiscence by an octogenarian patriarch who recalls that as a youth when about to be drafted he smashed his own arm with a huge stone, thus avoiding conscription:

> But even now on winter nights when the wind and the rain blow
> From evening on till day's dawn I cannot sleep for pain.
> Not sleeping for pain is a small thing to bear,
> Compared with the joy of being alive when all the rest are dead ...

Po relates the story, lets it stand, does not judge; he would perhaps be equally impartial if writing about American youths emigrating to Canada.

Since his quatrain is titled "Written in the year Chi-Hai" or 879 A.D., we have exact dating for an epigram by Tsao Sung (Davis, p. 28), perhaps the most widely-known short anti-war poem in Chinese literature:

> The submerged country, river and hill, is a battleground.
> How can common people enjoy their woodcutting and their
>   fuelgathering?
> I charge you, Sir, not to talk of high honors;
> A single general achieves fame on the rotting bones of
>   ten thousand.

Some Chinese scholars dismiss the nine centuries following A.D. 1000 as imitative and undistinguished in verse production despite the thousands of poems by hundreds of poets crowding these dynasties. The Poe-esquely surrealistic mood of Hsu Chao's

"The Locust Swarm," dated from the early 13th century, is therefore the more exceptional and haunting (Rexroth, p. 135):

> Locusts laid their eggs in the corpse
> Of a soldier. When the worms were
> Mature, they took wing. Their drone
> Was ominous, their shells hard . . .
> When the wife of the soldier
> Saw them, she turned pale, her breath
> Failed her. She knew he was dead
> In battle, his corpse lost in
> The desert. That night she dreamed
> She rode a white horse, so swift
> It left no footprints, and came
> To where he lay in the sand.
> She looked at his face, eaten
> By the locusts, and tears of
> Blood filled her eyes. Ever after
> She would not let her children
> Injure any insect which
> Might have fed on the dead. She
> Would lift her face to the sky
> And say, "O locusts, if you
> Are seeking a place to winter,
> You can find shelter in my heart."

What about the twentieth century in China? Forty-odd years ago, as a teen-age son of a missionary in Canton, I spent a terrified night on top of our mission home across the Pearl River from a city partly in flames; I'd armed myself with wet burlap and a waterbucket, to quench burning bits of debris dropping on to our roof. It was the night of the abortive Red Rebellion of December, 1927. Two days later I rode a rickshaw through blackened and looted Canton streets, nauseated at sight of hundreds of dead bodies—shot or axed—almost all of them communist rebels slaughtered by the Chinese war-lord who'd regained control. I'm perhaps one among few Americans today who saw then with my own eyes a bit of what a young Chinese poet in America agonizedly wrote about in his booklet titled "Poems of the Chinese Revolution" published in 1929 with a foreword by Upton Sinclair, and then forgotten. Tsiang's frenetic protests are too long to quote, but I wonder whatever happened to that unhappy young revolutionary exile . . . ?

Many poems by Chinese in our century, then, have been antagonistic to the status quo even before the Communist takeover in 1949. A poet whose pen-name was Ma Fan-t'o wrote during 1947 a poignant monolog (Hsu, p. 410) wherein an old woman tells what she did to save her son from conscription:

> I cried my eyes dry, dreading the arrival of dawn,
> For at dawn my son was to report to the army camp.
>
> While my son was asleep,
> And the neighborhood lay in total silence,
> "Ah, my son,
> Don't blame your mother for being too cruel . . ."
>
> I took needles,
> Two steel needles,
> And plunged them into my son's eyes.
> He screamed and the blood spurted out.
> "Ah, my son, they don't take a blind man in the army."

And we can go back to the 1920's when Wen Yi-tuo, a Chinese scholar and poet of increasingly leftist sympathies (he was murdered by Kuomintang soldiers in 1946), wrote this ironic protest, "Early Summer Night," with its ending lines (Payne, p. 300):

> A fire-swallowing, mist-spitting dragon climbs the iron stairway
> With "War" engraved on the gray uniform, hoarsely shouting, sobbing.
> The clapper of a great bell comforts the world,
> Saying, "Sleep in Peace," but who believes in the bell?
> O God, knowing the pass the world has come to,
> Are you not shuddering, O most benevolent God in the skies?

Mao Tse-tung himself has been a poet, usually belligerent in theme but traditional in form; yet in the final stanza of at least one poem, "Kunlun," of 1935 (Wong Man, p. 35) with a spirit uniquely tranquil and optimistic he addresses the huge, snowy mountain:

> To Kunlun now I say:
> Neither all that height

>   Nor that much of snow are needed.
> Could I but draw the precious sword that leant upon the sky
>   To slice you into three bits,
>   Giving one to Europe,
>   One to America,
>   And leaving one in China;
>   That peace may come,
>   Your warmth and coolness shared by all.

Well known in the 40's and 50's in China was Ai Ch'ing, a vigorous revolutionary who, however, took too literally the "hundred flowers" era of vocal freedom during certain years of the Mao regime and was "purged" in 1957. Composed around 1939, his long symbolic poem "Snow Falls on China" (Shimer, p. 99-100) ends in sympathy with the common folk he assisted:

> O China
> On this lampless night,
> Can my weak lines
> Give you a little warmth?

Since the 1940's, as the Australian scholar A. R. Davis grimly puts it (p. lxx), "poetry, like other literary forms in China, has been firmly harnessed to the propaganda machine." Examination of a dozen issues of the Peking English-language magazine *Chinese Literature* reveals an almost uninterrupted parade of poems shouting "Long live Chairman Mao" or "Mao Tse-tung thought gives me strength." Ai Ch'ing and certain other modern revolutionary Chinese poets with imagination and creativity appear nowhere in these pages, obviously.

When I turn to the island empire of Japan, I must first heed a warning by Donald Keene, who (in his letter to me of Oct. 10, 1970) reminds us that in classic Japan "there was really no tradition of expressing oneself on intellectual ideas in poetry," which was thus "written in the approved modes with the approved poetic diction, and these modes did not include mention of war in any connection." Yet in the great early Nipponese anthology, the *Manyoshu*, plaints by frontier-guards do touch on the human condition even if without disloyalty to their emperor. For instance, in 755 A.D., a guard named Akimochi pens this *tanka* (No. 764, p. 250):

> The dread imperial command
> I have received: from tomorrow
> I will sleep with the grass,
> No wife being with me.

During the period when Bashō and other poets made the 17-syllable *haiku* popular centuries later, "there were no wars in Japan, internal or external" (as Harold Henderson puts it, in his letter to me of Oct. 7, 1970); "so there seems to have been no urge to write *haiku* (which deal primarily with 'this moment') on the 'war/peace' motif." Actually, Bashō's famous epigram (Blyth, III, p. 309),

> Ah! summer grasses!
> All that remains
> Of the warriors' dreams,

stemmed from the poet's visit to a site where the medieval hero Yoshitsune had committed suicide 500 years before. However, a later *senryu* or ironic *haiku* by Ryomei (Blyth, p. 492) may bring acutely to mind the not infrequent occasions during the 1960's when strafing or bombing by American planes inadvertently killed our own G.I.'s in Vietnam:

> He died
> From the fire of his own troops
> And of the enemy.

Japan's Emperor Meiji, who over a century ago abolished the Shogunate and restored imperial power, wrote many thousand poems of which a few meditate on the peace theme, like this one composed during the Russo-Japanese war in 1904 (Asataro, p. 537):

> Surely in this world men are brothers all,
> One family!
> Then why do winds and waves on all the seas
> Rage stormily?

As Dr. Henderson recalls, "From 1941 on, anti-war *haiku* were suppressed by the government, and many anti-war poets were arrested." This poem by Kaneko Mitsuharu could not have been published during that period, but does serve to testify that not all Japanese youth were whole-souled in favor of the Second World War (Bownas and Thwaite, p. 199):

> Today is execution day for the pacifists.
> Escaping from the gunfire as their corpses topple,
> Their souls have ascended to heaven,
> To proclaim injustice and iniquity . . .

Reaction to an American air raid is the theme of a sequence of three *haiku* by Katō Shuson (Shimer, p. 125), who in a headnote recalls the context: "Carrying my sick brother on my back I wandered in the flames with my wife in search of our children." Out of such horror he distills this:

> In the depths of the flames
> I saw how a peony
> Crumbles to pieces . . .

Since the morning of August 6, 1945, when the A-bomb took the lives of (by Japanese statistics) almost 200,000 men, women, and children—mostly civilians in Hiroshima, thousands of poems by poets of all nations have expressed a world's horror and revulsion; but the Japanese victims themselves surely deserve the first right to be heard. Some of the writers of these unpolished *haiku* died later of wounds or leukemia:

> The spot where the bomb fell
>   Looks like
> A speechless eye.

> Undressing to the waist,
>   "It's too hot, Mama,"
> And he spoke no more.

> In Hiroshima
>   Salvias are in bloom,
> Believing in mankind.

One citizen, Shineo Shoda, wrote seventy *tanka* about the Hiroshima disaster, of which this one is representative:

> These big bones
> must be the teacher's.
> Around them,
> gathering in a circle,
> little skulls are found.

Using a libretto adapted from the poems of the most noted A-bomb poet-sufferer, Sankichi Toge (who lingered until 1953 before he died from the bomb's after-effects), an ambitious cantata was staged in Hiroshima in 1962. One section was titled "At a First-Aid Post"; it begins,

> You
> Who have no channels for tears when you weep
> No lips through which words can issue when you howl
> No skin for your fingers to grip with when you write in
>   torment . . .

and continues through broken lines of appalling clinical detail, to end:

> Here with your fellow creatures who one by one gradually
>   stop moving
> Remembering
> Those days when
> You were daughters of mankind.

And from a longer poem by Eisaku Yoneda, "The Sand on August 6," come these disturbing images (Ohara, pp. 14-16):

> The blood of men and women has soaked into everything, into
>   every grain,
> And the grains are their very bones ground into atoms.
> As the bell begins to toll,
> Each grain of sand will start to breathe its hot breath.
> They are fanned to fire, like so many sparks.
> Or are they stirring? are they starting to revive?

As Yoneda ends his poem, each grain is seen to symbolize a call for world peace. Indeed, in later years emerge some Japanese poems which express a measure of hope and prayer for the future. For example, Chiyoko Machida, wife of a husband dead in the holocaust, sublimates her grief thus:

> As I wandered through
>   the spring meadows
>   remembering the days with him . . .
> I met an orphan who
>   in a dirty hand
>   held a fragrant lotus-flower.

This severely abridged citing of Japanese poetic responses to the war/peace theme may be appropriately climaxed by quotation from a short but haunting poem by Murano Shirō, noted professional critic and poet (Bownas and Thwaite, p. 210); it's titled "Black Song":

>From eyes, from ears,
>Blackness pours;
>Melted in the night,
>Flesh gushing from my mouth,
>What can it be,
>This black song?
>
>Here no dawn reaches:
>A vacuum . . .
>
>And here, a heart
>That will not die,
>That will not sleep,
>Singing, singing.
>Friends of the world,
>Listen to its song,
>Black song of peace.

Now an appended glimpse at poems from seven centuries in the history of a small Indo-Chinese nation currently prone from the ravages of sickening war: Vietnam, of whose human beings north and south over a million have been killed since 1954. The 13th century poet Ly Dao Tai (Bich, p. 361) wrote "Pity for Prisoners" (ironically, the enemy during these eras was China):

>They write letters with their blood, to send news home.
>A lone wild goose flaps through the clouds.
>How many families are weeping under this same moon?
>The same thought wandering how far apart?

(It's sadly unnecessary to point out the modern timeliness of this plaint.) During the 18th century the poet Nguyen Du, in the course of a long poem titled "Calling the Lost Souls," addresses in one stanza the Chinese overlords who were then oppressing Vietnam (Raffel, p. 37):

> You sat and planned out battles,
> Schemed for command,
> Blew up thunder and lightning,
> Killed millions to make your glory.
> Battles turned wrong, a stray arrow, a chance bullet,
> And your blood on the field, your flesh rots,
> You hover near the sea, in distant lands,
> Your bones unclaimed, lying who knows where . . . ?

From Vietnamese poets I've been as yet unable to uncover a single serious poem supporting the conflict of the 1960's, but articulate Vietnamese voices, braving censorship and threats, have been increasingly heard crying out against the war. A vocal "third front" is represented by this manifesto (Bich, p. 5) from Tru Vu:

> I am neither a communist
> nor a nationalist:
> I am a Vietnamese.
> Is it not enough?
> For thousands of years
> that's what I've been:
> don't you think that's enough?
> And Vietnam in flames
> and mothers who weep
> and youngsters who suffer
> and all the terminology we use to kill each other!
> O River,
> we stand on our respective banks,
> our fallen tears mingling.

Sardonic thrusts like this ending from Thai Luan's poem, "Life," published early in the past decade, and addressed to us Americans—

> O people who never fear hunger and death,
> Come, to be our advisers and to help us to kill us—

and lyrics even more indignant could be quoted by the pageful; but I regard the "ubi sunt" wistfulness of the poem titled "Devastated," by a young poet, Truong Sinh (*Fellowship*, p. 15) as basically more significant—it was published just a few months ago:

> Bamboo creaking in the wind,
> Smoke hanging in the air,
> Whose voice in the wind
> Is whispering what?
>
> The jackfruit out in the garden,
> The lime tree in front of the gate,
> Withered leaves falling,
> Desolation, darkness, silence . . .
>
> Of the noise of the chickens hopping about the nest,
> Of the squeals of the hungry pigs,
> Of the hum of the fans winnowing rice,
> Not an echo.
>
> One heap of ashes, charcoal,
> Lying still, not speaking,
> Thinking of the beam, the roof,
> Seeing only the sad pillars standing alone.
>
> Gone the dragonflies,
> The birds and their greetings.
> Gone the charming voice
> Of the showy magpie.
>
> Gone the young girl
> Washing garments by the brook.
> Gone the youngsters
> And the summer noon song.

The scant three dozen poems and excerpts quoted in this survey (winnowed as they were from some 200 other verse-reactions to two millenia of wars in Asia) differ widely in range, emotional depth, intellectual acuteness, and degree of analysis or protest; but I think a few cautious generalizations can be offered. First, among the many thousands of Asian poems before the 20th century available in English translation, only a minuscule number seriously confront the phenomenon of "war" *per se*. Perhaps our translators have affected the percentages by frequent avoidance of Asian poems focused on this somber theme. Second, it is usually the by-products of war—wounds, desolation, bereavement, conscription, broken hearts—which enlist the distress or irony or outright protest of the more outspoken poets: not the basic concept of use of armed force. Third, certain poets who were magistrates or officers or other Establishment personnel could dip their brushes in agonized consideration of war's effects and yet continue in their positions or sinecures, not contemplating activist pacifism, etc., but nonetheless honest in their passive revulsion. As E. A. Robinson put it in another sense, "Their way was even as ours . . . "

I conclude with this second superb poem (p. 37) by Thich Nhat Hanh, whose verse introduced this paper:

> Promise me this day,
> promise me now
> while the sun is overhead
> exactly at the zenith,
> promise me.
>
> Even as they
> strike you down
> with a mountain of hate and violence,
> even as they
> step on your life and crush it
> like a worm,
> even as they dismember, disembowel you,
> remember, brother,
> remember
> man is not our enemy.

NOTE:
Chinese poems excerpted or quoted above come from the following anthologies: G. L. Anderson, *Masterpieces of the Orient* (Norton, 1961); Scott Bates, *Poems of War Resistance* (Crossman, 1969); Robert Cromie, *Where Steel Winds Blow* (David McKay, 1968); A. R. Davis, *Penguin Book of Chinese Verse* (Baltimore: Penguin, 1960); Frodsham, J. D., and Ch'eng Hsi, *Anthology of Chinese Verse* (London: Oxford, 1967); Henry Hart, *The Hundred Names* (California, 1933); Kai Yu Hsu, *Twentieth Century Chinese Poetry* (Anchor, 1964); William Hung, *Tu Fu, China's Greatest Poet* (Harvard, 1952); James Miller, R. O'Neal, and H. McDonnell, *Literature of the Eastern World* (Scott, Foresman, 1970); Robert Payne, *The White Pony* (New American Library, 1947); Kenneth Rexroth, *100 Poems from the Chinese* (New Directions, 1970); Eric Sackheim, *The Silent Zero* (Grossman, 1968); Dorothy Shimer, *The Mentor Book of Modern Asian Literature* (New American Library, 1969); Arthur Waley, ed. *One Hundred and Seventy Chinese Poems* (Knopf, 1919); Henry Wells, *Ancient Poetry from China, Japan, and India* (South Carolina, 1968); Wong Man, *Poems of Mao Tse-tung* (Hong Kong: Eastern Horizon Press, 1966); John D. Yohannan, *A Treasury of Asian Literature* (New American Library, 1956).

Japanese poems cited come from the following books: Miyamori Asataro, *Masterpieces of Japanese Poetry Ancient and Modern* (Tokyo: Taiseido Shobo, 1936); R. H. Blyth, ed. *Haiku,* in 4 volumes (Tokyo: Hokuseido, 1948); R. H. Blyth, *Japanese Life and Character in Senryu* (Tokyo: Hokuseido, 1960); Geoffrey Bownas and Anthony Thwaite, *Penguin Book of Japanese Verse* (Baltimore: Penguin, 1964); *The Manyoshu,* ed. Dept. History, Columbia U. (Columbia, 1965); Miyao Ohara, *The Songs of Hiroshima* (Hiroshima: Asano Library, 1967); Shimer (see above).

The three anonymous *haiku* by sufferers from the Hiroshima A-bomb, translated by Takahashi Horioka, were provided in typescript by Miss Lynne Shivers, World Friendship House, Hiroshima. The *tanka* by Shineo Shoda is from an undated booklet (ed. Sankichi Toge), "Genshi-Gu mo no Shita Yori" (Hiroshima: Aoki Shoten). Sankichi Toge's poem is from his cantata, "Give Back the Human," produced in Hiroshima in 1962, reprinted in *Poetry Nippon,* No. 11 (summer, 1970), pp. 2-3, translation by James Kirkup and Fumiko Mirua. Chiyoko Machida's poem is in a xerox pamphlet, *100 Poems by 100 Poets of Peace* (1949, Swarthmore College Peace Collection).

Vietnamese poems cited come from the following sources: Nguyen Ngoc Bich, "War Poems from the Vietnamese," *Hudson Review,* (Autumn, 1967), and "The Poetry of Vietnam," *Asia* (Spring, 1969); Burton Raffel, *From the Vietnamese: Ten Centuries of Poetry* (October House, 1968); Thich Nhat Hanh, *The Cry of Vietnam* (Santa Barbara: Unicorn Press, 1968); Thai Luan's poem was received in typescript, source untraced; Truong Sinh's poem appeared in *Fellowship* (July, 1969), p. 15.

赤裸裸而来
POSSESS NOTHING • OWN NONE •
NAKEDLY COME • NAKEDLY GO •
WANG • HUI-MING

Metaphors

Sally McNall

Perhaps
they are trying to tell us
something
the botched babies
the one with flippers
the one with
                the long split tongue
the one
      with his heart outside
                         his rib cage
About ocean
about
    language
about a world so gentle—

To Frank

David V. Quemada

Today I sat with your son
under a willow
brittle and bare
under a charcoal sky.
He said you died last night
without even your wife's knowing
sometime between the late news
and the late late show.
I wanted to visit you last week
when I heard you took to bed.
But I raked my yard heaped with leaves
then caulked my whistling windows
tight against the wind.
I had thought of bringing you a chicken dish
fit for a mandarin.

Round Lake

Janet Kauffman

I tell an easy story, all lies,
at parties. Ask me what I like,
I say digging pits, scrubbing sticks.
Ask me am I married. Easy.
I say no, divorced. You wonder
do I work. Sure I drill two exact
pinholes in a block of steel.

You I'll tell two things: the summer
I was 12 I saw the rich men from Detroit
without their wives unravel sails
with the care I'd seen them count their cash.
Their hair was white and grey and brushed.
The big sails hooked a wind and then two boats
with even-handed men slipped by,
slipped straight in a hush into blue.
I knew that they were making deals out there.
I thought I'd swim sometime to check
but everybody else said, Oh yeah
they'll hack some waves and yell,
back to your shack, girl. Git, git, git.
But I was sure the men would simply be precise:
Look, we'll tell you this, and this.

I learned to manage pretty well. And next:
when I was 17 and pregnant, I saw fire
spread across the lake in whorls,
the flames low, swirled, a richness
like embroidery, or golden robes.
I saw this for myself. And again
that winter, looking down through ice
in calms, in paths of blackened fish,
the sparks careened. A few like mica
flecked at the shores of eyes.

The lake steadied itself with lights
every season after.

                    Without leaving home
or reading anything I understood
I knew what traveling could do.
Here I am with square knots tying lies
when all along it was the lake,
its blue and white and gold geometry,
the dressy fire, that took me in.

Two Poems

GREG FIELD

Home Cooking Cafe

We are in Wieser, Idaho
Two young chicks
trot into the bus-depot-cafe
Three long-haired dudes
pitch pennies against its west wall
An old man puts a cheese sandwich together
Such is the entertainment

Midnight in Anchorage

the lady driver
is drunk, hot, and bloody
a cop comes silently

Absent Star

for my brother John

QUINTON DUVAL

After you left, I took the green
marbles that were your eyes. Lying
there in a suit with no back. I thought
the strange silk touched your shoulders
and buttocks like women's underwear.
The sad shoes that looked fine but
split down the back, harelipped,
cheating my father.

Once I twisted your arm so hard
I swear I felt my own break.
The turkish moon I banged in your
forehead with a stone, has caught me
like an invisible hook and teases me
until I break down and cry.

The woman you married over
and over again lives on. She counts
the minutes like money and looks at me
as if to demand payment.
I do what you would have wanted:
Look away and name everything I see.
I shake my own hand and pretend
we are making up for good.

She Pleads Guilty

ADRIAN OKTENBERG

A woman of seventy-one years
stands before strangers
and whispers her plea
She does not ask for mercy
She knows she is a criminal
and the bar of justice is austere
Her daughter stands up with her
and strokes her hair

Not the harridan drape of her dress
not her bag, or its emptiness
not the young grocer who pressed the charge
not the poverty
not the judge, nor the law
for none bears animosity
But the embarrassment
She cries openly

Brecht might have
brought a crowd into the street
Neruda might have
woven a garland for her of wheat
Lorca might have
torn out his heart to offer its wingbeat
She needed less
Thirteen dollars worth of vegetables and meat

Satyr

Marya Mannes

Rocking and rolling locked on tumbled bed,
priapic penis plunged in vaginal deep,
withdrawn and plunged again as exultant head
looms over face of woman whose fingers keep
pressing on urgent buttocks or sweating nape,
here is the playful, lustful, prideful male
in favorite exercise and fittest shape,
wanting no more from woman than her tail.
Wanting no more? Who knows? She wants his own,
wisely not waiting for any tender word
other than genital. Each is alone
except when the lust they share is undeterred
by consideration of love. The moment is all,
and the blind anonymity of sexual thrall.

Your Father Is Awake Shaking

Olivia Martin

Your father is awake shaking
like an angry fist.

The summers passed like buried ships.

He doesn't really know who you are.
He still loves you like another good idea.

You are trembling at his bed side.
His hair turns white before your eyes.
His teeth chatter and break his words.

You stand at his bed side and wait...

Consolation

JIM BARNES

Listen. That wind outside is yours:
your eyes ride it across jungles,
each yellow leaf a parachute.
You cannot go down:
the wind is for riding,
your eyes know.

Just listen. There is no dying in that,
though he is dead. The wind riddles
but it does not lie.
You can go on the wind
and come back here.

And listen. Take my hand. I offer
it to you to warm your breasts
while your dead airman's bones
talk to the wind we both know.

After Fire

KEN FIFER

First it was comical, then it was touching,
then it was tiring, then it was tired.
I stood on a roof already on fire.
Every man is a beast in that light.
I was not thinking of Vesuvius,
I was thinking of the fire in my house,
and a few thousand words, and a woman
I love, and all my scorched, familiar scars.

Two Poems

ALFRED STARR HAMILTON

Awesome

Is there any way I can lose my life
Is there any way I can lose my likeness
Is there any way I can lose my face
Is there any way I can lose my mistaken identity
Is there any way I can lose my likeness to the blue sky

rain

wasn't it drizzling
the last time I saw you
wasn't it in Chinatown
weren't our faces shining in the rain
weren't the city lights glimmering
wasn't it a white Chinese chickie
the last time I saw you in the rain

Judy Ray

Lilac Feeling

Richard Eberhart

Scent of the lilacs instills insouciance,
They gave to the daylight.
    This scent held onto air
    Like the poet's stare.

It was too sensual to rule,
And did not;
    Already the fragrance dies,
    As it reifies.

But at least they came late
Up here in the cold country;
    As we clip their tops
    We think time stops.

Judy Ray

poem for a "divorced" daughter

HORACE COLEMAN

if some nosey body asks "well,
is you got a daddy?"
give them the look that
writes "fool" on their face

if that aint enough & they
got to say "where he at?"
tell 'em "where he be!"

& if they *so* simple they
haven't got it yet & try
to stay in your business
to the degree of "well,
if he love you then how
come he aint here?"
you just sigh

poke your lip out low
ball your hands up on
your hips and let it
slip: "He loves me
where he *is*"
      cause i do
      where i am

Separate Courses

Henry H. Roth

I

When had the idea of a Memorial Day picnic begun?

Over coffee, one unusually warm winter evening on the sagging porch overlooking withered, frail trees and piles of dead leaves. There was an undeniable sense of times past, time moving too damn fast. Martha had turned to Jonathan and pointed out they never saw any old friends anymore. He had asked — You want to have a massive reunion? Yes — she said.

What plans were made?

A few days later they began writing letters, making calls, trying to locate their friends and choose a convenient date.

Why couldn't it have been enough just contacting old friends?

A few years before that it would have sufficed. But Jonathan and Martha were in their mid-thirties. What they were now is what they will be forever. Or so it seemed. Failure was like one's next breath. Deidre, thirteen, had already drifted away, at times the child was overtly hostile, daily flashing clear signs of alienation. Now they desired peer friends to touch and see.

Did they accept Deidre's actions, true part of childhood seeking its own place and role?

Oh, they accepted it, but surely would have preferred not being completely shut out. Deidre would no longer have any meals with them and kept her bedroom door locked. Martha had not entered in more than six months.

Why was Memorial Day such an advantageous date?

Because most of their friends taught and the college year was over, the battle for tenure put aside until the fall. For everyone, Memorial Day was a beginning toward good summer momentum.

How many times has the picnic been held?

This will be the fourth year.

Why has it become so difficult?

Martha and Jonathan have very little money; one unexpected illness, one car overhaul enough to topple them into sleepless, sullen days and bankrupt nights. In order to insure the Picnic's success, dozens of expensive, long distance calls have to be made and God knows how many stamped letters written. And then there is the enervating frightening potential of bad weather. What if it rains? Or is a cloudy, windy day? Jonathan and Martha have a tiny wooden frame house, a lot of land, but very little room at the inn. And there are other less abstract problems.

Doesn't the appearance of so many old friends who wish to retain old links make it all worthwhile?

Frankly, it has become quite a drag.

II

What is the day like?

Even at six everything is bright and clear like the super color TV set. And the birds are singing the hit tune about the singular pleasure of perfect day for a picnic. Thank God!

What actions have Martha and Jonathan taken to insure the day's success?

Each guest has been assigned a dish for the buffet table. There are no substitutes. Meat dishes are allotted to those who are more affluent. For desserts the best cooks are asked to contribute pies and cakes. Martha has been writing letters for the past year arranging all the dishes, Jonathan has phoned up till two days ago to finalize everything. Martha has contributed a bean salad. Jonathan has scythed the backyard.

From how many states do they come?

Thirteen.

Who is the first to arrive?

Always those who live furthest away arrive first. Jerry and

Claire, Mike and Donna, Sandor and Delores, it will be one of those couples. Jerry and Claire have been assigned a Virginia ham, Mike and Donna will bring two apple pies and a huge chunk of cheddar cheese. Sandor and Delores will bring 10 pounds of German potato salad.

Is Martha happy to see them?

She is relieved that they have brought what the list has them down for.

Is Jonathan happy to see them?

Jerry, Mike and Delores are college classmates. Jerry and Jonathan were quite friendly sophomore year but that was eighteen years ago. Soon snapshots of children will be passed around.

Who brings the pot?

Tony and Edna still live in the city and have the best contacts. Months ago each guest mailed two dollars to Tony toward the common goal of many bags of quality grass. There is always plenty of the weed and no one has ever asked for any strict accounting. But Martha evily wonders sometimes if Tony makes any money on the deal or hides some of the grass. He is very shrewd, the only one of their friends who is in advertising.

What time does the last guest arrive?

One fifteen. Maurice, now divorced, and very irresponsible, arrives with a very young and beautiful girl. Maurice has brought packaged Italian bread (not his assignment) and Martha is furious.

Why is this buffet different from the others?

Everyone has brought too much; it's almost sinful, what gluttons they have all become.

What is the image flashed to Jonathan?

He feels he has suddenly sold out, that he is fascist eating himself into stupor while peasants eat dirt.

What image flashes to Martha?

Two of the men here were lovers years ago, she tries to picture them as lean, attractive men and fails . . .

Why are children never invited?

Jonathan and Martha agreed years ago children would only be a pain.

Any humorous incidents?

Four years ago Jerry fell out of a tree and when he finally stumbled to his feet, tried to climb the tree again — but that was four years ago.

Any old songs sung?

Goodnight Irene and Teen Angel.

What new songs?

None.

Why did Diedre suddenly show?

Diedre's stoned out of her skull and sure she could handle sixty-seven adults. And she did, giggling and doing Yoga, though she wore no underwear, shocking the hell out of Martha.

List some items eaten?

No. Enough to say it had been too grandiose. Yet nothing is left. They have brought tons of food and eaten it all, which is more shocking. Four garbage baggies sag with bones and waste.

III

Dear Friends,

Jonathan and I pondered for quite awhile how to begin our salutation. Friends is not as warm as a first name greeting but remember this is a form letter that has been xeroxed free of charge by one of the community college's kind secretaries.

We have decided to formally end the PICNIC. Such an overwhelming success this time, how could we possibly top it? But it wasn't supposed to be a gourmet extravaganza. Initially, we did in past years draw upon some gossip and, occasionally, after too much sangría, leaning against a sturdy beech tree, someone did mumble words of bitter truth. But it's not enough, friends.

Our truth is that the Picnic has become too difficult for us. Our own life is too much right now to bear up under a year of planning. Jonathan claims the letter is cold and computerized but he is too and so am I and so is our child and so is the Picnic. Nothing warrants a longer run.

We are settling for TV talk shows, movies, and non-fiction;

we desire natural order and sure limits, as we dance to erotic fantasies. Most of us have succeeded partially in our goals; we'll press on, but not with the same vigor and though we may get no further, we are no longer humbled by lack of upward mobility. Predictably, we inspire half-truths on the phone and in person, our eyes show savage times and our drooping lips sneer our happy lives. We leave each other abruptly in the middle of a moan or sentence . . . it is sort of conversational interruptus, a painful but necessary withdrawal to abort any truth foetus. Abused, we use each other one afternoon and half an evening a year. We are the great pretenders playing in a movie that no one attends.

My daughter, the mysterious Deidre, whom you finally have seen, tells me I hate youth because I envy them beyond all reason. She adds I'm afraid of her and other children. Jonathan insists I omit the last two lines because it's a personal confession and has no general significance. How do you know that Jonathan? Are we the only failures with our children? And I want to be more personal and more universal, more anything.

A final personal anecdote, we went to a swinging party. An orgy, as the tabloids would headline. Instead of a marriage counsellor we went to an orgy. Jonathan wants no part of this, he's not smiling, he mutters no one will understand why we're shutting off their good time. Sure they will. Things are bad, friends. We sit here halfway up a mountain in an idyllic setting with pie all over our faces . . . creamy concoctions bombard and splatter us continually. Bills, broken promises, bad dreams, chase us and play cruel saloogie with our souls. The picnic stinks, we merely overplay our roles, drip sweat and bite our lips, afraid to cry out — *enough, I'm scared*. We want no more of you. You are the shallow fragments of the rainbow image, the hoax that good things are always happening. But we failed you and you didn't help either. Neither did the swinging.

It was a select group from all over the country chosen by the head of our progressive school board and a leading feminine ecologist. We met at the rented Legion Hall; were all introduced perfunctorily, the lights were snapped off, a patient voice explained in three hours a timed clock would ring, fifteen minutes later another warning buzz and then lights on. During the hours of darkness I was fondled and fondled in return many shadows; it was the penultimate sexual nightmare. In retrospect, friends, it was like the picnic — many strangers keeping to themselves as they huddled into one another.

When we got back home Jonathan and I stayed up all night watching TV movie after TV movie.

If Jonathan and I do not divorce, we will live separate lives. We do that right now but for change we'll voice our decisions about our own lives aloud. Our house lends itself to isolation. Jonathan confessed something astonishing yesterday, he no longer subscribes to any magazines, he either reads them at the library or lugs them home and he told me the reason he'd given up all subscriptions is that he always expects to cut and run the next day. Steady, reliable Jonathan only dreams of running away and I just found out two days ago. Brothers and sisters, that is the way we are now. Untogether is the way, the way is untogether.

Please do not take our refusal to hold the picnic any longer a challenge for one of you to pick up the gauntlet. Half day communes if not nightmares become ciphers. Stay home and lie to one another, it's less demanding. Thanks for coming the last four years, of course we have loved many moments, but that's it gang. Soon, soon we'll even forget one another and discover one day in a syndicated obit page that we have all died.

IV

Inside the yellow, yellowing kitchen, is an appropriate scene for an unusually honest picture postcard celebrating HAPPY HOLIDAY SEASONS: instead of the phony framed group portrait smiling very dumbly, here is a family unit huddling intently across a chipped table stuffing Xeroxed letters into envelopes. The mailing assembly line continues unabated as they share wine, a few joints . . . and Martha also prepares a zesty chicken soup. Observe Jonathan's long beard and Zeus-like appearance and Martha's gaunt, beautiful but sad, pioneer woman's stance, include Deidre's pleasant small features but detached air, hinting she is always somewhere else. Such a cursory glance might make this a radical mailing of position papers defending revolutions and eclectic bombings.

Three years before Deidre had been directly involved with her family. Oh the discussion that preceded that final decision! Martha definitely unwilling to bear another child, besides they couldn't afford such an extravagance; they leveled with their daughter, spoke openly as usual and more than suggested it wasn't a hundred percent sure daddy's seed had flowered inside mommy. But so be it. Either way it didn't matter for the little house along the big hillside just couldn't tolerate another presence. They just wanted another accomplice to rubber stamp their choice of abortion. "Oh kill the damn kid," Deidre had shouted out. They shuddered, explained how that was the wrong outcry, so Deidre obediently okayed the yea vote and still felt guilty being drawn and quartered by private adult machinations.

While today Deidre sucks in an excellent joint, feels invincible and giggles throughout the afternoon. Not saying aloud how crazy, telling all your friends to screw off because they're not going to get many new pals or better ones at their age . . . wisely she didn't also add, you don't even like each other anymore so don't mail the screwy letters, don't kill all your friends too . . . Jonathan holding the master letter asks Martha whether she wants her original framed — she modestly desires it placed in the file box with the stock certificates, insurance papers and wills.

Deidre slinks to the floor, tiring of stuffing and licking and proclaims the whole damn family plays without a full deck. They study Deidre carefully, trying to fully fathom the darted insult, but their daughter is smiling, not scowling or pouting, so the mother and father relax. Next Deidre announces she will continue working part time at Hamburger Palace to buy her Honda. Jonathan thinks both his wife and daughter look equally fierce.

Outside he scans the brittle sky and sees no hope of rain. Really worrying about the well he looks nervously to the right and left and only sees what he always sees, fat lush trees, wild thick bushes and reckless vines and wild flowers. When he steps back inside the house, Deidre and Martha are side by side laughing; like dynamite twins they finish off the mailing; he hauls the bundle of packets and tosses them into the back of his car as if it was just another bundle of supermarket staples.

Deidre suddenly asks her mother if she ever felt empty after the abortion. Martha hastily answers no. Later in retrospect she will think more deeply about the question, but can only honestly comment on the most recent events, such as the marvelous time when they were all together severing too many silly ties; it was a homey time and odor, the wonderful kitchen smelling mod, yet reeking of the past as grass and chicken soup were mixing it up . . .

V

Another cycle, another lousy epoch as the well dries up and the sewer line splits and now evil polluted water drips from kitchen and bathroom taps. Plumbers, the landlord, Roto Rooter folk center-stage the land and keep showing for premature curtain calls. The following days bring thunderstorms and monsoon and brackish foul looking water flows into the sinks gagging everyone. Days are terrible but nights even worse because no repair work is possible and there is no possible miracle of things clearing up until a next morning. Jonathan drowsy from wasted days, goes to bed early as if to hide but only dreams of telegrams and letters and notes and telegrams and phone calls demanding money and his surrender. One evening as Martha slides next to his tossing form Jonathan mutters and stutters, "Nothing changes ever" . . . she hisses into his ear "Screw it, screw you." Jonathan awakes with a bewildering start, "Huh, what?" She lies back grimly, not replying, then Martha clearly hears Deidre's eerie laughter. She leaps from the bed, he half turns, asks "Can't you sleep?" "I can't sleep when our damn daughter mocks us all night with her rotten humor."

"Deidre's sleeping at a friend's house. Don't you remember?" But Martha doesn't believe either of them. She clenches her hands, leans against the bedroom wall. They both hear the howling. "See what lousy rotten lives we live." Jonathan says, "It's something else, the wind. Take a tranquilizer."

Martha discovers the hooting comes from the barn where an ancient door hanging on faulty hinges grates into an ugly wilderness. The ground smells of sweet rotting overripe fruit, Martha runs back into the house and its strange, waiting rooms where unfamiliar possessions litter her path. Only the kitchen pounds with good memory.

While waiting for the coffee to perk, Martha actively attempts to recapture the human instant of a few weeks ago . . . she tries vainly to recapture the bittersweet nearness, the gluey taste of stamps and envelope flaps. She drinks her coffee, again tries to seize even one passionate second . . . tries again. And again.

Two Poems

Duff Bigger

IT IS WHEN THE TRIBE IS GONE
and I sit within the circle of stones
and maintain the fire.
A dog gnaws on a bone
      at my side.
The woods are full of deer.
That tapping that I hear is from my thumb
      on my bow when I hear something
move. We are not safe here on this planet.
It is winter. The smoke above the fire
      is getting dim.
On a night like this one Van Gogh dug in into his blanket
      and died

THE COMEDIAN SAID IT:
that talking to that girl
is like opening a door into the sea
and having the knob come off
      in your hand

Barbie
Harold Witt

You pull a string from her neck
and it slides back in as she says
"Would you like to go shopping?"
in a doll's hollow voice
as if from her rubbery head.

She hasn't any sex
except for her nippleless breasts
and is, in fact, all of a piece,
her vacuous face
after face after face
stamped by the money machine—

and her wardrobe's never complete—
each cute
fragile costume
costs what would feed
some rickety kid
for a week.

Over and over she asks,
thoughtless of hunger or bomb—
as her makers make toys,
too, for doomed boys:
hand grenades, almost real guns—
barbarous Barbie,
death's shallow mate—
"What shall I wear to the prom?"

Luz de Corral

Charles Itzin

Luz de Corral is Pancho Villa's widow who (if she is still alive) runs a Pancho Villa museum in Chihuahua City. Doreteo was Pancho Villa's christian name . . .

"Asi es como se perdio la guerra Villa."

I. The veterans

There are no children in the dust,
it is the same story, cross-grained,
this old house wandering into strange
cracks. One sparrow could not make
a summer, there was nothing more
to do. Always the sun has been a yo-yo,
the assassins are still at large.

I recall their shadows. In the
morning they come; friends, strangers,
movie-men. I do not ask, five pesos
a head, half-price for children. It
is all the same now. Sometimes old
men will take my arm. Luz, they will
say, I was with him, at Columbus,
in Mexico. Indeed, he spoke
of you often, I tell them. It
makes no difference. All old men
were there now. The ones with no ears,
no eyes, no arms, they do not come.

II. The Spirit Lamp

    You grow obscure, Doreteo.
    Lupe is bent, a broom maker keeping
    the dust from your eyes, scraping the rust,
    your crooked face growing unbearably white,
    the sun in a grain of sand,
    miles of desert. Mothers tell their children,
    Venga, hijo, the sun will make you black.
    They will call you nigger.

    The rings surround the isinglass moon,
    dissipate in mute patterns through
    the lattice, dance to their solitude
    in my liquid eyes. God knows the
    summer is over now, Doreteo. I count
    the pesos, turn them slowly between
    dry fingers, the dust settling
    from the moon.

    This is your house, I do not forget.
    When another day is locked behind
    the battle of Chihuahua,
    the bones of your armies, in the shadows
    of the spirit lamp your chalky eyes,
    leaden-hued, return, smashing my teeth,
    the butterfly drowning in the rooms
    of my mouth. Alone in a house of smoke,
    I rediscover the moments of our quick love,
    the crooked lines in the maps,
    the unsuccessful prison breaks.

Cattails

Greg Kuzma

No one ever comes here,
was what they said first
when we, nearing the crest
of the hill, first spied
them, there in the ditch,
those months ago. Now they
are all cut down.

Long palm leaves, then the
stalk, on top of which
the thing we used to make
a torch of, punks, or
smudges, to light our
cherry bombs. It's brown
on the outside, nearly
white inside, a sausage
packed with seeds. You
shake it down, once it's
ripe, it hangs a big umbrella
in the air, just like it's
sneezed.

They signalled, on that
small rise, in the middle
of those big dry fields,
beside that dusty road,
they signalled water in
the ditch. We got our
feet wet, cutting the
first of them.

Girl Floating On Air

Mary Crow

Lying on her back, hands raised
Above her head, she lies flat
On the bed of wire.

She seems to sleep, becalmed
In the moment's weather, waiting
For someone.

Now they are braiding
Something between her fingers,
Between her toes,

And wetting her stretched-out body—
Is it to purify?—
As she shivers there.

Her eyes are closed; no color
Hooks us in. This is the thing
As it is,

And we wait with her
(Imagining a better world?)
For the cattle prod.

Note In A Bottle

Gerald McCarthy

The Erie-Lackawanna trains are the ghosts
of summer nights. A town of freightyards,
tanning factories, timeclocks.
A town that smelled like leather.

I walk the ties through yards & loading docks,
remember crawling between rails, watching
the headlights of sheriff cars.

If I listen I can almost hear the sirens,
glimpse the smudge of orange sky beyond
the smokestacks. I push open the door
at Ernie's Grill on the North Side of town,
the Italian side.

His hands stained brown from shoe dye,
John Robinsky cursed the heat, swore
the union would never get in.

It never did. They quit making leather
from cowhide. They closed the factories,
laid-off the workers.

Robinsky raised pigeons because it was
something he could do. We used to watch
them lift off & carry those messages away.

Nobody answered, John. No one heard anything
but that flapping of wings. The gun lifted,
the glass raised. Soot filled years in the attic
with the wire cages; mornings in the steel vats,
the drying sheds. Nobody counted.

A town of mortgages, parking lots.
I turn away, walk home toward my father's house,
toward a light in the window of an upstairs room
that flickers & goes out.

The Dying of Frank Oldmixon

WYATT WYATT

It was a fundamental issue that brought Frank Oldmixon and me together.

I had quit my job, been divorced by my wife, and failed, for over a month, to satisfactorily move my bowels.

"That's some piece of constipation," Frank said. "You know what, I bet that's why you got divorced. A man gets full of shit, he forgets what love is."

I was feeling sorry for myself: "Love *is* shit," I said. "What are you in for?"

"Just the opposite of you."

He was a thin, wiry man draped in pajamas so loose on him he looked as if he were moulting. With his quick eyes, sharp beak of a nose, and feathery wisps of hair curling on his neck, he resembled nothing so much as a bedraggled old hawk.

I resisted him like a snake, but sharing a hospital room and its incumbent anxieties breaks down barriers, and we were soon friends, facing our common front away from the doctors, who practiced the dark side of medicine on us: complete rectal examinations. For three days they punched, probed, and photographed us both. And then let me go. Happily, I suffered from a psychosomatic block; I was only crazy.

But Frank had the misfortune to be sane, and when the surgeons cut him open to remove the obstruction, they found cancer all through him; instead of taking a piece of bowel out, they sewed him up again and added a piece on: a colostomy bag.

"Goddamn it, Barlow!" Frank marvelled. The doctors had already informed him of his terminal condition. "I ain't ever going to use my asshole again. I have to shit through my belly into a bag from now on. Stinks like holy hell, don't it?"

It did. But, like me, Frank was alone, so I ignored the smell and visited him often. An old con man, he got tougher as his body weakened, and never complained. Towards the end, the hospital, which he knew he was not going to leave, began to seem like a prison to him. I felt guilty in my freedom—a sentiment he shamelessly exploited—until at last I gave in and agreed to drive him to the west coast.

Frank said, "Just let me see the Gulf once more, Barlow, and buy me a drink of something stronger than hospital lemonade, and I'll die happy."

He was a natural charlatan, and kept me thinking all the way over that in spite of the heat and the smell, he was feeling fine. But we had not been out on the beach an hour when Frank suddenly vomited bile and blood, and all the false flush of health his transfusion had given him drained from his face. I watched horrified as he straightened up, wiped his mouth with a handkerchief, and showed me a weak grin. "Now I think I'm ready for that drink."

Cursing myself—we were three hours from Orlando—I got him back into the station wagon, where he passed out, falling into a dead sleep I was afraid he might never come out of. His mouth gaped, the breath gargled in his throat. His whole face seemed to collapse. Cheekbones, nose, eye sockets—all were like blunt blades barely sheathed in the worn, frail leather of his skin.

I crossed the bridge as fast as I dared and fought my way through the Petersburg rush-hour traffic to the Interstate, where I pushed the station wagon up to top speed, seventy-five; above that the front end shimmied, the engine knocked, the steering wheel rattled in my hands. I was afraid it would blow up if I went any faster, and that Frank would die before we reached the hospital if I went any slower. Once again, though, he fooled me. On the other side of Tampa near Plant City his mouth closed, he wiped the spittle off his lips, and sat up straight. "Turn off here," he said.

"No, Frank."

"You promised."

"Don't hold me to it."

"I'm dry as a turnip. I got to have me that drink. Come on."

"Goddamn it, Frank, this is a dirty trick. You're trying to die on me."

"I thought we had a deal," he said.

"Your part of the deal was that you would stay alive."

"I am alive, and we been to the beach, so all that's left is the drink."

"No. I'm taking you back to the hospital."

"Pull over then. Let me out here. I'll hitchhike."

"Frank, goddamn it. Please."

"My last drink," he said. "There's got to be something you gain from dying; we get a last request, don't we? Next week you can get drunk if you want to, and the week after that, and the one after that. But not me. It's my only chance. I won't ever again have the taste of whiskey on my tongue. Ever."

"This is a sob story. A cheap soap opera."

"Never ever."

"All right. Shit. I give up. You're a goddamned sentimental old man and stubborn as hell, but you'd better not die on me. I've had as much of that as I can take."

"That's exactly how much we all of us get."

I took the next exit and stopped at the first place we came to, a squat concrete block building on the side of the road with a naked woman painted in Da-Glo on the wall and a sign: *Great Go-Go Girls! Continuous!* It was one of those dark, marginal bars no one goes into unless he has already had two or three drinks. A woman with heavy wrists and ankles was dancing on the bar. It was late afternoon, a bad time to see her. Her coy look was plastered on her face like her powder and eye shadow, too thickly, and failed to hide the despair underneath. Her naked breasts sagged. Her thighs jiggled.

Frank was oblivious. He was performing an enormous act of will, dragging his nine-tenths dead body inside for a ritual drink. It was romantic defiance, a role he played so intensely that he created not only his own person but the setting around him as well. From the way he acted, it could have been the Ritz we had walked into. The illusion was startling. He had swelled himself up in pride and plumage to full size, a swaggerer, a roughneck. He winked at the dancer. He flirted with the barmaid. He glowered at a customer who moved aside too slowly. I thought for a moment he was going to start a fight, which I would have to finish.

"I'm no fighter," I told him. "Don't you start anything."

"What are you afraid of, those two guys? Shit, Barlow, we could take them." He was looking at the two men in a booth across the room, one of them with a dumb, placid look on his face as though he had been hit in the back of the head. It was the other, smaller man who made me uneasy. He had a thick neck and a truculent face, and was exactly the kind of bad character one avoids looking directly at in bars. He had spotted Frank, too, and stopped talking. His small, mean eyes fixed us like insects against the barstools.

"Let's get what we came for," I said, and turned Frank around.

He ordered a whiskey, double. "I always wanted to do that. All my life I been a beer drinker, not because I liked it, but because I was so damned timid. You know I never been in a barroom fight in my life?"

"Well you sure have the instinct for it. You couldn't have picked a worse guy to face down than that cretin across the room."

"A punk. I'd like to see him start something."

"What would you do, die in his arms and make him feel guilty?"

"Now that would be going out in style," Frank said.

The bartender set our drinks down before us, two double whiskeys. Frank picked his up and sipped it. His eyes watered.

"You don't have to finish it, you know."

"Shit, I'm all right, I'm having a good time. Maybe I'll have you get me a woman, too."

It was costing him a lot to carry it off. His forehead had broken out in big drops of sweat, and his fingers trembled so that the glass shook. To keep it from showing he steadied it against his teeth when he drank and lowered it quickly to the bar between swallows. The other hand was pressed against his shirt, supporting the colostomy bag, which seemed to be causing him some trouble. He sat up very straight and tall, and in the dim light of the bar must have looked to others as healthy as anyone else, but he was like a tree eaten up by termites from the inside out, a firm structure in appearance, ready to collapse and crumble into a powder in the hand at the first touch. I was watching him so closely that I didn't see the two guys across the room get up and leave their booth. It was not until I heard them that I knew they were there. The voice came suddenly from behind as though it had been thrown from a mop bucket.

"Sure stinks in here, don't it?"

"Sure does. You suppose one of these fellows is carrying a dead rat in his pocket?"

Frank spun his stool around slowly, drink in hand, and I had no choice but to turn with him. He was grinning. "Hello, boys," he said. "You must be talking about me. It takes a real man to smell as strong as I do."

The shorter of the two men had a chunky suntanned face like a piece of tough meat. He grinned back. "If I couldn't see you," he said, "but was to know you was in the room just by smelling your stink, I would've guessed you was one of those hippies who don't take baths. You're not one of them, are you?"

"No," Frank said, "I'm sure not."

"I guess I owe you a drink, Johnny," meat-face said.

"He's not a hippy, huh?"

"That's what he claims."

I swelled myself up as big as I could, but knew even as I did that my size would not intimidate either one of them. Johnny, the dumb one, was just as big as I, and I recognized meat-face as the kind of stocky ex-highschool athlete with a trunk like a tackling dummy who had made a career out of cutting down guys bigger than himself. A bluff was useless; I had to try to cool the whole thing. "Can we buy you two a drink?" I asked.

"He's not a hippy. What do you think it is, then, Johnny? You think he shit his pants?"

Frank laughed, and downed the rest of his drink like a shot of strengthening medicine. He actually looked restored. "I can promise you it wasn't that," he said. "Hoo, boy, I wish it was."

Big dumb Johnny was the straight man. "Do you believe him? Sure smells like shit to me."

"Awful strong shit. The kind that's caked up and drawn flies. Maybe you shit your pants early this morning and forgot about it."

"Look, you guys," I said, "we don't want any trouble. Why don't you let us buy you a drink, and then we'll leave. All right?"

"You stay out of it, prick-nose, we're talking to your partner." His grin didn't change, nor did he look at me. It was the kind of disdain calculated to push a big man into a fight. Evidently, they had made up their minds before they had even come across the room. I had to think of some way to get Frank out of there. He had absolutely no fear of them; as he saw it, there was nothing they could do to him. I was afraid he might even start it himself.

Meat-face was not letting up. "Is that what happened? You make a mess this morning and forget about it? Been carrying a load around all day?"

"Longer than that," Frank said.

"I thought you said you didn't do it," Johnny said. "Were you lying to us?"

"I said I didn't shit in my pants. That's no lie."

"I don't believe you," meat-face said.

"I think he's lying to us," Johnny said. "I don't like liars, do you?"

"Leave him alone," I said.

Studiously, meat-face continued to ignore me. He was up on the balls of his feet, though; he must have felt I was about primed. "Looks like we're going to have to find out for ourselves," he said. "Drop your pants, shit-britches."

There was no way out of it. If they made one move towards him, Frank would take a swing at them and get himself killed. He was so weak a strong breath would knock him off his feet. I was going to have to handle them both, and that meant I had to get in the first blow. So I came down off the stool swinging, a roundhouse right with all my weight behind it, aimed not at meat-face but at Johnny, the bigger man, and caught him behind the ear. To my surprise, and to his, it knocked him cold, and he went down like a crumpled paper cup. It also did what I had hoped: it startled meat-face and put the first hint of doubt in his eyes. But his instincts were good. He came back at me fast, before I was set, and shot three quick blows into my stomach. They were short straight punches with his shoulders behind them. I was thankful for the vanity that had kept me running and doing sit-ups; if I had been any softer he would have punched right through me. His fists were like brick halves.

"Is that the best you can do?" I taunted. He backed off, charged again, and slammed me with a stiff thump, like a badly-caught pass in the solar plexus. But I got him one, too, a glancing blow off the side of his head that hurt my hand and put a tiny cut at the corner of his eye. It brought a hoot of appreciation from Frank and cheered me more than it should have. I had drawn first blood, but he had hit me a hell of a lot harder and hurt me worse. I only hoped he didn't know it.

Again, he came at me. We traded blows, missed, traded again, and finally clenched. We were both sweating and breathing hard. I was in better shape, but he was stronger; he was trying to crush the air out of me with his arms and I was straining against him. All at once he let go. I foolishly grabbed tighter, and then winced as he chopped me with his open hands in the kidneys. That sent me a step backwards in pain and anger, opening myself up stupidly. It was his chance to end the fight, and had he come in fast he could have finished me off. But I was lucky. He knew that I was hurt but guessed that Frank would come into the fight, and so made the mistake of looking back over his shoulder. I threw myself forward with a blow that sent a solid and satisfying shock up my forearm all the way to the shoulder and lifted meat-face right off his feet. It broke his nose and smashed his upper lip against his teeth, cutting it badly. He staggered, went down to one knee, shook his head, and came back up. I was dismayed. It had been the best I could give; I would never hit him that hard again.

Spitting blood, he came straight for me, a mean, tough fighter who was not going to quit. I hit him again, and then again. It didn't stop him. He was slowed down enough so that I could get to him, but I couldn't seem to hurt him more than I already had. Tossing off my blows, he worked his way in close and clenched. This time I held his arms farther down, guarding against the kidney chops, but he got me with his foot, first stomping my toes, then delivering a sharp kick to my knee. I went backwards too fast and fell down, and immediately he was on me. The toe of his boot caught my ribs, the small of my back, my chest, my arm, and finally came down hard on the back of my thigh and left a whopping charleyhorse. I rolled under a table and came up on the other side, favoring the leg. He reached for me, and caught the table in the pit of his stomach as I slammed it forward.

For a moment he was the one backing off, but in the center of the room he stopped, and we began slugging it out. I knew I was not going to outlast him. He was too strong. And it looked like no one was going to stop us. The other customers had not even bothered to get up; they watched us from their booths and from the bar. The topless dancer had her breasts in her hands and was chewing gum. There was a baseball bat in the hand of the bartender, but he stood quietly to the side waiting for one of us to save him the trouble. It didn't seem that he would have to wait much longer. My hands felt weighted; I could hardly hold them up, much less hit him with any force. But for the second time I was lucky. By accident I caught him in the adam's apple, not nearly hard enough to decommission him, but enough to hurt him again. That's when I should have followed up and gone forward, but I didn't have the strength. So I backed off, moving away to the bar where, I hoped, Frank might have the chance and the good sense and possibly the strength of arm to pick up a bottle and smash meat-face over the head with it. Because the bastard was not through with me, he was still coming. And now I knew I had made another bad mistake. My back was to the bar; there was no room to maneuver. The blows came at me harder and faster—he was sensing his victory—and it was all I could do to protect my head and face.

I had no right to any more luck and would never have believed there might be a third granting of it, but there was. His strongest blow yet caught me square in the forehead and did not hurt at all, though it lifted me half way onto the bar. Because it had moved my body with such force, he must have thought the blow had finished me. In any case, he paused to see if it had. So instead of coming down off the bar I let myself go on back, bringing my foot all the way up from the floor into his balls. Then I came back, swinging down with both fists onto the back of his head. And as he sank, I brought my knee up as hard as I could into his chin. He crumbled, and I, as much done in but still on my feet, fell back into the bar stool beside Frank.

"I told you we could take them," he said.

That was when I knew my luck had run out. The big guy, Johnny, was shaking his head and getting up. He looked at me and then at meat-face, and finally helped his friend to his feet.

"Hand me a bottle," meat-face said.

And big dumb Johnny, who knew his partner well and understood what was wanted, picked up a beer bottle and smashed it over the edge of the bar, and put the jagged neck of it into meat-face's hand. "Now," meat-face said, "we'll see what the sonovabitch is made of." They both came towards me at once.

Behind them the bartender was moving forward with his baseball bat, but I knew he would never reach them in time. My life was going to end as stupidly and meaninglessly as it possibly could. A rough hot gash across the throat, the blood pumping out, perhaps a wet gasp and sputter of breath, and then the long soft fall into sleep. Meat-face and Johnny stalked me. I watched the bottle neck advance, the baseball bat rise behind them, and Frank, next to me, unbutton his shirt.

"You shit-heads didn't really think you could whip us, did you?" he said. And he ripped off his colostomy bag and sprayed them full in the face.

The stink was gagging, more powerful than a shot of straight ammonia. I came sharp alert and lept down off the bar stool. At the same time the baseball bat came down on meat-face and then again on Johnny, a mercy for them both, blinded and staggering with their faces full of Frank's cancerous blood and shit. They sank to the floor, and Frank and I, laughing like lunatics, held each other up in a staggering run for the station wagon. We made it out of the parking lot to the street not thirty seconds before the police car came roaring around the corner, its sirens screaming.

"Oh shit—" Frank said. He was laughing so hard he couldn't speak. "I thought—when he came at you with the bottle—"

"What?"

"I thought—by god, I was going—to outlive all of you."

"That's—you won't—you won't believe this, but—" I, too, was helpless with laughter.

"What?" Frank said.

"I was so scared that—"

"What?"

"—so scared that I—"

"What?"

"—that I shit my pants."

II

We might have laughed ourselves to death if I hadn't come to my senses. I pulled the station wagon over to the curb and turned off the ignition.

"Hoo, boy," Frank said, "I wouldn't have missed that for anything in the world." The look on his face was one I had never seen before. His eyes, though directed at me, were focused inward on some inevitable process of decay, and it was clear, even though he was still laughing, that he hated whatever it was he saw.

"I'd better get you back," I said.

"Yeah. I guess so."

This exchange ended our laughter. We both understood what it meant. Without saying anything more, I swung the station wagon away from the curb and headed for the highway. Not the Interstate this time, but U.S. 92; I was thinking that there were several towns we had to pass through where one might make an emergency stop. Frank was still putting up a good front, but he was visibly sinking. I watched him pull up his trouser leg to rub his shin and saw that the swelling had gone out of his legs as well as his stomach; it almost seemed a miracle, until I realized it was collecting as fluid in his lungs. His breathing had become thick and labored. I slowed down and reached over to roll down the window for him so he could get more air. He seemed grateful, but did not try to speak. It was only after we passed the junction with U.S. 17 and were entering Winter Haven that he broke the grim silence.

"What I hate is the damned indignity of it," he wheezed. "Weak as wet toilet paper and smelling like a shit house. Listen, Barlow . . ."

"What is it?"

"I hate to ask you this."

"Go ahead."

"I want you to stop and get me cleaned up before we go back to the hospital. I can't promise you I'll make it this time, but I don't want to check in like this."

"We don't have to go there if you don't want to. You can come to my house, or we can go to another hospital right here in Winter Haven."

"No. It might make trouble for you if I don't get back. Besides," he said, and smiled weakly, "they got a nurse back there I wouldn't mind looking at one more time."

"I don't know how we'll do it. I stink like a dead hog myself. Who'd let us in?"

"Now that's what I mean," Frank said. "How can I go back in this miserable mess, driven by a chauffeur with his pants full of shit? Damn, nobody ought to have to die like that."

I could understand his not wanting to meet death in such total disarray, his dignity collapsed. And I was ready enough to do something about myself. Not since primary school had I felt the humiliating grainy dampness of sitting in my own shit. On the outskirts of town I found a motel that looked as if it might not turn us away. It was a 1940's motor inn with garages and kitchenettes, a flat stuccoed structure that had been repainted a dozen times in war surplus paint, a bilious apple green. *Modern*, the sign said. *Phone in every room. Day rates. Vacancy.*

The proprietor was a retired army sergeant. After ringing the bell, I stood at the desk waiting for him and looking over the photographs, campaign ribbons, and citations he had covered the wall with. Dominant was the portrait of a slim, firm-jawed man about my age in an overseas cap tipped at a rakish angle. He had a cigar clamped between his teeth as though he were biting a bullet. Maybe I had picked the wrong place again. Out by the car, parked far enough away so that Frank would not be visible from the office, lay the turd that had rolled down my leg and fallen out the cuff. It felt as though another were breaking loose now. If it did, I couldn't blame the ex-sergeant for throwing me out the door with a shovel. Maybe the stink of me alone would be enough to infuriate him. As ancient and decrepit as it was, the motel seemed scrupulously clean.

There was a sound of footsteps outside, and then the front door opened. "Sorry," a voice said, "I was seeing to the coke machine, didn't hear you pull up." I breathed a sigh of relief. The ex-sergeant was old, bald, fat, and suffering from a miserable head cold.

"That's a nasty cold. I'll bet you can't smell a thing."

"It's the shits," he said, and wiped his nose with his finger. "What can I do for you?"

"I want a room for two with a bath. I'll pay in advance."

I couldn't remember the number on the license plate, so I made one up. The ex-sergeant didn't notice, or if he did, didn't care. He took the key down and put it in my hand, a newly-cut one in bright metallic red, his one apparent renovation. It was attached by a metal ring to a flat coffin-shaped piece of plastic that had the room number printed on it. "Coke machine at the end of the row," he said. "You get your ice here in the office."

"Thanks. You'd better take something for that cold."

"It's a bitch. I catch one every year. I ask you now, what's the good of moving to Florida if you still have to suffer these bitching colds?"

"It beats me," I said.

The room was down near the coke-machine end of the motel. As far as I could see, only one other room had been taken, two doors up from us. There a customized older car with an unnaturally high rear end stuck out of the garage like a bull backing up. We pulled up and parked just as the door of that room opened and a high school boy with a sheepish grin on his face came out leading by the hand a small blond girl in a cheerleading sweater. She looked as though she couldn't have been older than thirteen.

"By god, Barlow, you know how to pick the places," Frank said. "While I'm in the tub you bring me a girl just like that one."

"Frank, you are a depraved and dirty old man."

"I always wanted somebody to say that about me."

For all his bluffing talk, Frank was about used up and knew it. He let me almost carry him into the room, his feet touching the ground only in a kind of token walking. I got him onto the bed and pulled his clothes off, then went into the bathroom and cleaned myself up first. My trousers I threw into the trash. The shirt still had a spot of meat-face's blood on it, but it would do.

"You're wearing my pants," Frank said when I came out. "What am I going to put on?"

"Don't worry. I'll take care of that. Right now let's get you in the tub."

His body was as light as a child's, and I was shocked by the secret frailty of it. It was as though his bones were hollow, his flesh made of styrofoam. I put him down in the water gingerly, afraid he would break if I were not careful.

"Hoo, that feels good," he said. "I haven't had anything wetter than a washcloth on me since I went into the hospital. A sponge bath—that has to be one of the most unsatisfying things in the world."

I put the soap into his hand. "Can you manage now?"

"I think so. Man, this is fine. I wish I could have a haircut and shoeshine, too."

"I'm leaving a towel on the toilet stool. If I don't get back right away, you think you can dry yourself off and get into bed?"

"Where are you going?"

"I'm going to get you some new clothes."

He grinned like a boy. "Nothing too conservative," he said.

On the way out I picked up his shoes and put them in the car with the intention of having them shined, if I could find a place. Then a better idea occurred to me. The first shop I found open was a small boutique with the fitting name of *The Living End*. The salesman, a young man with long hair and a green velvet shirt, looked over my baggy clothes with poorly concealed distaste.

"May I help you?"

"Do you have shoes here?"

"Yes we do, right over there. But I'm not sure you'll find the sort of thing you want."

"I think I will. Show me your shirts and trousers first."

Yawning, he led me to a rack of expensive and dull trousers in plain colors. "These have only a slight flare," he said. "I'm afraid we don't have anything in the style you have on."

"What about those over there?" I pointed to a series of pigeon hole shelves against the wall full of stacked bell bottoms. In Frank's size they had one pair that was bright pink, three or four blue and white tie-dies, and several others I rejected as too ordinary. The tie-dies were better than the pink ones, but I was afraid Frank would think bleach had been spilled on them accidentally. Then I saw at the bottom of the stack the perfect ones. Shimmering silver cotton velveteen bell bottoms. They looked like polished metal, and would flash light three blocks away.

"Those?"

"Perfect. It's Christmas time in the city."

"Sir?"

"Silver bells. Now let's see a shirt."

With new respect he took me at once to the rack of soft collarless sweater shirts with pop appliqués. I debated over a superman shirt and one that said in star-spangled letters *Fuck Off!*, but compromised at last on a purple sweater with a red velvet heart on the chest, broken in half and dripping red velvet tears.

"Far out," the salesman said. He was completely won over, and when I asked for shoes brought out a bright red phony-alligator leather pair, and told me they would go smashingly with the heart.

"You're right, you have good taste. Pick out a belt and socks for me, too."

The bill came to more than I had, but he was happy to put it on my Master Charge card. I left with everything wrapped up in one big package and stopped at the drugstore to pick up a pair of scissors and some after shave lotion. Then I hurried back to the motel.

Frank was still in the lukewarm water, and he looked miserable. His hands gripped the curved porcelain edge of the tub like talons, and he seemed to be holding himself up with great effort.

"I tried," he said weakly. "I couldn't get out by myself. Barlow, I'm a little scared."

"Never mind that. You're going to make it all the way back. You're going to go out in style, Frank. I'll help you."

He let me pick him up and dry him off like a two-year-old child, turning when I asked. I set him down on the toilet seat, wrapped in the thin motel towels, and took out the scissors I had bought to trim his hair. His face, grim and determined, looked like it belonged to a very old man. The skin was wrinkled and thin, and his nearly fleshless lips had drawn into a permanent grimace that could have been either a smile or a suppressed wince. Now, as the wisps of hair on his neck began to fall away and his sideburns thinned out, he took on a curiously youthful appearance. I brushed the loose hair off his shoulders with a towel, followed his instructions to irrigate his colostomy, and then splashed him with after shave.

"I didn't think I would ever smell this good again," he said. "They won't even know me."

"Wait till you see the clothes. You're going to look so good Death might not take you. He'll think he made some mistake."

"He did make a mistake, by god. He should have picked on somebody his own size."

I had to carry him into the other room, but when I had unwrapped the package and he saw his clothes he got to his feet and let the towels fall away. His eyes were bright. "I don't know what to say, Barlow."

"Let's put them on."

It was horrible, seeing Frank standing naked in the middle of the room; he looked like a photograph of Dauchau: bones covered with skin like a sack, deep eyes from which all ignorance had forever disappeared; and yet—it made me weep to see it— he was smiling. I set him down on the bed and helped him into the silver trousers, tied the red shoes on his feet, pulled the bleeding-heart shirt over his head and raised arms. "There. Frank, you look so good the hospital won't even admit you."

"I want to see."

I helped him up, but he pulled his arm away and made it to the mirror on his own.

"You like it?"

"Holy shit yes," he said. "Now I'm fit to kill."

III

It was dark and gloomy outside when we left the motel, the kind of night that seems tethered to the earth. Frank, who claimed he did not want to wrinkle his new clothes, insisted on lying down in the back of the station wagon. I hated the way this turned the car into an ambulance and maybe, before we arrived, even a hearse. All the way back I drove in silence, straining to hear Frank's breath, which alarmed me by its gargling irregularity.

When we reached the hospital, though, he sat up. His face was yellow, as pale as the leathery skin would ever get, and the shortness of his breath took away the last of his bluff. He couldn't hide his anxiety now. I half carried him as far as the front desk, but there he made one last near-superhuman effort to stand all alone.

"I'm back," he told the girl at the desk, touching his shirt and trousers and clearly hoping she would say something about the new clothes.

She was very young, and confused by Frank's gaudy appearance. Wasn't a hospital, after all, the most serious place one knew? "What was your name, sir?"

"*Is*," Frank said.

"Sir?"

"*Is*, dammit, I'm not dead yet. My name *is*—not was—Frank Oldmixon."

"Yes, sir, I'm sorry." The blush was becoming to the girl, with her starched blouse and small clean hands, and made her look like a child. She was flustered by Frank's clothes and his manner and, as she at last noticed, his impending collapse. She was even more flustered when she found the card in her records.

"There must be some mistake."

"You bet your sweet ass there is," Frank said.

"Miss, please. We have to get him inside, you can see that. He's already registered. Room 333. Frank Oldmixon."

"Yes, sir. There *was* a Mr. Oldmixon in that room, but he passed away this morning."

Somehow Frank got enough air into his lungs to burst out laughing. "Hoo," he said weakly, "they sure hurry you along, don't they?"

"You'll have to fill out these forms."

"Has anyone else been assigned to the room?" I asked.

"No sir, not yet. But—"

"Look. You can see the shape he's in, can't you?"

She could. Holding the card over her mouth, she looked at me and then at Frank. I could tell from her eyes that we had put her in a terrible dilemma. The merely sick and the injured she knew how to handle, but Frank was obviously dying, and though she wasn't certain of it, dying might take precedence over bookkeeping. It was enough hesitation for me.

"Come on," I said, and picked him up bodily and carried him to the elevator. We ascended slowly.

"Barlow, boy, this is not my idea of fun. I always thought I'd have a big scene with friends and relatives crowded around the bed, the room all dim and full of the sound of weeping, and some pretty girl holding my hand, and—"

"Shhh, Frank. Take it easy." Speech was robbing him of breath; every third word was a gasp.

He ignored me, though, and was still talking and gasping when the elevator stopped and I carried him in my arms down the hall to his room. The bed had been stripped. I lay him down on the mattress.

"Let's get out of those clothes now."

"No. Let me go out in style." He managed a weak grin. "I want to die with my red alligator shoes on."

"I'm getting the doctor."

"Not yet. Ox . . ."

"What?" I bent closer.

"Oxygen," he whispered.

Plugged directly into the wall, the plastic oxygen tube ran up through a filtering bottle of water and then looped down in a coil hanging on a hook. I straightened it out and rigged the clip to Frank's nose, turned the dial, and heard the hiss of the gas through the tube. The bottle of water bubbled, and Frank sighed and relaxed. "That's better," he said. "Hoo. Hey. I made it, didn't I?"

"You made it, Frank."

"You look terrible, you know it?"

"Yeah, well I don't feel so good either."

"I'll tell you what's wrong, it's all this dying you've been around. You're not cut out for that stuff, Barlow."

"You rest now, Frank."

"Rest. That's what they always say to us dying people, isn't it? *You rest now.* As if we had any choice."

But, then, after a fit of coughing that made the tendons in his neck stand out like tightened cords, he gave up trying to talk and did rest. The oxygen hissed steadily into his nose, and he breathed more regularly. I pulled a chair over to the bed and sat beside him. For an hour or two he slept without moving. About two in the morning, without waking, he tossed onto his side and drew up his legs, and I came out of my daze and realized it was getting cool in the room. There were some blankets in the closet. I got one of them down and had just spread it over him when the nurse came in. Nodding at me, she sat on the edge of his bed and took Frank's pulse.

"Not much longer," she said.

I wondered if she were the nurse Frank had hoped to see once more. She had big breasts and strong hands and a stern, impersonal manner that hid any feeling she might have. So far as I could tell, she was not surprised to find Frank still alive and back in the room, nor to have him dying, officially, for the second time. Maybe in hospitals, with all their ceaseless comings and goings, there were no surprises, and one really did get used to death.

"How much longer?" I asked her.

"I'm no doctor."

"Do you think you should get one?"

"In time." She lay Frank's thin wrist on the blanket and left. Like all his limbs, his pale bony arm had shrunk, its substance fed to the cannibalism of the cancer. Looking at it made me furious with the hunger that ate and ate, devouring his flesh until he was a poor child's body stretched over a man's skeleton. I put his frail arm back under the blanket and pulled it up to his chin.

After that, I must have fallen asleep myself. Shortly before dawn I woke up with a stiff neck and back and pains all over my body, some of them reminiscences of the fight in the bar, others contributed by the hard chair I had fallen asleep in. Frank was still asleep, and still breathing, though even with the oxygen his breath sounded hoarse and labored. I turned the dial to give him a bit more, and then went over to the window and stretched, trying to work the soreness out of my limbs. Outside, the sky was a fine delicate grey shading into blue and orange. As I looked, the edge of the sun broke like the blade of a gold shovel digging into sky.

It was beautiful, and I wished Frank could see it; he was sentimental enough to love the dawn.

"Pensacola," he said weakly.

I hurried over to the bed. "What is it, Frank?"

"Put it in the bag."

"Put what in the bag?"

"The cat food."

"I will. I will."

He opened his eyes and looked at me, but without recognition. Then he said, still in the coma, ". . . carpets, floor, furniture, anything . . . best suction . . ."

"That's right, Frank. It's the best."

"Pensacola. We'll clean up."

"Yes we will."

"All right then."

He slept again. About eight, the same nurse came in with a tray of food and put it down on the table. "Breakfast," she said cheerily. Frank opened his eyes and smiled. "You help me," the nurse said to me. "Hold him up while I feed him. Come on, now, I want you to take this juice."

I put my arm around his back and lifted him up to a sitting position; he felt light, the spine and all the bones delicate and

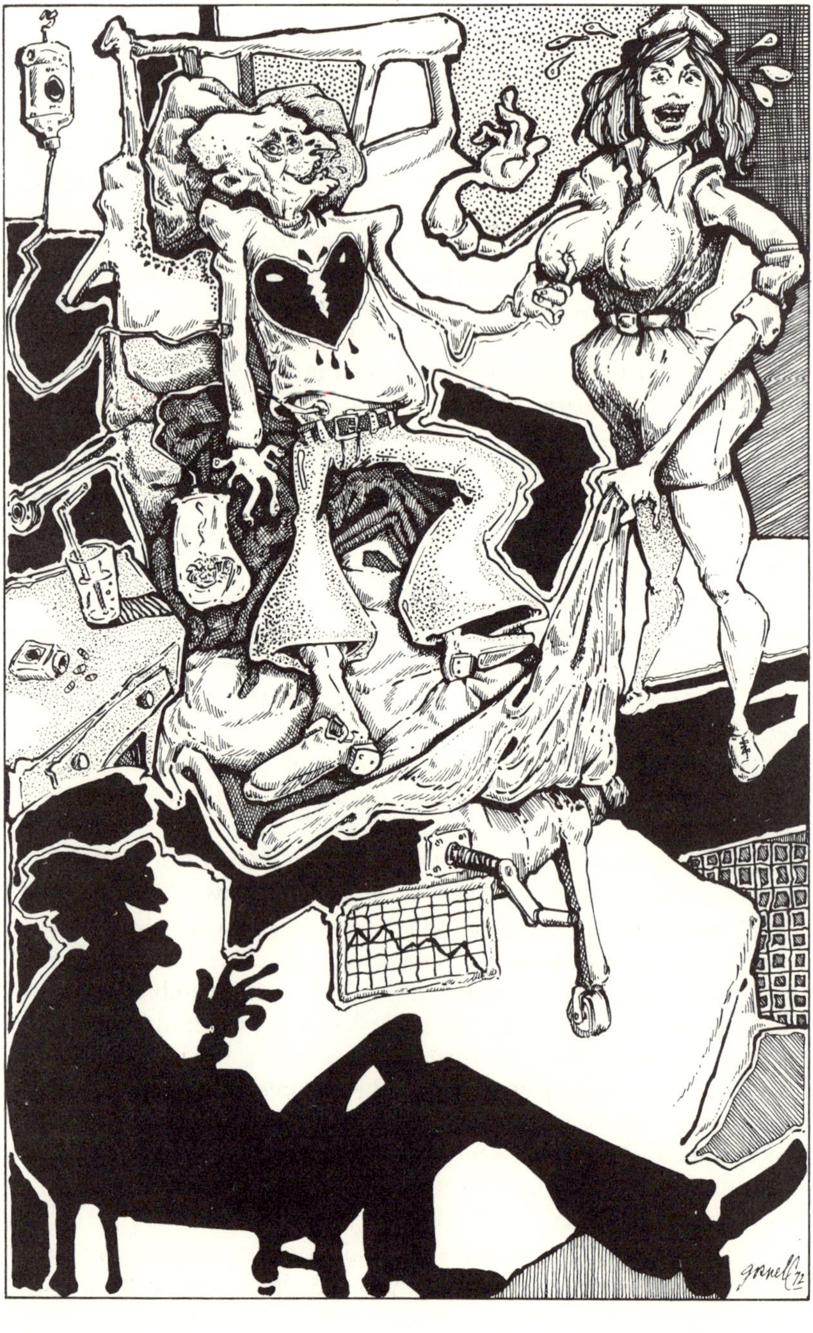
gornell 72

hollow, and even though he seemed to recognize us, he was as helpless as a baby. It was difficult for me to resist talking to him as though he were one. The nurse didn't try to resist it. "Come on, now," she said, "be a big boy. Swallow it down. Dat's it. Goo' for you."

He was taking the juice through a straw, sucking like an infant on a nipple. After he had finished, the nurse leaned closer and patted him on the back. "Do you expect him to burp?" I asked. I thought Frank was beyond noticing either one of us, but he shocked me with a wink and the faint ghost of a smile, and reached his hand up and gave a squeeze to the nurse's big breast.

"Dat's it," I said. "Goo' for you."

To her credit, the nurse was not embarrassed. She patted Frank's hand, and then helped me lower him back to the bed. "He doesn't need this," she said, and pulled the blanket off, revealing Frank's satin heart and silver bell bottoms in all their glory. For a moment she stood looking down at him, and then grinned and shook her head. "You old reprobate," she said. The next minute she was gathering up the tray with crisp efficiency and bustling out of the room, but I loved her for allowing that tiny crack in the surface of her professional impersonality. Frank, weak as he was, beamed, and he fell asleep still smiling.

The end came a few minutes past ten. He woke up with a clear, startled look in his eyes. "This is it, Barlow," he said.

I took hold of his hand and bent to hear what else he was saying, but he had lapsed at once back into coma, and his words made no sense. He mumbled something about hamburgers and then trees. "Trees know," he said. "Give it to the dog." There was more about fish and carrots and a white sidewall tire, and then his eyes came open again and he stopped talking and looked at me. His voice was a pale breath; it had no strength to it, but he spoke clearly. "You know what death is?"

"No, Frank."

"Shit."

I don't know if the nurse heard this or not, but at the moment he said it she came through the door with a doctor, a young intern with soft cheeks and long sideburns and a frightened look on his face. The timing was eerie. Right on cue, Frank looked into my face.

That's the way he went. Nothing changed, only his chest stopped rising, and the oxygen hissed cruelly into the still holes of his nose. The scared young doctor bent over him and pressed his stethoscope to the poor collapsed bird-chest, listened hard, and rose, shaking his head. The nurse nodded and reached her hand towards Frank's open eyes.

"I'll do that," I said. I don't know why. I had never done anything like it before, but suddenly I felt I had to. Frank had held out to the last minute, and then gone in style; I couldn't let him down now. So I reached out and closed his eyes both at once with my two fingers the way I had always imagined people doing it. They stayed closed, and I left him like that.

David Ray

Collected Poems
E. L. MAYO

E. L. Mayo's poems shine with a wit and wonder and intelligence that make them truly remarkable.
—ROBERT DANA

A *New Letters* Book

Ohio University Press/Swallow Press
Athens, Ohio 45701

Ohio University Press/Swallow Press
Athens, Ohio 45701

India
An Anthology of Contemporary Writing

Edited by
DAVID RAY and AMRITJIT SINGH

1983   277 pp.   6 x 9   illus. $10.95